JESUS AND PHILOSOPHY

What, if anything, does Jesus of Nazareth have to do with philosophy? This question motivates this collection of new essays from leading theologians, philosophers, and biblical scholars. Part I portrays Jesus in his first-century intellectual and historical context, attending to intellectual influences and contributions and contemporaneous similar patterns of thought. Part II examines how Jesus influenced two of the most prominent medieval philosophers. It considers the seeming conceptual shift from Hebraic categories of thought to distinctively Greco-Roman ones in later Christian philosophers. Part III considers the significance of Jesus for some prominent contemporary philosophical topics, including epistemology and the meaning of life. The focus is not so much on how Christianity figures in such topics as on how Jesus makes distinctive contributions to such topics.

Paul K. Moser is professor and chair of philosophy at Loyola University Chicago. He is author most recently of *The Elusive God: Reorienting Religious Epistemology* (Cambridge University Press, 2008) and coeditor of *Divine Hiddenness* (Cambridge University Press, 2001). He is also editor of *The Oxford Handbook of Epistemology* (2005), general editor of the book series *Oxford Handbooks of Philosophy*, and editor of the journal *American Philosophical Quarterly*.

Jesus and Philosophy

New Essays

Edited by

PAUL K. MOSER
Loyola University Chicago

CAMBRIDGE
UNIVERSITY PRESS

CAMBRIDGE UNIVERSITY PRESS
Cambridge, New York, Melbourne, Madrid, Cape Town, Singapore, São Paulo, Delhi

Cambridge University Press
32 Avenue of the Americas, New York, NY 10013-2473, USA

www.cambridge.org
Information on this title: www.cambridge.org/9780521694865

First published 2009

Printed in the United States of America

A catalog record for this publication is available from the British Library.

Library of Congress Cataloging in Publication Data

Jesus and philosophy : new essays / edited by Paul K. Moser.
p.   cm.
Includes bibliographical references and index.
ISBN 978-0-521-87336-9 (hardback) – ISBN 978-0-521-69486-5 (pbk.)
1. Jesus Christ.   2. Jesus Christ – Influence.   3. Philosophy.   4. Philosophy and religion.
I. Moser, Paul K., 1957–   II. Title.
BT205.J43   2008
232.9′04–dc22   2008031948

ISBN   978-0-521-87336-9 hardback
ISBN   978-0-521-69486-5 paperback

Contents

Preface

What, if anything, does Jesus of Nazareth, the founder of the Christian movement, have to do with philosophy? This question motivates this book and its essays. Even though Jesus has had a profound impact on many philosophers and on many philosophies, no substantial scholarly book has been devoted to the topic of Jesus and philosophy. Perhaps philosophers have been unwilling, for some unclear reason or other, to take up the philosophical relevance of Jesus. In any case, this book fills this gap in the literature of philosophy. Of course, no single book could be altogether comprehensive on the topic of Jesus and philosophy, but the present book offers wide-ranging substantial coverage that will be of interest to philosophers and to other readers, including scholars and students in theology, religious studies, and history.

The book is divided into three main parts: I. *Jesus in His First-Century Thought Context*; II. *Jesus in Medieval Philosophy*; and III. *Jesus in Contemporary Philosophy*. Part I portrays Jesus in his first-century context, attending to intellectual influences and contributions and contemporaneous similar patterns of thought. It sets an intellectual and historical context for examining the book's subsequent reflections on Jesus. Part II examines how Jesus influenced some of the most prominent medieval philosophers. It attends to what seems to be a conceptual shift from largely Hebraic categories of thought in Jesus to distinctively Greco-Roman categories in later Christian philosophers. Part III considers the significance of Jesus for some prominent contemporary philosophical topics, including epistemology and the meaning of life. The focus is not so much on how "Christianity" figures in such topics as on how Jesus makes distinctive contributions to such topics. His contributions, as the book illustrates, are distinctive and enduring indeed.

I thank Andy Beck, commissioning editor at Cambridge University Press, for his kind help and patience with the project, and Greg Wolcott, my Loyola

University Chicago research assistant, for his reliable help preparing the manuscript and the index.

Paul K. Moser
Chicago, Illinois

Contributors

William J. Abraham University Distinguished Professor, Perkins School of Theology, Southern Methodist University

James L. Crenshaw Robert Flowers Professor of Old Testament, Duke Divinity School

Craig A. Evans Payzant Distinguished Professor of New Testament, Acadia University, Canada

David F. Ford Regius Professor of Divinity, University of Cambridge

Paul W. Gooch Professor of Philosophy and President of Victoria University in the University of Toronto

Luke Timothy Johnson Robert Woodruff Professor of New Testament & Christian Origins, Emory University

Brian Leftow Nolloth Professor of Philosophy, Oxford University

Gareth B. Matthews Professor of Philosophy, University of Massachusetts, Amherst

Paul K. Moser Professor and Chair of Philosophy, Loyola University Chicago

Charles Taliaferro Professor of Philosophy, St. Olaf College

Nicholas Wolterstorff Noah Porter Professor of Philosophical Theology, Yale University

Introduction: Jesus and Philosophy

Paul K. Moser

How are Jesus and philosophy related? How should they be related? Such questions about the relevance of Jesus to philosophy take us back and forth between philosophy and theology in a way suggesting that the two disciplines are importantly related, at least regarding various topics of interest to philosophers and theologians. Contemporary philosophers seldom tread on theological ground, perhaps owing to general uneasiness with things theological. In any case, inquirers about the relevance of Jesus to philosophy shouldn't hesitate to cross disciplinary boundaries when explanation, knowledge, and truth are served. We shall proceed accordingly.

1. FROM ATHENS TO JERUSALEM

We may begin, for the sake of adequate context, with a question broader than that of the relevance of Jesus himself to philosophy: what, if anything, does Jerusalem, as the center of the earliest Jewish-Christian movement of Jesus's disciples, have to do with Athens, as the center of Western philosophy in its inception? Do they share *intellectual goals*, and if so, do they share *means* to achieving their common intellectual goals? The two questions demand *yes* answers, because Jerusalem and Athens both aim to achieve *truth* (perhaps among other things), and they aim to achieve truth via *knowledge* of truth. These two factors play a significant role in what defines Jerusalem and Athens, and thus Jerusalem and Athens share something significant, however much they differ and even avoid or fear each other.

Of course, aiming for truth via knowledge of truth doesn't set Jerusalem and Athens apart from many other influential movements. The later natural and social sciences, for example, aim for truth via knowledge, but they aren't original citizens of either Jerusalem or Athens. The earliest philosophy characteristic of Athens seeks a kind of philosophical truth whose discovery

1

didn't wait for the later empirical work of the natural and social sciences. Accordingly, Socrates and Plato pursued their philosophical work vigorously even though the natural and social sciences were at best immature, if they existed at all. Similarly, the theology characteristic of the earliest Christian movement in Jerusalem didn't wait for the empirical work of the later natural and social sciences. Its theology of the Good News of God's redemptive intervention in Jesus as God's self-giving Son for humans approached the wider world without relying on the natural and social sciences. So, the founding philosophers and theologians from Athens and Jerusalem didn't need to draw from the natural or social sciences to launch their respective traditions of seeking truth via knowledge.

What *distinguishes* Jerusalem from Athens? We may begin with the rough observation that Socrates and Plato started a *wisdom movement* that characterized humans as cognitive and moral agents in pursuit of the good life. The wisdom movement of Socrates and Plato focused on death as well as life: " . . . those who really apply themselves in the right way to philosophy are directly and of their own accord preparing themselves for dying and death" (*Phaedo* 64a). Death, according to Socrates and Plato, is the release of the soul from the body, and this release enables the soul to attain finally, without bodily interference, to unadulterated truth and clear thinking. Persons of wisdom (philosophers) welcome death as an opportunity for intellectual purification from the physical, sensory, and emotional pollution of the present transitory world. Plato's *Phaedo* promotes this philosophy of intellectual enlightenment characteristic of ancient Athens as the birthplace of Western philosophy.

In contrast to the philosophers of Athens, Jesus and his follower Paul of Tarsus promoted a *Good News power movement* that offered people the power of spiritual, moral, and even bodily redemption by God.[1] The heart of this redemption is offered as a gift of gracious reconciliation of humans to God, including fellowship with God, at God's expense (see, for example, Lk. 15:11–24, 24:1–35, 1 Cor. 1:9, 15:12–32, 2 Cor. 5:16–21). Jesus and Paul, as devout Jews, proceeded in the theological light of such ancient Hebrew prophets as Isaiah, Jeremiah, Ezekiel, Daniel, and Hosea, and drew their general idea of divine Good News from the book of Isaiah (cf. Isa. 52:7, 61:1).[2] The promise of

---

[1] On the unifying idea of a Good News proclamation among the New Testament writers, see Eugene Lemcio, "The Unifying Kerygma of the New Testament," in Lemcio, *The Past of Jesus in the Gospels* (Cambridge: Cambridge University Press, 1991), 115–31. Cf. Lemcio, "The Gospels within the New Testament Canon," in C. G. Bartholomew, ed., *Canon and Biblical Interpretation* (London: Paternoster, 2006), 123–45.

[2] On the contribution of the book of Isaiah to the Good News message in the New Testament, see Otto Betz, "Jesus' Gospel of the Kingdom," in Peter Stuhlmacher, ed., *The Gospel and*

divine redemption preached by Jesus and Paul included a promise of *bodily* resurrection that isn't to be confused either with resuscitation of a dead person or with immortality.

Socrates and Plato hoped for immortality for at least some humans, but they had no place for bodily resurrection in their hope. The human body, in their story, obstructs human purification as intellectual enlightenment and thus is an impediment to the kind of mental and moral goodness offered (at least in principle) by our impending death. In contrast, Jesus and Paul taught, in the tradition of Genesis 1–2, that God's creation of the physical world was initially good, and not a mere impediment to our intellectual purification. They embraced and extended the reported divine promise to some of the ancient Hebrew prophets that the people of God would be raised from the dead, even bodily. Without such resurrection, they assumed, human redemption would be gravely incomplete, because God intended humans to be embodied. Full resurrection, in their eyes, thus included embodiment; accordingly, Paul and various other early followers of Jesus preached the actual bodily resurrection of Jesus and, for the future, of his followers too (see 1 Cor. 15:1–15).[3] Jerusalem thus contradicts Athens, and the two won't be united in their attitudes toward either the value of the physical world or what humans ultimately need.

According to the apostle Paul, the Good News movement stems from God's redemptive self-revelation in the life, death, and resurrection of Jesus. More specifically, this movement is founded on "the power of God for salvation for everyone who trusts [God]" (Rom. 1:16; cf. 1 Cor. 1:18), and this divine power is perfectly exemplified in the human Jesus (2 Cor. 4:4, 5:19; cf. Phil. 2:6). Paul thought of (a) the obedient death-by-crucifixion undergone by Jesus and (b) God's resurrection of Jesus from the dead as two decisively related moments in a single life-giving, redemptive movement by the one true God of authoritative righteous love (*agape*). The resurrection of Jesus was central to Paul's understanding of salvation as divine redemption from evil and death; he thus held: " . . . [I]f Christ has not been raised [from the dead by God], your faith is futile and you are still in your sins" (1 Cor. 15:17). In addition, Paul speaks of the kind of "knowing Christ" who is essential to

---

the Gospels (Grand Rapids, MI: Eerdmans, 1991), 53–74, Rikki Watts, *New Exodus and Mark* (Tübingen: Mohr Siebeck, 1997), chap. 4, and Graham Stanton, "Jesus and Gospel," in Stanton, *Jesus and Gospel* (Cambridge: Cambridge University Press, 2004), 9–62.

[3] On the place of resurrection in the earliest Christian preaching, see Floyd V. Filson, *Jesus Christ the Risen Lord* (Nashville: Abingdon, 1956), Rowan Williams, *Resurrection* (London: Darton, 1982), and Markus Bockmuehl, "Resurrection," in Bockmuehl, ed., *The Cambridge Companion to Jesus* (Cambridge: Cambridge University Press, 2001), 102–18.

salvation as involving our knowing "the power of his resurrection" via our being conformed to Jesus's death (Phil. 3:10). Paul thus proclaimed the death-by-crucifixion of Jesus *because* he also proclaimed the resurrection-by-God of Jesus for divine redemptive purposes. The two, according to Paul, must be portrayed together to capture God's redemptive Good News movement (see, for example, Rom. 3–6).

The divine power central to the Good News movement of Jerusalem is, in Paul's perspective, cognitively as well as morally and spiritually important. Many philosophers of religion have overlooked this perspective, and hence its distinctive underlying epistemology has rarely surfaced in philosophy. Paul holds that he knows the risen Jesus on the basis of his knowing firsthand the power of Jesus's resurrection by God (cf. Phil. 3:8–11). Redemption, according to Paul, consists in knowing firsthand the divine power of Jesus's divine resurrection in virtue of being transformed by it to conform to Jesus's self-giving death, in volitional fellowship with the God who raised Jesus from death.

Joseph Fitzmyer has characterized the relevant power and corresponding knowledge, as follows:

> This "power" is not limited to the influence of the risen Jesus on the Christian, but includes a reference to the origin of that influence in [God] the Father himself. The knowledge, then, that Paul seeks to attain, the knowledge that he regards as transforming the life of a Christian and his/her sufferings, must be understood as encompassing the full ambit of that power. It emanates from the Father, raises Jesus from the dead at his resurrection, endows him with a new vitality, and finally proceeds from him as the life-giving, vitalizing force of the "new creation" [cf. 2 Cor. 5:17] and of the new life that Christians in union with Christ experience and live ... [T]he knowledge of [this power], emanating from Christian faith, is the transforming force that vitalizes Christian life and molds the suffering of the Christian to the pattern which is Christ.[4]

This characterization of resurrection power fits with Paul's aforementioned view that the Good News of what God has done through Jesus is "the power of *God*" for human salvation (Rom. 1:16; cf. Eph. 1:19–20). As a result, the Good News Jesus movement advanced by Paul is no narrow Jesus cult, but is rather offered as a power movement of the one true God of the whole

---

[4] Joseph Fitzmyer, "'To Know Him and the Power of His Resurrection' (Phil. 3:10)," in Fitzmyer, *To Advance the Gospel*, 2nd ed. (Grand Rapids, MI: Eerdmans, 1998), 208–9.

world, including Gentiles as well as Jews (Rom. 3:29, 15:15–17).[5] This fits with the focus on God in the ministry of Jesus himself (see, for example, Mk. 1:15, 12:29–30).

In Paul's perspective on the earliest Jesus movement, God's intervening Spirit supplies the needed *power* of resurrection, including the power that raised Jesus (Rom. 1:4). The same Spirit, according to Paul, supplies the needed firsthand authoritative *evidence* and *knowledge* of this power to willing recipients (see Rom. 5:5, 8:15–16, 1 Cor. 2:9–12). Such an approach to evidence and knowledge of divine reality acknowledges *purposively available* evidence of divine reality that is offered in accordance with divine redemptive purposes. This kind of cognitive perspective on knowledge of divine reality was evidently influenced by Jesus himself (see Mk. 4:2–12, Matt. 11:25–30). With regard to evidence of divine reality, philosophers of religion and theologians often leave inquirers, without an authoritative volitional challenge, at the level of merely theoretical assessment of propositional evidence, including historical propositional evidence. At this level, one can't make good sense of the revolutionary Good News movement launched by Jerusalem, particularly by Jesus and, in his wake, Paul. Such a life-transforming revolution needs an authoritative volitional anchor deeper than merely theoretical assessment of propositional evidence, including historical propositional evidence.[6] Jesus and Paul (following Jesus) redirect religious epistemology accordingly, to authoritative divine evidence that offers the needed volitional challenge to humans and thus moves beyond merely theoretical assessment.

In contrast with the Jerusalem of Jesus, Athens yields an intellectual-enlightenment wisdom movement that holds out no hope or even desire of lasting life via bodily resurrection. Contemporary Western philosophy largely follows suit, particularly as a result of its widespread abandonment of robust theism. Following Jesus, Jerusalem offers a Good News power movement of redemption as fellowship with God and eventual deliverance by God from both evil and death into lasting life, including bodily resurrection. The resurrection of Jesus is thereby proclaimed, by Paul and other early disciples, as the victory inauguration of this revolutionary movement of God's intervening Spirit. The movement, as represented by Jesus, focuses on the

---

[5] See Dunn, "Christology as an Aspect of Theology," in A. J. Malherbe and W. A. Meeks, eds., *The Future of Christology* (Minneapolis: Fortress, 1993), 202–12.

[6] On this point, in connection with theoretical historical evidence for the resurrection of Jesus, see Paul Minear, *The Bible and the Historian* (Nashville: Abingdon, 2002), chap. 5, Dale Allison, *Resurrecting Jesus: The Earliest Christian Tradition and its Interpreters* (London: T&T Clark. 2005), and Paul Moser, *The Elusive God: Reorienting Religious Epistemology* (New York: Cambridge University Press, 2008), chap. 3.

gracious redemptive intervention of a divine Spirit that empowers lasting life in divine-human fellowship, including human freedom to love all people, even enemies. Life, according to this Good News movement, can offer, via divine empowerment, progressive moral and spiritual renewal toward God's character of unselfish love and, in the future, bodily resurrection.

The central question from Athens to Jerusalem is cognitive, if often skeptical: How can one *know* that the redemptive promise of the Good News movement is actually reliable rather than just wishful thinking? Jerusalem's answer, represented by Jesus and Paul, is widely neglected: by volitionally knowing firsthand the promise-*Giver*, via one's willing participation in the available power of God's life-giving and life-transforming Spirit. The question from Jerusalem to Athens is thus, as always, volitional: Are we humans sincerely *willing* to participate in the powerful life of a perfectly loving God, thereby giving up our selfish lives for the sake of lasting lives in God's unselfish love, even toward enemies? Jesus himself was not particularly optimistic about the answer to the latter question (see, for example, Lk. 18:8).

2. GOOD NEWS FOR PHILOSOPHY

The Good News movement underwent a striking shift, after the crucifixion of Jesus, that resulted in the preaching, by Paul and others, of the bodily resurrection of Jesus by God. Jesus as the preacher of the Good News about God's arriving kingdom, under formative influence from the book of Isaiah, became *an object of focus* in the preaching of the Good News by his earliest, Jewish disciples. The *preacher* thus became *a central part of the preached*; the *proclaimer* became integral to the *proclaimed*, as many New Testament scholars have noted.[7]

In one of the earliest statements of the Good News in the New Testament, Paul writes:

> For I delivered to you of first importance what I have received: that Christ died for our sins according to the Scriptures, that he was buried, that he was raised on the third day according to the Scriptures, and that he appeared to Peter, and then to the twelve. After that, he appeared to more than five hundred brothers at the same time, most of whom remain until now, but some have fallen asleep. Then he appeared to James, then to all the apostles, and last of all he appeared also to me, as to one untimely born.... If Christ has not been raised, our preaching is futile and your faith is futile too. We are

[7] On this theme, see Filson, *Jesus Christ the Risen Lord*, and Klyne Snodgrass, "The Gospel of Jesus," in Markus Bockmuehl and Donald Hagner, eds., *The Written Gospel* (Cambridge: Cambridge University Press), 31–44. Cf. Betz, "Jesus' Gospel of the Kingdom."

also then found to be false witnesses about God, because we have testified about God that he raised Christ from the dead.... If Christ has not been raised, your faith is futile; you are still in your sins.... If we have hope in Christ only for this life, we are to be pitied more than all men. But Christ has been raised from the dead, the firstfruits of those who have fallen asleep (1 Cor. 15:3–8, 14–15, 17, 19–20).

Paul had unmatched influence in clarifying the Good News movement after the death of Jesus. The Goods News, according to Paul, includes that "Christ died for our sins" and was raised from the dead. Paul regards the Good News as false and futile in the absence of the resurrection of Jesus by God. In particular, he links the resurrection of Jesus by God to the divine forgiveness of human sins in such a way that if there is no resurrection of Jesus, "you are still in your sins."

According to various New Testament writers, a central theme of the Good News movement is that God forgives human sins, and humans are thereby offered reconciliation and fellowship with God, in connection with the life, death, and resurrection of Jesus. What exactly this connection involves has been a topic of controversy among philosophers of religion and theologians. If we think of *atonement* as divine-human reconciliation that suitably deals with human sin as resistance to divine unselfish love and fellowship, we may understand the heart of this controversy about the life, death, and resurrection of Jesus as a debate about atonement. How exactly do the life, death, and resurrection of Jesus figure in (the intended) divine-human atonement? How, in addition, is such atonement to be appropriated by humans? Furthermore, is such atonement actually needed by humans? If so, why is it needed? These are among many questions that emerge regarding the person and mission of Jesus, and they have generated controversy in philosophical theology and in philosophy of religion.

We do well not to portray Jesus as a typical teacher of Jewish wisdom. At the Last Supper, according to Matthew's Gospel (26:28), Jesus announced that he will die "for the forgiveness of sins." The atoning sacrifice of Jesus as God's sinless offering for sinful humans is, at least according to Matthew's Jesus, at the center of God's redemptive work. Among other New Testament writings, John's Gospel (cf. Jn. 1:36) and Paul's undisputed epistles (cf. 1 Cor. 5:7, 2 Cor. 5:21, Rom. 3:24–26) concur on this lesson about atonement. This unique role attributed to Jesus in divine-human atonement sets him apart from Abraham, Moses, Paul, Confucius, Krishna, Gautama the Buddha, Muhammad, the Dalai Lama, and every other known religious leader. Only Jesus, as portrayed at least by Matthew, John, and Paul, offered himself as God's atoning sacrifice to God for wayward humans. Only Jesus, therefore, emerged as the human center of the first-century Good News of God's intended redemption of wayward humans.

Many philosophers of religion and theologians share the apostle Peter's initial denial that the death of Jesus is central to the divine plan of reconciliation of humans to God (see Mk. 8:31–32). In fact, they doubt that the crucifixion of the obedient Son of God would be compatible with God's merciful love, at least toward Jesus. Paul faced similar doubts about the cross of Jesus among the earliest Christians in Corinth, and he responded straightforwardly: "I resolved to know nothing while I was with you except Jesus Christ *and him crucified*" (1 Cor. 2:2, italics added). The obedient death of Jesus is, in Paul's portrait of the Good News, as important as his resurrection for divine-human reconciliation.

The Roman crucifixion of Jesus seems to seal his fate as a dismal failure, perhaps even as one "cursed" before God (see Gal. 3:13, Deut. 21:23). Even so, the cross of Jesus is announced by Paul, Matthew, and John, among other New Testament writers, as a central place of God's atoning sacrifice and turnaround redemptive victory on behalf of humans. Out of the evident defeat of Jesus, according to the Good News movement, God brought a unique manifestation of divine love and forgiveness toward humans, even toward God's enemies. The fatal cross of Jesus is proclaimed as a central part of God's intended grand reversal of the dark human tragedy of alienation from fellowship with God. This reversal, according to the proclamation of the Good News movement, aims at divine-human reconciliation, or atonement, by means of a stark but powerful manifestation of God's righteous and merciful character as exemplified in Jesus.

The Good News movement founded by Jesus offers a *divine manifest-offering* approach to divine-human atonement. According to its unique message, what is being made *manifest* is God's character of righteous and merciful love, and what is being *offered*, in agreement with that character, is lasting divine-human fellowship as a gracious divine gift on the basis of (a) the forgiveness manifested and offered via God's atoning sacrifice in Jesus and (b) God's resurrection of Jesus as Lord and as Giver of God's Spirit. The manifestation of God's self-giving character in Jesus reveals the kind of God who is thereby offering lasting divine-human forgiveness and fellowship to humans. Although the death of Jesus can't bring about divine-human reconciliation by itself, it is presented, by Jesus, Paul, and others, as supplying God's distinctive means of intended implementation of reconciliation via divine manifestation and offering. For the sake of actual divine-human reconciliation, according to Jesus and Paul, humans must *receive* the manifest-offering via grounded trust and obedience (cf. Matt. 7: 21–23, Rom. 5:1–2).

Paul acknowledges that the message of the cross of Jesus as central to divine-human atonement appears to some people to be utter nonsense:

> [T]he message of the cross is foolishness to those perishing, but to us being saved it is the power of God.... Jews request signs and Greeks look for wisdom, but we preach Christ crucified, a stumbling block to Jews and foolishness to Gentiles, but to those called [by God], both Jews and Greeks, Christ the power of God and the wisdom of God. For the foolishness of God is wiser than human wisdom, and the weakness of God is stronger than human strength (1 Cor. 1:18, 22–25).

The power and wisdom of God's morally righteous and merciful character are manifested, according to Paul, in the crucified Jesus, whom God approvingly raised as Lord from death by crucifixion. Such divine power and wisdom, in Paul's Good News message, overcome even death, thereby surpassing any human power or wisdom, including the human power of evil. According to the Good News offered by Jesus and Paul, God sent God's own beloved Son, Jesus, to live and to die and to be resurrected by God. The divine aim was to manifest God's forgiving and righteous love for all people, even God's enemies (Rom. 5:6–8), and thereby to offer people lasting divine-human fellowship under Jesus as Lord who offers God's empowering Spirit (1 Cor. 1:9, 1 Thess. 5:10). The Good News message of Jesus and Paul implies that Jesus came from God to identify with humans in their weakness and trouble, while he represented his divine Father in righteous and merciful self-giving love. As divinely appointed mediator, Jesus thus aims to serve as a personal bridge between God *and* humans by seeking to reconcile humans to his Father with the divine gift of fellowship anchored in merciful, forgiving love and God's own intervening Spirit.

A central theme of the Good News message is that Jesus's obedient death on the cross, commanded of him by God (see Rom. 3:25, 1 Cor. 5:7, Phil. 2:8; cf. Mk. 14:23–24, Jn. 18:11), aims to manifest how far he and his Father will go, even to gruesome death, to offer divine forgiveness and fellowship to alienated humans. According to this message, Jesus gives humans all he has, avowedly from his Father's love, to manifest that God mercifully and righteously loves humans to the fullest extent and offers humans the gracious gift of unearned fellowship and membership in God's everlasting family via reception of God's own empowering Spirit (cf. Rom. 5:8, Jn. 3:16–17). This is the heart of the Good News that emerges from the Jerusalem of Jesus and Paul and goes far beyond anything offered in the wisdom movement from Athens.

The Good News movement reports that God uses the crucifixion of the willingly obedient Jesus as the episode whereby selfish human rebellion against

God is mercifully judged and forgiven by God. This claim does *not* imply that God punished Jesus, and no New Testament writer teaches otherwise, contrary to some subsequent, less careful theologians. (Some theologians might be inclined to counter with Mk. 14:27 or Gal. 3:13, but neither passage implies that God punished Jesus.) According to the Good News, God sent Jesus into the rebellious human world to undergo, willingly and obediently, suffering and death that God would deem adequate for dealing justly, under divine righteousness, with human rebellion against God and God's unselfish love. Jesus thus pays the price on behalf of selfish humans for righteous divine reconciliation of humans and thereby removes any need for selfish fear, condemnation, anxiety, guilt, and punishment among humans in relation to God (see Rom. 8:1).

In the writings of Paul, Matthew, and John, among other New Testament writers, the crucified Jesus is the manifest power and mirror image of a perfectly loving God. Specifically, according to Paul, the foundational motive for the crucifixion of Jesus is his Father's *righteous love* for humans:

> Now apart from law, a righteousness of God has been manifested, to which the Law and the Prophets bear witness. This righteousness of God comes through trust in Jesus Christ to all who trust [in him]. There is no difference, for all have sinned and fall short of the glory of God, and are justified freely by his grace through the redemption in Christ Jesus, whom God put forth as an atoning sacrifice, through trust, in his blood. He did this to manifest his righteousness, because in his forbearance he had passed over the sins previously committed. He did this to manifest his righteousness in the current time, in order to be righteous and the one who justifies those who trust in Jesus (Rom. 3:21–26).

Paul identifies three times here the *manifestation* of God's righteousness as central to God's redemptive plan involving Jesus, including his death. In addition, Paul twice suggests that this divine manifestation is aimed at God's graciously justifying, or reconciling, humans before God via trust in Jesus. This passage thus repeatedly endorses a divine manifest-offering approach to atonement via Jesus. God's graciously forgiving offer of divine-human reconciliation, according to Paul, comes with a manifestation of God's righteousness in the crucified Jesus.

Unlike many later theologians, Paul decisively links divine righteousness, or justice, with God's love: "God manifests his own love (*agape*) for us in that while we were yet sinners, Christ died for us.... Since we have now been justified by his blood, how much more shall we be saved by him from the wrath [of God].... [W]hile we were enemies [of God], we were reconciled to God through the death of his Son" (Rom. 5:8–10). God thus takes the initiative and the crucial means through Jesus in offering a gracious gift of divine-human reconciliation. Paul, accordingly, takes the sacrificial death of Jesus to manifest divine love and righteousness. He seems, accordingly, to have thought of divine love as *righteous love*.

Famously, Paul denies that the divinely offered gift of reconciliation can be earned by human "works" that obligate God to redeem humans (Rom. 4:4), because humans have fallen short of the divine standard of perfect love (Rom. 3:10–12, 23). Still, obedience as internal volitional submission to God's authoritative call to repentance and divine-human fellowship is central to appropriating the offered gift (Rom. 1:5, 6:16, 16:26, 2 Thess. 1:8; cf. Matt. 7:21–25). Such appropriating, however, differs from earning a reward, because the divine gift of righteousness to humans comes not by human earning but rather by divine gracious reckoning of a gift via human trust, which includes volitional yielding, toward the Gift-Giver (see Rom. 4:5–11, 10:8–10). As a result, human prideful boasting, or taking of self-credit, before God with regard to the Good News of reconciliation is altogether misplaced (Rom. 3:27).

According to the Good News movement of Jesus and Paul, the God of perfect love, who is the Father of Jesus, is also a God of *righteous wrath and judgment* (Rom. 1:18, 2:2–8).[8] The pertinent idea is this: (a) *because* God is inherently loving toward all other persons, God loves all sinners, including God's enemies, and (b) *because* God loves all sinners, God has wrath and judgment toward sin, given that sin leads to death (as separation from God) rather than life (as obedient fellowship with God). God as perfectly loving seeks to reconcile humans to God, even via judgment, in a way that exceeds mere divine forgiveness and satisfies God's standard of morally perfect love in divine-human reconciliation and fellowship (see Rom. 11:15, 30–32).

Divine forgiveness of humans wouldn't by itself adequately deal with the source of the wrongdoing that called for such forgiveness, namely, human neglect of divine authority (on which see Rom. 1:21, 28; cf. Matt. 7:21–27). In judging the source of wrongdoing, according to the Good News movement, God upholds perfect moral integrity in divine redemption of humans, without condoning wrongdoing or evil. More specifically, through the loving self-sacrifice of Jesus, *God* meets the standard of morally perfect love *for humans*

---

[8] On the place of divine judgment in the message of Jesus and Paul, see Marius Reiser, *Jesus and Judgment*, trans. L. M. Maloney (Minneapolis: Fortress, 1997), and Edward Meadors, *Idolatry and the Hardening of the Heart* (London: T&T Clark, 2006).

(when they wouldn't), and then God offers this gracious gift of divinely provided righteousness to humans, as God's Passover lamb for humans (1 Cor. 5:7; cf. Matt. 26:26–29, Jn. 1:29), to be received by trust in Jesus and God as redeeming Gift-Givers. Otherwise, human prospects for meeting the standard of divine perfect love would be dim indeed.[9]

Paul reports that "God was, in Christ, reconciling the world to Himself," not counting our sins against us (2 Cor. 5:19). This redemptive theme is at the heart of the Good News message of Jesus and Paul. The motivation of undergoing crucifixion for Jesus was his *obedience* to his Father on behalf of humans for the sake of divine-human reconciliation. He expressed the centrality of obedience to his Father in Gethsemane at a pivotal moment: "Not what I will, but what You will" (Mk. 14:35–36; cf. Mk. 14:22–25). Likewise, Paul identified the crucial role of Jesus's obedience: "Christ Jesus, who, being in the form of God, did not consider equality with God something to be grasped, but he emptied himself, taking the form of a servant, being made in human likeness. Being found in appearance as a man, he humbled himself and became *obedient* to death, even death on a cross" (Phil. 2:6–8, italics added; cf. Rom. 5:18–19). The acknowledged obedience of Jesus in his death is obedience to the Good News redemptive mission of his Father, who reportedly gave Jesus his cup of suffering and death (Rom. 8:3–4; cf. Jn. 18:11).

Paul presents Jesus as God's Passover lamb on behalf of humans, that is, as God's own atoning sacrifice to God for humans (Rom. 3:25), because he was perfectly obedient in the eyes of his perfectly righteous Father. Jesus's perfectly obedient life toward God, according to at least Paul, Matthew, and John, is an acceptable sacrifice to God for humans and is offered on behalf of humans by Jesus and God. Gethsemane and the Last Supper manifest these central lessons about Jesus's obedience toward God. Gethsemane shows Jesus passionately resolving to put his Father's will first, even in the face of death, and the Last Supper has Jesus portraying, with the bread and the wine as emblematic of his body and his blood, the ultimate self-sacrifice pleasing to his Father on behalf of humans. The idea of a Passover sacrifice has roots in ancient Judaism (see Ex. 12:1–27), but it continued to figure in the Good News of redemption preached, at least by Paul, Matthew, and John, among the earliest Christians. Their Good News message rests on a perfectly righteous divine character and a divine redemptive plan for the world (as identified

---

[9] On gift-righteousness as central to Paul's thought, see Stephen Westerholm, *Perspectives Old and New on Paul* (Grand Rapids, MI: Eerdmans, 2004), chap. 15. Cf. Peter Stuhlmacher, *Reconciliation, Law, and Righteousness: Essays in Biblical Theology*, trans. E. R. Kalin (Philadelphia: Fortress, 1986), chaps. 3, 5. For parallels in Jesus, see David Wenham, *Paul: Follower of Jesus or Founder of Christianity?* (Grand Rapids, MI: Eerdmans, 1995).

in Isaiah, for instance) rather than abstract principles of justice or love that typically misrepresent the motivation for what Paul calls God's "redemption in Christ Jesus" (Rom. 3:24; cf. Rom. 5:10–11).

The Good News redemptive mission of Jesus, as proclaimed by Jesus, Paul, and many other first-century Jews, included not only his death but also his resurrection by God. The aforementioned divine manifest-offering approach to atonement captures this fact by acknowledging the divine gracious offering of *lasting* divine-human fellowship under Jesus as Lord. Such offered fellowship requires, of course, that Jesus be *alive* to be Lord lastingly on behalf of humans. This illuminates Paul's otherwise puzzling remarks that Jesus "was raised for our justification" and that "we shall be saved by his life" (Rom. 4:25, 5:10), once we acknowledge that justification and salvation from death are, like forgiveness, for the sake of lasting divine-human fellowship under Jesus as Lord (cf. 1 Thess. 5:10).

The resurrection of Jesus, as proclaimed in the Good News message, is offered as God's indelible signature of approval and even exaltation on God's obedient, crucified Son, the atoning sacrifice from God for humans (see Phil. 2:9–11). The resurrection of Jesus thus gets some of its crucial significance from the cross, where Jesus gave full obedience to his Father in order to supply a manifest-offering of divine-human reconciliation to humans via trust in God. In his full, life-surrendering obedience, Jesus manifests his authoritative Father's worthiness of complete trust and obedience, even when death ensues. More generally, Jesus confirms through his perfect obedience the preeminent authority of his Father for the sake of redeeming humans, and his Father, in turn, approvingly authorizes and exalts Jesus, likewise for the sake of redeeming humans. Both Jesus and his divine Father thus have, according to the Good News movement, crucial roles in the divine manifest-offering aimed at the atoning redemption of humans.

3. PHILOSOPHY AS A KERYGMATIC DISCIPLINE

Given the Good News movement advanced by Jesus, Paul, and others, Jesus bears on philosophy to the extent that divine redemption of humans bears on philosophy. Clearly, this movement prompts a wide range of philosophical questions, including conceptual, metaphysical, epistemological, and ethical questions. Philosophical theology and the philosophy of religion have pursued such questions at length, and their pursuit continues in strength. Still, does Jesus make any *disciplinary* difference to philosophy? It seems so, given his distinctive approach to human priorities, which bears on philosophy as well as other truth-seeking disciplines.

Drawing from the Hebrew scriptures, Jesus summarized the divine love commands in the following way:

> [O]ne of the scribes came up and heard them disputing with one another, and seeing that he [Jesus] answered them well, asked him, "Which commandment is the first of all?" Jesus answered, "The first is, 'Hear, O Israel: The Lord our God, the Lord is one; and you shall love the Lord your God with all your heart, and with all your soul, and with all your mind, and with all your strength.' The second is this: 'You shall love your neighbor as yourself.' There is no other commandment greater than these" (Mk. 12:28–31, RSV; cf. Deut. 6:4, Lev. 19:18).

These commands, found in the Hebrew scriptures and in the Christian New Testament, give a priority ranking to what humans should love. They imply that at the very top of a ranking of what we humans love should be, first, God and, second, our neighbor (as well as ourselves). They thus imply that any opposing ranking is morally unacceptable. More specifically, they imply that human projects, including intellectual and philosophical projects, are acceptable only to the extent that they contribute to satisfying the divine love commands. Let's consider briefly how this lesson bears on philosophy as a discipline.

Loving God and our neighbor requires *eagerly serving* God and our neighbor for their best interests. Characterized broadly, our eagerly serving God and our neighbor requires (a) our eagerly obeying God to the best of our ability and (b) our eagerly contributing, so far as we are able, to the life-sustaining needs of our neighbor. Such eager serving is central to love as *agape*, the New Testament kind of merciful love that is incompatible with selfishness or harmfulness toward others. Of course, we shouldn't confuse our neighbors' best interests or life-sustaining needs with *mere preferences* expressed by our neighbors. Otherwise, we would risk making love servile in a manner that benefits no one.

We humans, of course, have limited resources, in terms of time and energy for pursuing our projects. We thus must *choose* how to spend our time and energy in ways that pursue some projects and exclude others. If I eagerly choose projects that exclude my eagerly serving the life-sustaining needs of my neighbor (when I could have undertaken the latter), I thereby fail to love my neighbor. I also thereby fail to obey God's command, as represented by Jesus, to give priority to my eagerly serving the life-sustaining needs of my neighbor, and, to that extent, I fail to love God and my neighbor (cf. 1 Jn. 4:20–21). The divine love commands don't allow us to love God to the exclusion of loving our neighbor.

The lesson about failing to love applies directly to typical pursuit of philosophical questions. If my typical eager pursuit of philosophical questions blocks my eagerly serving the life-sustaining needs of my neighbor (when I could have undertaken the latter), I thereby fail to love my neighbor. I also fail then to obey the divine love command regarding my neighbor. In this case, my eager pursuit of philosophical questions will result in my failing to love God and my neighbor as God has commanded, at least in the commands summarized by Jesus. The failing would be a moral deficiency in serving God and my neighbor, owing to my choosing to serve other purposes instead, namely, philosophical purposes independent of loving God and others.

Even if a philosophical purpose is truth-seeking, including seeking after truths about God and divine love, it could run afoul of the divine love commands. It could advance a philosophical concern, even a truth-seeking philosophical concern, at the expense of eagerly serving God and one's neighbor. For instance, I could eagerly pursue an intriguing, if esoteric, metaphysical truth in ways that disregard eager service toward God and my neighbor. Not all truth-seeking, then, proceeds in agreement with the divine love commands. This lesson applies equally to philosophy, theology, and any other truth-seeking discipline.

The divine love commands, as summarized by Jesus, don't exempt any capable person or group of capable people, not even truth-seeking philosophers. Their purpose is to call *all* capable people to reflect the morally perfect character of God, who is their perfectly authoritative and loving creator. Jesus identifies this purpose in the Sermon on the Mount, after calling his followers to love even their enemies (see Matt. 5:44–45, 48; cf. Lk. 6:35–36). Given that all capable people are created by God to be obedient creatures relative to God, all capable people are called to reflect God's moral character of self-giving love. As a result, no capable person is exempt from the divine command to love God and neighbors. In the presence of the perfectly loving God represented by Jesus, truth-seeking, including philosophical truth-seeking, doesn't trump the requirement to love others, because it doesn't override the requirement to mirror God's perfectly loving character. An assumption of the exemption of philosophers relative to the love commands conflicts with a divine redemptive purpose for capable humans to become loving as God is loving.

Jesus offers the divine love commands within a context agreeable to the following approach to the Good News message of divine redemption:

> Jesus Christ has a twofold meaning for the religious experience of mankind. He is God's call to the world to take history with absolute [moral] seriousness, and he is God's sign in history that [this] invocation has [God's] eternal

benediction. Those who hear the invocation without the benediction are either fatigued by the prospect of realizing anything ultimate in history or inflamed by the desire to do so on their own terms. The whole Gospel [or, Good News] is not at hand, however, until it is known that in Christ God gives what he commands. That knowledge is the ground of repentance for the rebellious and the resigned alike.[10]

The notion of God's offering, as a gracious and powerful gift, what the divine love commands require of humans is central to Paul's aforementioned presentation of the Good News of God's invitation to redemption as "the power of God for salvation to everyone who has faith" (Rom. 1:16, RSV; cf. 1 Cor. 4:20, Phil. 2:12–13). In addition, this notion fits with the emphasis of Jesus on God's gratuitous provision toward humans (Matt. 20:1–16, Lk. 15:11–32). That provision intends to save people from being "either fatigued by the prospect of realizing anything ultimate in history or inflamed by the desire to do so on their own terms." More specifically, the provision acknowledges that the divine love commands require a kind of power among humans, the power of self-giving love, which only a perfectly loving God can provide to receptive humans.

The divine love commands issued by Jesus aren't ordinary moral rules that concern only actions. They call for volitional *fellowship relationships* of unselfish love between oneself and God and between oneself and other humans. Such relationships go beyond mere actions to attitudes and to volitional fellowship, friendship, and communion between and among personal agents, with God at the center as the personal source of power needed for unselfish love. The background, foreground, and center of Jesus's divine love commands are thoroughly and irreducibly *person*-oriented and *person*-focused. They direct hearers to persons and fellowship relationships with persons, particularly with God and other humans. The love commands can't be reduced, then, to familiar standards of right action. They cut much deeper than any such standards, into who we are and how we exist in the presence of a person-oriented divine standard of unselfish love.

The divine love commands (a) correctively judge humans by calling them up short by a morally perfect divine standard, and then (b) call humans to obedient self-redefinition, even "new creation," by a gracious and powerful divine redemptive gift of volitional fellowship with a perfectly loving God as manifested by Jesus (cf. Jn. 3:1–12). Willing humans move beyond discussion, then, to personal transformation via obedience, in a relationship of volitional

[10] Carl Michalson, "Christianity and the Finality of Faith," in Michalson, *Worldly Theology* (New York: Scribner, 1967), 192.

fellowship with the God who commands unselfish love as supremely life-giving. In such transformation, pride, even intellectual pride, gives way to the humility of obedience to the divine love commands and their personal powerful source.

How, then, is Jesus relevant to philosophy as a discipline? Philosophy in its normal mode, without being receptive to an authoritative divine challenge stemming from divine love commands, leaves humans in a discussion mode, short of an obedience mode under divine authority. Philosophical questions naturally prompt metaphilosophical questions about philosophical questions, and this launches a parade of higher-order, or at least related, questions, with no end to philosophical discussion. Hence, the questions of philosophy are, notoriously, perennial. As divinely appointed Lord, in contrast, Jesus commands humans to move, for their own good, to an obedience mode of existence relative to divine love commands. He thereby points humans to his perfectly loving Father who ultimately underwrites the divine love commands for humans, for the sake of divine-human fellowship. Accordingly, humans need to transcend a normal discussion mode, and thus philosophical discussion itself, to face with sincerity the personal Authority who commands what humans need: faithful obedience to the perfectly loving Giver of divine love commands, for the sake of divine-human fellowship. Such obedience of the heart, involving the conforming of a human will to a divine will, is just the way humans are truly to *receive* the gift of divine redemptive love. Insofar as the discipline of philosophy becomes guided, in terms of its pursuits, by that gift on offer, it becomes kerygma-oriented in virtue of becoming an enabler of the aforementioned Good News message of Jesus.[11] According to Jesus, humans, including philosophers, were intended by God to live in faithful obedience to the divine love commands, whereby they enter into volitional fellowship with God and, on that basis, with others.

Many philosophers are very uneasy with Jesus, because he himself transcends any familiar, honorific discussion mode and demands that they do the same. Still, there's no suggestion here of being thoughtless, anti-intellectual, or unreasonable on the part of Jesus or his right-minded disciples. Philosophical discussion becomes advisable and permissible, under the divine love commands, if and only if it genuinely honors those commands by sincere compliance with them. Jesus calls people, in any case, to move beyond discussion to faithful obedience to his perfectly loving Father. He commands love from us toward God and others *beyond* discussion and the acquisition of truth, even philosophical truth. He thereby cleanses the temple of philosophy

---

[11] For elaboration on this approach to philosophy, see Moser, *The Elusive God*, chap. 4.

and turns over our self-crediting tables of mere philosophical discussion. He pronounces judgment on this long-standing self-made temple, in genuine love for its wayward builders. His corrective judgment purportedly brings us what humans truly need to flourish in lasting community with God and other humans, including philosophers: the demand of a life infused with faithful obedience of the heart to a perfectly loving Giver of love commands. At any rate, we can now see that Jesus bears significantly on philosophy as a discipline. This book's selections further clarify the bearing of Jesus on philosophy.

4. THE SELECTIONS

Craig A. Evans addresses two issues in his essay "Jesus: Sources of Self-Understanding." First, to which sources can we appeal to gain reliable historical information about Jesus? Second, what can we hope to learn about Jesus's self-understanding in these sources? Surveying Christian, Jewish, and pagan sources, Evans concludes that these sources point to the historical Jesus, to events of his life, and to a lasting impact on his followers. More specifically, Evans concludes that the New Testament (in particular, its Gospels) is the clearest and most precise source of evidence for learning of Jesus's self-understanding. By "self-understanding," Evans means not Jesus's psychological state or personality, but rather Jesus's appreciation of his role within the history of Israel and of his purpose in his life and his deliberate activities.

Evans argues that Jesus understood himself not merely as a prophet, but as a divinely ordained eschatological agent through whom God would enact the restoration of Israel according to divine rule. Furthermore, Evans argues that Jesus understood his death as the basis for a new covenant with Israel. Importantly, Evans distinguishes Jesus's self-understanding from later developments in Christology.

In "Sipping from the Cup of Wisdom," James Crenshaw examines the evolution of conceptions of deity in the Mesopotamian world up to the writings of the Gospels, with a special emphasis on the Wisdom traditions. Beginning with the idea of human beings created in the image of a deity, including covenantal relationships with such a deity (or deities), Crenshaw identifies a number of conflicting conceptions of humans' relationship to and knowledge of the divine. For example, how does one reconcile a god who destroys and punishes people with a god who shares in human concerns? In addition, how is one to understand the divine plans? Is God a mystery, or can we know something of God's desires? Questions of theodicy abound, and Crenshaw examines their influence on Jesus's teachings. Despite some tendencies to view God as distant and obscure in the ancient world, Crenshaw concludes that the insights from Wisdom of Solomon and Neoplatonic views of immortality helped to influence the Gospel writers' understanding of Jesus as the divine word and to incorporate Jesus's death and call for universal love into a renewed concept of an anthropomorphized deity.

In "The Jesus of the Gospels and Philosophy," Luke Timothy Johnson considers four philosophically significant approaches to the reading of the Gospels. First, one can understand Jesus as a sage and thus situate him within the historical tradition of other philosophical wisdom sources (such as Socrates or Epictetus). Second, one can situate Jesus in the tradition of character ethics by emphasizing his role as a moral exemplar. Third, one can consider the mythic quality of Jesus, thus facilitating a rich discussion of ontological considerations involving his being considered divine and human, as well as capturing the historical-philosophical tradition and imagination surrounding this approach. Fourth, one can take a narrative approach to the Gospels in order to capture the epiphenomenal character of the Gospels as an art.

Johnson laments the reduction of Jesus scholarship to post-Enlightenment historical and empirical research, and instead argues for a robust commitment to each of the aforementioned approaches, with a special emphasis on the moral exemplar and ontological approaches. Given such a commitment and emphasis, according to Johnson, we can understand how radical both the event of Jesus (including his life, mission, and relationship with God) and the call for discipleship (especially in the transformative role of discipleship) were and are, and thus we can avoid partial (and possibly inaccurate) representations of Jesus and the loss of the central truth of the Gospels.

In "Paul, the Mind of Christ, and Philosophy," Paul W. Gooch proposes that an adequate understanding of the role of philosophy in the Christian faith tradition requires an appreciation of Paul's experiences and teachings on the mind of Christ. Gooch argues that we must understand Paul's putative rejection of philosophy contextually. Specifically, Paul's critique of philosophy and worldly wisdom in his letters to the Corinthian community, for example, are warnings against epistemological hubris and not, specifically, against natural theistic knowledge. Gooch's argument rests upon the premise that had not human beings *some* capacity for knowledge of God, then Paul's message to spread the good news of salvation to all – Gentiles and Jews alike – would be futile. Gooch affirms nonetheless that philosophy remains woefully inadequate for the requisite spiritual knowledge of revelation and divine purposes.

Gooch identifies an instrumental, indirect role for philosophy in the Pauline tradition. Beyond the message to be Christlike in one's activities (a message that is not concerned solely with the activity of philosophy, but that applies universally to all human endeavors), Gooch argues that we need the rigor and resources of philosophy to engage and to reflect upon Christian beliefs, practices, and concepts. Paul did not shy away from raising metaphysical and epistemological questions concerning Christ and God, and philosophers now have the opportunity to take the mantle of trying to understand and elucidate key concepts in the attempt to know the mind of Christ. Gooch suggests that current philosophers have an advantage over Paul: as Paul sought to understand the mind of Christ through his revelatory experience, we now have both the mind of Jesus and the mind of Paul, as well as our predecessors' history, as resources to assist our seeking of the mind of Christ.

In "Jesus and Augustine," Gareth B. Matthews starts with the observation that problems concerning how words are learned initially, without reference to other words, can give rise to a theory of ostension. Even so, a problem of ambiguity plagues the view that language is acquired by ostension. Augustine, as Matthews explains, saw a solution to such problems of meaning in a theory of illumination implying that Christ is the Inner Teacher. Matthews argues that this theory can help underscore Augustine's theory of inner-life ethics as well.

Placing Augustine's ethical theory within the virtue ethics tradition, Matthews distinguishes Augustine's approach to the development of a virtuous character from Kantian and utilitarian approaches to ethics. The concept of a "complete sin" in Augustine's philosophy takes its roots in acts that have three parts: suggestion, pleasure, and consent, in keeping with Jesus's admonitions in the Sermon on the Mount about sins committed in one's heart. Having located sin not in the act but in its constitutive parts, however, Augustine must address the sins of the dreaming mind, for example, and any other situations where the acts are never consummated. Matthews points here to the special role of the Inner Teacher in fostering a virtuous character and suggests that Augustine's inner-life ethics, as inaugurated by Jesus in the Sermon on the Mount, may be a fruitful approach to ethical theory.

In "Jesus and Aquinas," Brian Leftow argues for a significant, yet indirect, role for Christ in Thomas Aquinas's philosophy. Leftow takes as his starting point two fundamental premises that, when placed together, invite a Christian philosophy: first, that philosophy seeks truth, and second, that Jesus proclaimed, "I am the truth." In other words, if it is the job of philosophy to understand, explore, and expand upon knowledge in the realm of ultimate truth (that is, divine truth), and if God is the locus of such truth, then philosophers (knowingly or not) pursue divine truth.

Leftow contends that for Thomas, philosophy and faith don't just run parallel in pursuit of truth, but that faith, through revelation, completes the ascent toward truth where philosophy must fail. (Hence, we have the replacement of Aristotle's inadequate conception of God with the loving God as Father in Jesus.) Because, however, faith orients the questions philosophers pursue, philosophy still has a prominent role in explicating and comprehending the nature of the truths we are offered. Leftow draws a comparison between Thomas's method and the way that philosophers of science pursue scientific "facts": these philosophers begin with the data of science and provide philosophical explanations for them in the way that Thomas begins with revelation and provides philosophical explanations for the dicta of the faith. Leftow also explores Thomas's conceptions of human and divine singular reference in order to examine the complex relationship between God's knowledge of creation and God's causality. Leftow argues that Thomas understands God's causality in creation in a way that saves God's knowledge of evil without God's determination of evil, while saving human free agency and preventing God's knowledge of creation as dependent upon that creation.

In "The Epistemology of Jesus: An Initial Investigation," William Abraham identifies a number of problems surrounding the marriages between revelation and reason, theology and philosophy, and the divine and the human. Specifically, what, if anything, does Jesus have to do with epistemology? Attempts to incorporate the two present a particular paradox: if divine revelation dictates our epistemology, then we have no independent, nonarbitrary reasons for accepting one source of revelation over another. If, on the other hand, we allow reason to dictate our acceptance of revelation, we have placed the divine in the hands of the humane and the sacred in the hands of the profane.

Using Peter's confession of Jesus as Messiah from Mark's Gospel as his primary example, Abraham's solution to this paradox is to acknowledge, first, that we cannot begin any pursuit – theological, philosophical, or quotidian – without a tacit acceptance of the reliability of our current epistemic functions. We thus rely upon memory, sense perception, intuitions, reasoning capabilities, and so on, to pursue any task. However, no sophisticated task ends by christening our basic epistemic framework. Rather, experiences and new beliefs about those experiences force upon us a reevaluation of those epistemic foundations, thus clarifying our existing knowledge and expanding on that knowledge, often on the insistence of revelation's authority (in the case of the epistemology of theology). Hence, we may understand Peter's confession of Jesus as Messiah as founded on his antecedent beliefs about scripture, the redemption of Israel, and discipleship, as well as his natural reasoning capacities, all of which were further clarified and amplified by the diachronic experience of conversion and relationship with Jesus. Abraham concludes that this binary relationship between human cognitive capacities and divine revelation preserves human free agency and responsibility in light of God's assistance to us and his offer of fellowship to us.

In "Paul Ricouer: A Biblical Philosopher on Jesus," David F. Ford offers a comprehensive analysis of the Ricoeurian project with regard to Jesus and philosophy, specifically, a biblical philosophy. Ford argues that Ricouer, as a Christian philosopher, explores "all things" that revolve around the axis of *Logos*. Thus, his work, unlike Karl Barth's, is not specifically theological or doctrinal, but it does complement Christology insofar as all truths relate, ultimately, to God. Armed with the Prologue of John's Gospel, Ford analyzes the transformative process of the Spirit that accompanies the ambitious hermeneutical task of uncovering, exploring, and upending the texts that reveal Jesus as the "how much more" of God.

The approach in question seeks to marshal all available rational resources for the interpretative work of understanding and engaging the manifold metaphors, hyperboles, parables, narratives, and symbols of the scriptures and the resulting tradition. Because the aim of this approach is not directly theological, apologetics and doctrinal exposition are not the primary goals, and so it remains a philosophical enterprise that employs other disciplines. Still, this distinguishes Ricoeur from other philosophers in the Western tradition who have sharply divided faith and reason. By using this approach, however, Ricoeur aims to raise the possibilities of understanding truth – and the fullness of Jesus – beyond simply conventional and secular ways.

In "Jesus and Forgiveness," Nicholas Wolterstorff begins by examining two assertions by Hannah Arendt: first, that forgiveness plays a central role in human action by undoing the seemingly irreversible past, and second, that Jesus was the original advocate of forgiveness, especially in light of the backdrop of pagan antiquity and Jewish law. Wolterstorff argues that Arendt is mistaken in her view of what forgiveness accomplishes. Instead of "undoing" the past, forgiveness, when properly conceived, reconciles the victim with the wrongdoer by bridging the gap that the evil committed by the wrongdoer created. This is achieved through an act of love by the victim, not through an act of punishment. Forgiveness does not *forget*, for this would be tantamount to ignoring a moral judgment of an act as evil. Rather, forgiveness *foregoes* both resentment against the person who committed evil and also any claim to retribution that might restore a just balance. In this way, forgiveness entails an active component of love by requiring not only that a wrongdoer is shown mercy, but that the victim *do good* to the wrongdoer. Still, according to

Wolterstorff, Arendt was correct to identify Jesus as the principal discoverer of forgiveness in human action, because these characteristics of forgiveness that eschew retributive justice are unique to his "ethic of love." To make this apparent, Wolterstorff juxtaposes Jesus's understanding of forgiveness with the punishment-laden conceptions of mercy, clemency, and forgiveness as found in pagan figures such as Aristotle and Seneca. Wolterstorff concludes that these other notions of forgiveness preclude reconciliation, a key concept that Jesus's notion of forgiveness embraces.

In "Jesus Christ and the Meaning of Life," Charles Taliaferro contrasts three different standpoints with reference to the meaning of life: Christian theism, secular naturalism, and Thereavada Buddhism. It is sensible, Taliaferro claims, to seek to understand how any one of these metaphysical standpoints shapes and impacts questions about our activities, purposes, values, and beliefs. Taliaferro finds that though there may be many points of intersection between these three positions, there are radically different implications derived from each of them. Specifically, belief in Jesus Christ has immense normative significance in how we view our activities insofar as such belief both deepens their value and heightens our awareness of life's meaning.

Our internal states, especially our intentions and desires, affect in a subjective way that which we consider meaningful in life. However, Christian belief adds an external reference (in particular, the reality of the goodness of creation as a result of a loving and good Creator) that indicates that life itself is intrinsically meaningful *and* meaningful for God's purposes. Taliaferro takes this to mean *not* that our activities are only meaningful instrumentally, but that our activities take on a deeper dimension and that we are capable of rejoicing in this heightened metaphysical awareness of that meaning. Furthermore, the redemption that is found in relationship with Christ now becomes an integral answer to questions of life's meaning. This redemption is an invitation to be part of the Body of Christ, which Taliaferro believes includes five basic elements: cognition, intentions, a rite, an affective identification, and charity. Thus, the meaningfulness of one's activities depends in large measure on how these elements support or deny being a member of the Body of Christ.

PART ONE

JESUS IN HIS FIRST-CENTURY THOUGHT
CONTEXT

Jesus: Sources and Self-Understanding

Craig A. Evans

To come to any credible conclusion with respect to Jesus's self-understanding, one must have access to credible sources. Fortunately, such sources are available. Indeed, historians have a wealth of sources, whose great number poses almost as many problems as presents opportunities for productive critical research. The sources themselves must be critically sifted, following the canons recognized by historians in weighing the value of documents that survive from antiquity. Some of these canons are little more than common sense. Many of them are reflected in what Jesus researchers often refer to as the "criteria of authenticity."[1]

The aim of the present chapter is twofold: (1) to identify and assess the sources that purport to impart information about the historical Jesus, and (2) to deduce from the most reliable sources what the historian can know about how Jesus understood himself and his mission.

SOURCES FOR THE STUDY OF THE HISTORICAL JESUS

The late antique sources for Jesus fall into three categories: Christian, Jewish, and pagan. It is not always easy to decide which sources belong in which category. For example, although many scholars readily assign Gnostic writings

---

[1] The criteria of authenticity in Jesus research have been discussed in many studies. For very recent and judicious assessments, see J. P. Meier, *A Marginal Jew: Rethinking the Historical Jesus*. Vol. 1: *The Roots of the Problem and the Person* (ABRL; New York: Doubleday, 1991), 167–95; S. E. Porter, *The Criteria for Authenticity in Historical-Jesus Research: Previous Discussion and New Proposals* (JSNTSup 191; Sheffield: Sheffield Academic Press, 2000); and G. Theissen and D. Winter, *The Quest for the Plausible Jesus: The Question of Criteria* (Louisville: Westminster John Knox Press, 2002). The criteria are itemized, with a bibliography, in C. A. Evans, *Life of Jesus Research: An Annotated Bibliography* (NTTS 24; Leiden: Brill, 1996), 127–46.

to Christianity, I am inclined to assign most of them to paganism (more on this later). Moreover, there is some overlap between the Christian and Jewish categories, in that many early Christian sources also derive from Jewish authors and faith communities.

Christian Sources

As one would expect, the Christian sources are the most numerous. These comprise mainly the New Testament writings themselves, the most important being the Gospels of Matthew, Mark, Luke, and John. In some of his letters Paul refers to sayings of Jesus, though scholars are not always sure if the apostle is referring to public words of the historical Jesus or to private revelation.[2] There are a few other references here or there, as in 2 Peter 1:16–18, in reference to the Transfiguration. The letter attributed to James, "the Lord's brother" (Gal. 1:19), is replete with echoes of Jesus's teaching. Jude is yet another letter that is claimed to have been written by a brother of Jesus.[3]

Outside the New Testament there are several early Christian writings, some of them classified as the Apostolic Fathers. Preeminent among them is the *Didache*, which, as its names implies, has preserved a significant body of Jesus's teachings, whose relationship to the Synoptic tradition is not clear. We may have here a very early collection, at points independent from the literary sources used by the evangelists.[4] Closely related are the fragmentary remains of several Jewish-Christian – or Ebionite – Gospels, whose distinctive traditions bear an uncertain relationship to the Synoptics (esp. Matthew).[5]

We also have fragments of various harmonies and lost Gospels.[6] Among these one of the most interesting is the Oxyrhynchus Papyrus 840, which

---

[2] See J. D. G. Dunn, "Jesus Tradition in Paul," in *Studying the Historical Jesus: Evaluations of the State of Current Research*, eds. B. D. Chilton and C. A. Evans (NTTS 19; Leiden: Brill, 1994), 155–78.

[3] Recent scholarship shows greater openness to understanding James and Jude as authentic letters of the brothers of Jesus. See W. F. Brosend II, *James and Jude* (New Cambridge Bible Commentary; New York: Cambridge University Press, 2004); P. H. Davids, "Palestinian Traditions in the Epistle of James," in *James the Just and Christian Origins*, eds. B. D. Chilton and C. A. Evans (NovTSup 98; Leiden: Brill, 1999), 33–57; L. T. Johnson, *The Letter of James* (AB 37A; Garden City: Doubleday, 1995).

[4] See K. Niederwimmer, *The Didache* (Hermeneia; Minneapolis: Fortress, 1998); H. van de Sandt and D. Flusser, *The Didache: Its Jewish Sources and its Place in Early Judaism and Christianity* (CRINT 3.5; Assen: Van Gorcum; Minneapolis: Fortress, 2002).

[5] See C. A. Evans, "The Jewish Christian Gospel Tradition," in *Jewish Believers in Jesus: The Early Centuries*, eds. O. Skarsaune and R. Hvalvik (Peabody: Hendrickson, 2007), 241–77.

[6] The most important material is gathered in D. Lürhmann, with E. Schlarb, *Fragmente apokryph gewordener Evangelien in griechischer und lateinischer Sprache* (MTS 59; Marburg: N. G. Elwert, 2000).

narrates a dispute between Jesus and the ruling priest in the temple precincts. The Syrian church produced several writings, many of them focused on the disciple Thomas. Best known among these is the Gospel of Thomas, of which three Greek fragments and a complete Coptic translation were found in Egypt. Familiar with Tatian's *Diatessaron* (written c. 175) and other distinctively Syrian traditions, *Thomas* probably cannot be dated earlier than the end of the second century.[7] Notwithstanding this preponderance of evidence for a late date, some scholars – notably those associated with the Jesus Seminar – argue for a much earlier date, even assigning imagined "versions" of *Thomas* to the middle of the first century. This uncritical view is now widely challenged.

Other Christian Gospels are far more dubious. First, Papyrus Egerton 2, which should be dated to the middle of the second century, is probably an early example of a Gospel harmony. Attempts to date this document to the middle of the first century, independent of the Synoptic Gospels, are not persuasive.[8] Second, the Akhmîm Gospel fragment, which many scholars assume is the Gospel of Peter mentioned at the beginning of the third century by Bishop Serapion, is probably a much later Byzantine text.[9] In any case, its fantastic details (such as the talking cross that exits the tomb with the risen Jesus, whose head reaches above the heavens) argue for a date no earlier than the third or fourth century.[10] And finally, the so-called Secret Gospel of Mark, allegedly discovered by Morton Smith at the Mar Saba monastery in the

---

[7] N. Perrin, *Thomas and Tatian: The Relationship between the Gospel of Thomas and the Diatessaron* (Academia Biblica 5; Atlanta: Society of Biblical Literature, 2002); ibid., "NHC II, 2 and the Oxyrhynchus Fragments (P.Oxy 1, 654, 655): Overlooked Evidence for a Syriac *Gospel of Thomas*," *VC* 58 (2004), 138–51.

[8] One of the fragmentary stories in Papyrus Egerton 2 resembles a fantastic story in the *Infancy Gospel of Thomas* (no earlier than the end of the second century), where we are told of the boy Jesus who sowed a handful of seed that yielded a remarkable harvest (*Infan. Thom.* 10:1–2 [Latin version]).

[9] As is pointed out by P. Foster, "Are there any Early Fragments of the So-Called *Gospel of Peter*?" *NTS* 52 (2006), 1–28.

[10] Many scholars have concluded that the Akhmîm Gospel fragment presupposes most if not all of the New Testament Gospels. On this point, see K. Beyschlag, "Das Petrusevangelium," in *Die verborgene Überlieferung von Christus* (Munich and Hamburg: Siebenstern Taschenbuch, 1969), 27–64; and É. Massaux, *The Influence of the Gospel of Saint Matthew on Christian Literature before Saint Irenaeus*, ed. A. J. Bellinzoni (3 vols., NGS 5.1–3; Macon: Mercer University Press, 1990–93), 2:202–14. On the lateness of the fantastic details in the Akhmîm Gospel fragment, see C. L. Quarles, "The Gospel of Peter: Does It Contain a Precanonical Resurrection Narrative?" in *The Resurrection of Jesus: John Dominic Crossan and N. T. Wright in Dialogue*, ed. R. B. Stewart (Minneapolis: Fortress Press, 2006), 106–20. Quarles rightly concludes that this Gospel fragment (whether or not it really is the *Gospel of Peter*) does not contain a precanonical resurrection narrative.

Judean desert in 1958,[11] has been convincingly shown to be the work of Smith himself.[12]

There are several other late, fanciful works, such as the *Infancy Gospel*, the *Protevangelium of James* (which tells of the miraculous birth of Mary, her upbringing, and betrothal of Joseph), the *Acts of Pilate* (which among other things tells of Christ's descent into and triumph over Hell), and others.[13] These writings tell us much about popular piety and imagination in the second to fourth centuries; they tell us nothing about the historical Jesus and his self-understanding.

Jewish Sources

These include the various versions of Josephus and early rabbinic traditions. Because none of the rabbinic tradition regarding Jesus can with confidence be dated before the third century, it really has nothing of historical significance to offer.[14] Josephus, the first-century Jewish historian and apologist, is another matter.

Josephus mentions Jesus twice in his 20-volume work *Jewish Antiquities*. One passage concerns James, the brother of "Jesus called Christ" (*Ant.* 20.200). Although this passage provides useful information about James (i.e., the year

[11] For an account of the "discovery" of the Clementine letter containing the quotations of *Secret Mark*, along with text, notes, and commentary, see M. Smith, *Clement of Alexandria and a Secret Gospel of Mark* (Cambridge, MA: Harvard University Press, 1973); ibid., *The Secret Gospel: The Discovery and Interpretation of the Secret Gospel according to Mark* (New York: Harper & Row, 1973).

[12] Smith's hoax has been exposed beyond reasonable doubt through analysis of the handwriting, parallels with a popular mystery novel, Smith's knowledge of the distinctive elements of the text prior to the disovery of the text, and a myriad of other clues Smith playfully planted in the text. See S. C. Carlson, *The Gospel Hoax: Morton Smith's Invention of Secret Mark* (Waco, TX: Baylor University Press, 2005); P. Jeffrey, *The Secret Gospel of Mark Unveiled: Imagined Rituals of Sex, Death, and Madness in a Biblical Forgery* (New Haven: Yale University Press, 2007).

[13] These writings are conveniently gathered in J. K. Elliott, *The Apocryphal New Testament: A Collection of Apocryphal Christian Literature in an English Translation based on M. R. James* (Oxford: Clarendon Press, 1993); ibid., *The Apocryphal Jesus: Legends of the Early Church* (Oxford: Oxford University Press, 1996); W. Schneemelcher, ed., *New Testament Apocrypha. Volume One: Gospels and Related Writings* (rev. ed., Cambridge: James Clarke; Louisville: Westminster/John Knox Press, 1991).

[14] These traditions have been carefully assessed in R. T. Herford, *Christianity in Talmud and Midrash* (London: Williams and Norgate, 1903; repr., New York: Ktav, 1975); M. Goldstein, *Jesus in the Jewish Tradition* (New York: Macmillan, 1950); J. Maier, *Jesus von Nazareth in der talmudischen Überlieferung* (ErFor 82; Darmstadt: Wissenschaftliche Buchgesellschaft, 1978); G. Twelftree, "Jesus in Jewish Traditions," in *The Jesus Tradition Outside the Gospels*, ed. D. Wenham (Gospel Perspectives 5; Sheffield: JSOT Press, 1985), 289–342.

of his death, that he was regarded as a "lawbreaker"), it tells us nothing about Jesus. Of course, it does provide us with non-Christian attestation that Jesus had a brother named James. However, the second passage provides important corroboration of the main outline of Jesus's ministry, arrest, and execution, because these elements are found in the New Testament Gospels. The passage reads (*Ant.* 18.63–64):

> At this time there appeared Jesus, a wise man, *if indeed one ought to call him a man.* For he was a doer of amazing deeds, a teacher of persons who receive truth with pleasure. He won over many Jews and many of the Greeks. *He was the Messiah.* And when Pilate condemned him to the cross, the leading men among us having accused him, those who loved him from the first did not cease to do so. *For he appeared to them the third day alive again, the divine prophets having spoken these things and a myriad of other marvels concerning him.* And to the present the tribe of Christians, named after this person, has not disappeared.

The words placed in italics are widely recognized as Christian interpolations. The remainder of the passage, however, reflects the style and vocabulary of Josephus and coheres with the narrative context.[15] What we have here is likely independent of the New Testament Gospel narratives, yet like them, Josephus's account speaks of Jesus as teacher and wonderworker, accused by "the leading men" (i.e., the ruling priests) and handed over to Pilate, who condemns him to the cross. The testimony of Josephus tells strongly against claims made from time to time that the story of Jesus's being accused by Jewish ruling priests is a fiction produced by the New Testament evangelists in an attempt to shift blame for Jesus's death away from the Roman authority to the Jewish leaders.

There are additional passages in Josephus that refer to Jesus, to John the Baptist, and to other details related in one way or another in the New Testament Gospels. But these additional passages are found in the Slavonic version of *Jewish War* and in a Hebrew version of Josephus called the *Josippon.*[16] None of this material is early or of historical worth.

[15] See T. W. Manson, "The Life of Jesus: A Study of the Available Materials," *ExpTim* 53 (1942), 248–51; repr. in Manson, *Studies in the Gospels and Epistles,* ed. M. Black (Manchester: Manchester University Press, 1962), 13–27, cf. esp. 18–19: "It is difficult to imagine what sort of Christian could have deemed it woth his while to interpolate this cool, objective, patronising, and faintly contemptuous paragraph into the text of Josephus." For a more recent study, which supports the position taken here, see J. P. Meier, "Jesus in Josephus: A Modest Proposal," *CBQ* 52 (1990), 76–103.

[16] See D. Flusser, "Josippon, a Medieval Hebrew Version of Josephus," in *Josephus, Judaism, and Christianity,* eds. L. H. Feldman and G. Hata (Detroit: Wayne State University Press, 1987), 386–97.

Pagan Sources

Jesus is mentioned a few times in Greco-Roman sources. Julius Africanus (early third century) refers to one Thallus, who mentions the darkness at the time of Jesus's death (*Chronography* frag. 18). Mara bar Serapion (late first/early second century?) refers to Jesus as the wise king of the Jewish people (*bar Serapion's letter to his son*). Suetonius (c. 110) refers to the name *Chrestus*, by which he probably means Christ (*Claudius* 25.4), but he tells us nothing more. Pliny the Younger, governor of Bithynia, writes to Emperor Trajan (c. 110), saying that Christians sing hymns to "Christ as to a god" (*Epistles* 10.96). Tacitus (c. 112) explains: "Christus, the author of their name, had suffered the death penalty during the reign of Tiberius, by sentence of the procurator Pontius Pilate" (*Annals* 15.44). Celsus provides a series of slanders and distorted traditions in his polemic against Christianity (*apud* Origen, *Contra Celsum*). Justin Martyr quotes Trypho the Jew (c. 160), who describes Jesus as a "magician and deceiver of the people" (*Dialogue with Trypho* 69.7). Lucian of Samosata (c. 160) mockingly describes Christians as a people who worship "that crucified sophist" (*Peregrinus* 13), even "the man who was cruficied in Palestine" (*Peregrinus* 11). Some of this material contains a modicum of importance, but it adds nothing to what we have in the New Testament Gospels.

Finally, we have several Gnostic writings, many of them called "gospels" or "secret books." Here I have in mind especially the *Gospel of Philip*, the *Gospel of Mary*, and the recently published *Gospel of Judas*. It has become fashionable in some scholarly circles to refer to these writings as Christian and to claim that the various communities that stood behind them are lost "Christianities."[17] I think this is inaccurate and misleading. These writings reject the cardinal teaching of the early Christian movement, which firmly maintained that salvation was achieved through Jesus's death. Gnostics, however, taught that salvation was acquired through knowledge (*gnosis*) and that Jesus's death either did not take place at all (e.g., someone else died) or was nothing more than the means by which Jesus escaped the physical world to return to the heavenly world of light above. Gnosticism is nothing more than a form of paganism that adopted elements of the Christian story.[18]

---

[17] As seen, for example, in B. D. Ehrman, *Lost Christianities: The Battles for Scripture and the Faiths We Never Knew* (Oxford and New York: Oxford University Press, 2003). The "lost Christianities," of which Ehrman speaks, are various pagans and pagan movements in the second and third centuries that made use of aspects of Christian thought and the story of Jesus. Ehrman's work is marred by anachronism and confusion of categories.

[18] For survey and assessments of Jesus tradition outside Christianity, see C. A. Evans, "Jesus in non-Christian Sources," in *Studying the Historical Jesus*, eds. Chilton and Evans, 443–78;

After review of all of the material that is available, we may ask what is the earliest, most reliable, and most important for historical research? The overwhelming majority of New Testament scholars, as well as historians of late antiquity, have concluded that the New Testament writings, particularly the Gospels, are the best historical sources that we have.

In a recent study Martin Hengel has assessed the witnesses to the life of Jesus outside the New Testament Gospels.[19] He reviews Christian witnesses, such as Paul, Acts, Hebrews, 1 *Clement*, and James. He reviews non-Christian witnesses, such as Josephus, Tacitus, Pliny the Younger, Suetonius, Lucian of Samosata, Mara bar Serapion, and others. Hengel rightly concludes that the best historical sources available today are those that early Chrsitians wisely recognized and preserved, namely, the Gospels of Matthew, Mark, Luke, and John. Other sources have value, to be sure, and in some cases offer important corroboration. But the New Testament Gospels are by far the oldest and most reliable materials that we have.

JESUS'S SELF-UNDERSTANDING

Jesus wrote nothing. He left behind no journal, in which he might have revealed his thoughts, plans, and hopes. The mind of Jesus, or his self-understanding, must be inferred from his actions, his teachings, and his impact and influence on others. We must also recognize that by speaking of "self-understanding" we are not speaking of the *psychology* or *mental state* of Jesus. In a certain sense Rudolf Bultmann's famous dictum "We know basically nothing of his personality"[20] is quite correct. We can know nothing of Jesus's inner life and personality. Quests for a psychologically understood Jesus were misguided and were without hope of success.[21]

But there is reasonable hope for recovering the aims or purpose of Jesus and, to a limited degree, facets of his self-understanding. Did he see himself

---

R. E. Van Voorst, *Jesus Outside the New Testament: An Introduction to the Ancient Evidence* (Studying the Historical Jesus; Grand Rapids: Eerdmans, 2000).

[19] M. Hengel, "Jesuszeugnisse ausserhalb der Evangelien," in *Testimony and Interpretation: Early Christology in Its Judeo-Hellenistic Milieu. Studies in Honor of Petr Pokorný*, eds. J. Mrázek and J. Roskovec (LNTS 272; London and New York: T & T Clark, 2004), 143–58. Hengel comments that given the impressive testimony to the historicity of Jesus in early and diverse non-Christian writings, the radical skepticism of persons such as Bruno Bauer (i.e., to the effect that Jesus was not a historical personage) is wholly without justification.

[20] R. Bultmann, *Jesus* (Berlin: Deutsche Bibliothek, 1926), 12: "wir so gut wie nichts über seine Persönlichkeit wissen." See also the ET *Jesus and the Word* (New York: Scribner's Sons, 1934), 9.

[21] Albert Schweitzer was rightly critical of the romantic and psychologizing interpretations of Jesus, yet his own assessment attempted the same thing. See A. Schweitzer, *The Quest of the Historical Jesus* (New York: Macmillan, 1968), 350–97.

as an eschatological prophet? Or as Israel's Messiah? Or in some sense as God's Son? Did he anticipate his death in Jerusalem, and if he did, how did he understand it? Did he anticipate his resurrection, and if so, when did he think he would be raised up? In three days or perhaps in the time of Judgment? Our sources are such that it is possible to find reasonably supported, even compelling answers to these questions.

In his influential book *Jesus and Judaism*, E. P. Sanders identified eight facts or activities about which we may be relatively confident. They are as follows:

1. Jesus was baptized by John the Baptist.
2. Jesus was a Galilean who preached and healed.
3. Jesus called disciples and spoke of there being twelve.
4. Jesus confined his activity to Israel.
5. Jesus engaged in a controversy about the Temple.
6. Jesus was crucified outside Jerusalem by the Roman authorities.
7. After Jesus's death his followers continued as an identifiable movement.
8. At least some Jews persecuted at least parts of the new movement (Gal. 1:13, 22; Phil. 3:6), and it appears that this persecution endured at least to a time near the end of Paul's career (2 Cor. 11:24; Gal. 5:11, 6:12; cf. Matt. 23:34, 10:17).[22]

In his later, less technical work *The Historical Figure of Jesus*,[23] Sanders enumerates several other highly probable facts:

1. Jesus was born c. 4 BCE, at the approximate time of the death of Herod the Great.
2. Jesus grew up in Nazareth of Galilee.
3. Although Jesus taught in small villages and towns, he seems to have avoided cities.
4. Jesus ate a final meal with his disciples.
5. Jesus was arrested and interrogated by Jewish authorities, apparently by orders of the High Priest.
6. Although they abandoned Jesus after his arrest, the disciples later "saw" him after his death. This led the disciples to the belief that Jesus would return and found the kingdom.[24]

---

[22] E. P. Sanders, *Jesus and Judaism* (London: SCM Press; Philadelphia: Fortress, 1985), 11.

[23] E. P. Sanders, *The Historical Figure of Jesus* (London and New York: Penguin, 1993).

[24] For a helpful tabulation that compares the "almost indisputable facts" given by Sanders in his two books, see M. A. Powell, *Jesus as a Figure in History* (Louisville: Westminster John Knox Press, 1998), 117.

I am in essential agreement with Sanders, both with regard to this list and with regard to his emphasis on events and activities. Of course, Sanders has been criticized for giving priority to *facts*, as opposed to the *sayings* of Jesus, which is where most studies traditionally have begun.[25] I am not, however, impressed by this criticism; I believe that it is prudent historical procedure to attempt the construction of the basic framework, even sequence of events (as limited as that may be), in the light of which Jesus's teachings and practices should be studied. It is in the context of this framework that important insights into Jesus's self-understanding will be gained. The most important may now be considered briefly.

Baptism at the hands of John the Baptist and the appointment of the Twelve (Mk. 1.9–11; Matt. 3:13–17; Lk. 3:21–22; cf. Jn. 1:29–34). What does Jesus's baptism at the hands of John tell us about Jesus's self-understanding? At the very least it implies that Jesus was in essential agreement with the Baptist's agenda, an agenda that seems to have the restoration of Israel as its goal (through repentance and preparation for eschatological judgment). John's reference to "these stones" from which God is able to raise up sons to Abraham (Matt. 3:9 = Lk. 3:8) alludes to the twelve stones placed beside the Jordan River when the twelve tribes prepared to cross the river and enter the promised land (cf. Josh. 4:7). When Jesus himself subsequently appointed twelve apostles (Mk. 3:14; 6:7; cf. 1 Cor. 15:5) and spoke of the apostles judging the twelve tribes of Israel (Matt. 19:30 = Lk. 22:28–30), we have a continuation and development of this typology.

The proclamation of the rule of God (Mk. 1:14–15; Matt. 4:12–17). Consistent with John's ministry of restoration and the symbolism of the twelve employed by Jesus is the proclamation of the rule (or "kingdom") of God. His proclamation of God's rule as the "good news," as "fulfilled," and as "at hand" is consistent with his recognition as a prophet. It is also consistent with the theme of Isaiah 61 ("the Lord has anointed me to proclaim good news"), to which Jesus alludes in a tradition that surely is authentic (cf. Matt. 11:4–5 = Lk. 7:22).[26] Influence of Isaiah's theology is witnessed throughout Jesus's ministry:

---

[25] See Sanders, *Jesus and Judaism*, 10–22.

[26] Occurrences of "good news" or "gospel" are found in the second half of Isaiah. There are five passages in all (Isa. 40:1–11; 41:21–29; 52:7–12; 60:1–7; 61:1–11). The summary in Mark 1:15 betrays significant points of dictional coherence with the Aramaic paraphrase of some of these passages from Isaiah. In *Tg.* Isaiah 40:9 we read, "*The kingdom of* your God *is revealed!*" instead of "Here is your God!" Again, in *Tg.* Isa 52:7 we read, "*The kingdom of* your God *is revealed*" instead of "Your God reigns." The italicized words indicate the places where the Aramaic departs from the Hebrew. The Aramaic diction approximates the gist of Jesus's proclamation: "The time is fulfilled, the kingdom of God is at hand; repent, and believe in the good news."

the provision of food (Mk. 6:35–44; 8:1–10; cf. Isa. 25:6), healing (Mk. 1:29–31, 32–34, 40–45; 2:1–12; 3:1–6; cf. Isa. 35:5–6; 61:1–2), and even raising the dead (Mk. 5:35–43; Lk. 7:11–17; cf. Isa. 26:19). Although how much of this tradition derives from the actual activities of Jesus is debated, the contribution of Isaiah can hardly be gainsaid. An orientation toward Isaiah strongly suggests that Jesus understood his message and mission in terms of national restoration. The allusions and appeals to Isaiah 61, which speaks of one anointed by the Spirit of God, strongly suggest that Jesus understood himself as Israel's Messiah or one anointed by God. Although highly formulaic, Peter's confession of Jesus as Messiah (Mk. 8:27–30) should be viewed as an authentic fragment of this tradition. Jesus understood himself as Israel's Messiah, and his closest disciples recognized and encouraged this understanding.

Exorcisms and healings (e.g., Mk. 1:21–28, 32–34; Lk. 11:14–23). Any fair reading of the Gospels and other ancient sources (including Josephus)[27] inexorably leads to the conclusion that Jesus was well known in his time as a healer and exorcist. Historians need not be distracted by scientific and philosophical questions that inquire into the exact nature of these events. It is sufficient for historians to conclude that Jesus engaged in activities that led his contemporaries to view him as a healer and exorcist. Many scholars in recent years have adopted this view.[28]

What is especially significant in this context is that in his reply to those who have charged him with being in league with Satan (cf. Mk. 3:27), Jesus understands himself as one who has bound Satan (the "strong man" of the parable) and sacked his house. The claim is extraordinary. Combined with with his ubiquitous self-reference as the "son of man" (e.g., Mk. 2:28; 14:21, 41, 62), which unmistakably alludes to the vision of Dan 7:13–14, Jesus evidently understood himself as authorized by God himself to announce the rule of God and exercise "authority on earth" (cf. Mk. 2:10) in a variety of tasks, such as forgiving sins, making legal pronouncements (e.g., regarding what can and cannot be done on the Sabbath, what is clean), healing, cleansing, casting out unclean spirits, and, in general terms, redeeming and restoring Israel. Jesus understood himself as none other than the "one like a human being" (the meaning of "one like a son of man") described in Daniel 7, to whom kingly power and authority were given by God himself and to whom

---

[27] In the part of the so-called *Testimonium Flavianum* most scholars regard as authentic, Josephus describes Jesus as a "doer of amazing deeds [*paradoxon ergon poietes*]" (*Ant.* 18.63).

[28] Among others, see B. F. Meyer, *The Aims of Jesus* (London: SCM Press, 1979), 155; Sanders, *Jesus and Judaism*, 166; J. D. Crossan, *The Historical Jesus: The Life of a Jewish Mediterranean Peasant* (San Francisco: HarperCollins, 1991), 318–19; G. Twelftree, *Jesus the Exorcist: A Contribution to the Study of the Historical Jesus* (WUNT 2.54; Tübingen: Mohr [Siebeck], 1993), 98–113.

the nations would be obedient. This observation complements what was said earlier about Jesus's messianic self-understanding (and also what will be said in what follows).

One should also take into consideration the intriguing statements in which Jesus speaks as the incarnation of divine Wisdom.[29] We hear this when he says (Matt. 11:28–30):

> Come to me all who labor and are heavy laden, and I will give you rest. Take my yoke upon you, and learn from me; for I am gentle and lowly in heart, and you will find rest for your souls. For my yoke is easy, and my burden is light.

We hear it again when Jesus describes himself as "something greater than Solomon" (Matt. 12:42). It may also be implied, such as when the blind beggar appeals to Jesus: "Son of David, have mercy on me!" (Mk. 10:47, 48). As "son of David," Jesus functions as Solomon, David's famous son and successor, who possesses the wisdom and power to heal.

"I am; and you will see the Son of man seated at the right hand of Power, and coming with the clouds of heaven" (Mk. 14:62). Jesus affirms the high priest's question "Are you the Messiah, the Son of the Blessed [God]?" (Mk. 14:61). Although some skeptical critics doubt the historicity of this tradition, the crucifixion of Jesus as "king of the Jews" (Mk. 15:18, 26) lends important circumstantial support. From a religious perspective Jews viewed their true king (what Roman authority called the "king of the Jews") as the Messiah, Son of God.[30] The universal view among the followers of Jesus, in the post-Easter setting, that Jesus was the Messiah argues strongly for this view. It argues, moreover, that Jesus was recognized as the Messiah by his disciples (as in Mk. 8:27–30) before Easter and that the Resurrection was not the cause of the confession of Jesus as Messiah. The Resurrection – as amazing and

---

[29] This theme is pursued in detail in B. Witherington, *Jesus the Sage: The Pilgrimage of Wisdom* (Minneapolis: Fortress, 1994).

[30] At the prompting of Marcus Antonius the Roman Senate, and later emperor Augustus, recognized Herod the Great as "king of the Jews," or "king of Judea" (Josephus, *Ant.* 14.9, 280; 15.409; cf. *J.W.* 1.282–85). In the New Testament Gospels only Romans call Jesus "king of the Jews." In contrast, the mocking priests call Jesus "king of Israel" (Mk. 15:31–32). Christians, however, regarded Jesus as the Messiah, the Son of God, and never call him "king of the Jews." In view of these considerations I have to agree with the majority of scholars who accept the *titulus* and its wording as historical and genuine. G. Schneider, "The Political Charge," in *Jesus and the Politics of His Day*, eds. E. Bammel and C. F. D. Moule (Cambridge: Cambridge University Press, 1984), 403–14. On p. 403 Schneider comments that the *titulus* is "historically unimpeachable." So also E. Bammel, "The *titulus*," in *Jesus and the Politics of His Day*, eds. Bammel and Moule, 353–64. On p. 363 Bammel concludes that the "wording of the *titulus* as it is reported in the Gospels is in all likelihood authentic."

unexpected as it was – would not in itself have generated recognition of Jesus as the Messiah, unless that idea had taken hold in Jesus and his movement prior to Easter.

"This is my blood of the covenant, which is poured out for many" (Mk. 14:22–25). In his final meal with his disciples, which left an indelible imprint on the collective memory of his earliest followers, Jesus spoke of the coming of the kingdom and of "blood of the covenant." The full passage reads (Mk. 14:22–25):

> And as they were eating, he took bread, and blessed, and broke it, and gave it to them, and said, "Take; this is my body." And he took a cup, and when he had given thanks he gave it to them, and they all drank of it. And he said to them, "This is my blood of the covenant, which is poured out for many. Truly, I say to you, I shall not drink again of the fruit of the vine until that day when I drink it new in the kingdom of God."[31]

Although Jesus's understanding that his death would benefit his people is not without parallel in the traditions of the Jewish martyrs (among them especially the Maccabean martyrs),[32] his language, in which the shedding of his blood is compared to God's covenant with Israel (Exod. 24:8) and the promise of a new covenant (Jer. 31:31), is extraordinary. This extraordinary element is compounded with the phrase "which is poured out for many" (Mk. 14:24). Jesus appears to have alluded to Leviticus 8:15, where Moses "poured out the blood" of the sacrificial animal,[33] and to Isaiah 53:12, where the Servant of the Lord "poured out his soul to death . . . bore the sins of many, and made intercession for the transgressors."

These scriptural allusions suggest that Jesus understood his death in sacrificial terms, as inaugurating the promised new covenant whereby sinners may be forgiven.[34] Jesus saw himself not only as the Messiah, or Anointed One of

---

[31] In the parallels in Luke 22:20 and 1 Corinthians 11:25 the words are "new covenant in my blood."

[32] Eleazar, brother of Judas Maccabeus, "gave himself to save his people and to win for himself an everlasting name" (1 Macc. 6:44). For more examples, see 2 Maccabees 7:33, 37–38; Pseudo-Philo, *Bib. Ant.* 18:5; and *T. Moses* 9:6b–10:1. The latter is especially interesting, for following the death of the righteous priest and his sons the kingdom of God will arise and Satan "will have an end" (cf. Mk. 3:26: "And if Satan has risen up against himself and is divided, he cannot stand, but has an end").

[33] See also the interesting parallel in Sirach 50:15, where the "blood of the grape" is poured out. Recall that Jesus compared his blood to the *wine* of the Last Supper.

[34] In my view, Jesus anticipated his death some time before he spoke the Words of Institution at the Last Supper. This anticipation is preserved in the tradition as the so-called Passion Predictions, the first of which the Markan evangelist places at the midpoint of his narrative (i.e., at 8:31; cf. 9:31; 10:33–34). Although these Passion Predictions have been edited, multiplied,

the Lord, who as the figure described in the vision of Daniel 7 was invested with divine authority, but as the agent whose suffering would provide atonement and redemption for God's people. This teaching, and not the mere fact of Jesus's brutal execution, on the one hand, or the astounding event of the Resurrection, on the other, is what gave rise to early Christianity's interest in the meaning of Jesus's death (such as seen in the book of Hebrews).

CONCLUSION

Historians have at their disposal a wealth of source material, a good portion of it quite reliable, from which they may construct a reasonable portrait of the activities and teaching of Jesus of Nazareth, from the time he became a public figure to his death and what his disciples proclaimed about him after his death. From these activities and this teaching, the historian may deduce the aims of Jesus and, further, his self-understanding.

Consideration of these materials leads to a series of conclusions that may be stated in descending probability: First, it is virtually certain that Jesus was associated with John the Baptist and shared his vision of Israel's restoration and redemption. Second, it is virtually certain that Jesus proclaimed the rule of God as the power by which Israel's redemption would come about. Linked closely to this proclamation is the strong probability that Jesus demonstrated the truth of his proclamation of God's rule through works of power. Third, it is highly probable that Jesus understood himself as more than merely a proclaimer of God's rule and Israel's redemption. His remarkable pronouncements, his self-reference as "son of man," his surprising claims of authority, and his remarkable deeds strongly suggest that Jesus understood himself not simply as a prophet but as an eschatological agent through whom God was achieving his will on earth (as it had already been achieved "in heaven"). Given the post-Easter Church's universal proclamation of Jesus as Messiah, Son of God, and Savior, it is probable that the pre-Easter Jesus had understood himself and allowed his disciples to conclude that he was indeed Israel's Messiah and God's Son. Fourth, it is also probable that Jesus anticipated his death and sought to interpret the significance of his death. It seems that he understood this death in sacrificial terms, implying that Israel (and, in turn,

and predated to an earlier stage in the ministry, it is probable that Jesus in fact anticipated his death and spoke of it. Moreover, it is also probable that he tried to reassure his disciples by appealing to Hosea 6:2, when he spoke of being raised up "on the third day." For more on this, see C. A. Evans, "Did Jesus Predict His Death and Resurrection?" in *Resurrection*, eds. S. E. Porter, M. A. Hayes, and D. Tombs (JSNTSup 186; Sheffield: Sheffield Academic Press, 1999), 82–97.

Gentiles) would benefit through his death. His death would provide for the awaited new covenant, on the basis of which redemption could take place.

These aspects of Jesus's self-understanding, which here have been assessed with varying degrees of probability, enjoy the support of the criterion of outcome. That is, these aspects of Jesus's self-understanding explain the emergence of Christology as we find it in the New Testament writings. The universal confession that Jesus was the Messiah, the Son of God, and the world's Savior, whose death on the cross makes atonement for human sin possible has its roots in the teaching and activities of Jesus. To be sure, in the passage of time this early Christology would expand and gain further nuances (as, for example, we see in Trinitarian theology and its implications for Christology). But its essential elements, which are closely tied to Jesus's self-understanding, had their origin in the pre-Easter Jesus.

2

ॐ

Sipping from the Cup of Wisdom

James L. Crenshaw

Biblical sages never asked the question that is arguably the most divisive of all intellectual queries: "Does Being exist?" With one possible exception, the sayings of a non-Israelite named Agur in Proverbs 30:1–14, they joined their ancient Near Eastern counterparts in taking the existence of a supreme power as a given.[1] Indeed, the intelligentsia in Egypt and Mesopotamia assumed that a host of lesser gods made up a pantheon, which modern scholars identify as a Divine Council. Biblical wise men appear to have found this understanding of reality acceptable, for the prologue to the book of Job describes such an assembly of gods. In this regard, the sages merely adopted the prevailing views of the day, like the unknown author of Genesis 6:1–4, who mentions lustful sons of God who descended to earth and cohabited with women.

The belief in heavenly beings who functioned as a royal court occurs in several biblical texts and often reinforces ethical ideals, as in Deuteronomy 32:8 and Psalm 82, which allude to patron gods of the nations and their abdication of responsibility to maintain justice on earth. Other references to the Divine Council involve a semi-Platonic notion of events in heaven that are subsequently enacted on earth (1 Kgs. 22:19), add drama to a prophetic vision involving a chilling vocation (Isa. 6:1–13), or convey a sense of grandeur to the description of Yahweh as creator and savior (Isa. 40–55). The few

---

[1] The initial remark by Agur, *le'iti'el le'iti'el we'ukāl*, has been understood as an expression of exhaustion spoken to an individual whose name was Ithiel and as a denial of theism that robbed the speaker of ability. Scholars disagree about the language, whether Hebrew or Aramaic, and tend to view the extent of the literary unit as either minimal (verses 1–4) or maximal (verses 1–14). They also question the integrity of the unit, sometimes recognizing an internal debate between a skeptic and a dogmatist. The possibilities are examined in James L. Crenshaw, "Clanging Symbols," in *Justice and the Holy*, eds. Douglas A. Knight and Peter J. Paris (Philadelphia: Fortress Press, 1989), 51–64, reprinted in James L. Crenshaw, *Urgent Advice and Probing Questions: Collected Writings on Old Testament Wisdom* (Macon, GA: Mercer University Press, 1995), 371–82.

dissidents who are mentioned in the book of Psalms become objects of ridicule for their lack of faith and are burdened with the label "Fool" (Pss. 14:1 and 53:1) even when divine silence encourages such radical thoughts (Ps. 10:4, 11).

Now if the authors of canonical wisdom – Proverbs, Ecclesiastes, Job, Sirach [Ecclesiasticus], and Wisdom of Solomon – failed to ponder whether or not God exists, they did, however, raise the most penetrating question of all: "Am I accountable to a higher power than earthly monarchs?" "Given the existence of a transcendent being," they asked, "what difference does that make in daily experience?" Stated differently, "Does the divine countenance present a smile or a frown when humans come to mind?" Not knowing the answer, they devoted their efforts to discovering how to gain the favor of the Supreme Being, whom they identified as creator of the universe.

I. MADE IN THE IMAGE OF GOD

They began by postulating a principle of similarity between humans and deity, by no means an obvious assumption at the time.[2] The long history of veneration of deities in nonhuman form, beautifully analyzed by Thorkild Jacobsen in *The Treasures of Darkness: A History of Mesopotamian Religion*,[3] could not easily be erased from memory, especially when in popular imagination nature's potency was witnessed season after season. The secret to harnessing this energy was gradually unveiled as a consequence of the rise of city-states and the surging of political ambition; as the sovereign domain of a nation expanded, so did the god's territorial claim. Thus the benevolent deeds

---

[2] Karel van der Toorn, "Sources in Heaven: Revelation as a Scholarly Construct in Second Temple Judaism," in *Kein Land für sich allein: Studien zum Kulturkontakt in Kanaan, Israel/Palästina und Ebirnâri für Manfred Weippert zum 65. Geburtstag*, hrsg. Ulrich Hübner und Ernst Axel Knauf (Freiburg: Universitätsverlag Freiburg und Göttingen: Vandenhoeck & Ruprecht, 2002), 265–77, has argued that the collapse of a worldview based on the principle that the gods resembled humans led to the idea of revelation and to elitism. If gods and humans were inherently different, all knowledge of deity must have come from revelation, which lifted its recipients above everyone else. When written texts were involved, elitism increased, for very few people could read. (James L. Crenshaw, *Education in Ancient Israel: Across the Deadening Silence* [New York: Doubleday, 1998], and David M. Carr, *Writing on the Tablet of the Heart: Origins of Scripture and Literature* [Oxford/New York: Oxford University Press, 2005].)

[3] (New Haven: Yale University Press, 1976). Jacobsen applies three adjectives – natural, royal, and familial – to successive millennia of religious development in Mesopotamia. With the emergence of city-states and strong rulers, the tendency to view gods as embodiments of nature itself gave way to terminology involving kings. This practice declined when families gained influence amid growing concern for gods with parental attributes.

that had been ascribed to patron deities were credited to the god of the dominant earthly power. That process also explains the ascendancy of the biblical Yahweh, who slowly took on the features of deities whose city-states fell to a stronger Israel and Judah during the brief period of a monarchy (roughly the tenth through the first decade of the sixth century BCE). This personalization of the gods brought with it the possibility of imagining a relationship between them and humans that was ultimately akin to the way women and men relate to one another. In sociopolitical language, these bonds were called treaties. Religious associations of like-minded people were said to have been linked by covenants.

Nowhere does the idea of similarity between gods and humans occur more clearly than in Genesis 1:26–27, which describes Elohim's intentions to create a being "in our image," here articulated within the Divine Council, and reports the implementation of the plan that results in "male and female," who are nevertheless said to bear the imprint of their creator. It is not necessary to resolve the issue of the exact meaning of this language about the image of God, which must certainly imply in the narrative context a physical likeness but much more, including any one, or all, of the following possibilities: self-transcendence, a verbal capacity, and dominance over other creatures. It is noteworthy that this priestly author, who was probably active during the early post-exilic period (after 539 BCE), avoids hubris by having this notion of a similarity between humans and God originate with deity rather than with mortals. The only other clear reference to this idea within canonical literature (Sir. 17:3) completely divests it of the slightest hint of pride, for Ben Sira states it within the context of human mortality and divine majesty, where the benefits of likeness to the divine, spelled out as dominance over creatures and intellectual capacity, pale before life's brevity and the reminder that dust is the substance from which mortals were formed and will be their sure future as well.

This dual aspect, likeness to deity and kinship with dust, rendered humans the object of intellectual ambivalence, occasionally eliciting wonder, as in Psalm 8, but also satire when vulnerability encompasses miserable victims of flesh and blood, as in Job 7:17–21. Belief in such elevation to a status approaching divinity partially explains the several myths that recount the heroic efforts on the part of exceptional individuals to achieve full divinity.

The best-known example of this failed endeavor from Mesopotamia involves a certain Adapa, the most perfect of mortals, whose ascent to the assembly of the gods did not achieve the desired end because Ea, the god of wisdom, tricked him into refusing an offer of food that would have made him immortal.[4] Although the biblical story of the first couple lacks an ascent to the heavens, it nevertheless describes their frustrated attempt to attain equality with Elohim, which the narrative glosses as knowing good and evil. The two words, "good and evil," appear to function as a merism connoting "everything."[5] The presence of a second tree in the midst of the Garden of Eden suggests that the myth did not limit equality with Elohim to the cognitive realm but also embraced the temporal, or rather its transcendence. Access to the tree of life meant the possibility of sloughing off mortal robes for eternal apparel. The operative word here is "possibility," for just as the hero Gilgamesh was robbed of a branch from the tree of life by a serpent, so Adam and Eve, having succumbed to the seductive rhetoric of a clever serpent, incurred divine wrath that resulted in their expulsion from the garden and loss of access to the tree of life. The author does not question the couple's choice of fruit from the tree of knowledge, when sampling the produce from the tree of life nearby would have given them immortality. After all, myths must ring true; humans possess knowledge, not immortality.[6]

Not surprisingly, the gods were believed to be protective of their unique status. Thus we hear about Ea's willingness to deceive even favored individuals like Adapa, who had every reason to trust the god of wisdom. The biblical Elohim is not entirely above blame either, for the serpent owes its presence

---

[4] "The gods may lie, cheat, steal, and deceive each other, the very actions that humans may be punished for. These possibilities make for a certain drama in the universe, if at the same time for a certain moral bleakness" (Benjamin R. Foster, *From Distant Days: Myths, Tales, and Poetry of Ancient Mesopotamia* [Bethesda, MD: CDL Press, 1995], 2). Although given a moral rationale, the biblical account of the flood implicitly indicts Yahweh for perpetuating violence and authorizes Sovereignty as if the deity were above challenge for what would clearly be a moral outrage if done by humans.

[5] A striking similarity occurs in the Gilgamesh Epic, where a harlot who has introduced Enkidu to the wonders of sex informs him as follows: "Thou art wise, Enkidu, art become like a god!" (James B. Pritchard, ed., *Ancient Near Eastern Texts Relating to the Old Testament* [Princeton, NJ: Princeton University Press, 1969], 75 [hereafter *ANET*]).

[6] James Barr, *Biblical Faith and Natural Theology: The Gifford Lectures for 1991* (Oxford: Clarendon Press, 1993), makes a persuasive argument for viewing the biblical story as implying that Adam and Eve were mortal prior to their disobedience. The Ugaritic "Tale of Aqhatu" has its hero reject an offer of immortality by Anatu with these words:

> "Fib not to me, O Maiden;
> For to a Youth thy fibbing is loathsome.
> Further life – how can mortal attain it?
> How can mortal attain life enduring?
> Glaze will be poured [on] my head,
> Plaster upon my pate;
> And I'll die as everyone dies,
> I too shall assuredly die" (*ANET*, 151).

in the garden to the creator.[7] For some inexplicable reason, the acquisition of knowledge, presumably the salutary result of asserting personal freedom, poses a threat that must be immediately suppressed. The outcome, at least in the eyes of the narrator, is the permanent closing of the door to full equality with God.

That closed door, however, did not prevent Levitical teachers from admonishing Israelites to pattern their lives after the Lord, whom they worshipped as a partner in a covenantal relationship, as Erich Fromm's *You Shall Be As God* recognizes.[8] The later theological term for the object of this appeal, *imitatio Dei*, acknowledges both the extraordinary potential within humans to scale ethical heights and the wide gulf separating God and mortals. Ironically, the promise placed in the mouth of the serpent in Eden became the desired destination of individuals who aspired to holiness.

For at least two reasons, this compulsion to imitate the deity approaches the ironic. First, because the gods themselves were thought to have been subject to death, a belief that found expression in myths about gods who died and rose from the dead as perfect symbols for seasonal changes that brought new vegetation, only to see it replaced in due time by barren earth.[9] Psalm 82 offers another explanation for the death of the gods, specifically their failure to protect widows, orphans, the weak, and the needy from compassionless citizens with "strong elbows." Second, because the very possibility of rising above self-absorption was denied by learned teachers. This low opinion of human beings seems to have been widespread, at least among the intelligentsia, judging from such texts as "The Babylonian Theodicy" and an apparent proverbial saying attributed to the prophet Jeremiah. The former text has the Job-like sufferer lay full responsibility for mortals' lying ways on the gods. In Benjamin Foster's felicitous translation, the text reads:

> Enlil, king of the gods, who created teeming mankind,
> Majestic Ea, who pinched off their clay,

---

[7] Biblical literature reveals varying degrees of willingness to attribute responsibility for evil to Yahweh, even when forced to do so by an emerging sense of monotheism (James L. Crenshaw, *Defending God: Biblical Responses to the Problem of Evil* [Oxford and New York: Oxford University Press, 2005]). Hence the emergence of the figure who eventually was given a personal name: Satan. At first an official in divine service, Satan eventually was removed from the role of certifying authentic loyalty and became an antagonist. Nevertheless, Satan was always thought to be subject to God's authority.

[8] (Greenwich, CT: Fawcett Publishing Inc., 1966).

[9] Jonathan Z. Smith has challenged the very notion of dying/rising gods as inaccurate ("Dying and Rising Gods," in *The Encyclopedia of Religion*, ed. Mircea Eliade [New York: Collier Macmillan Publishers, 1987], and *Drudgery Divine: On the Comparison of Early Christianities and the Religions of Late Antiquity* [Chicago: University of Chicago Press, 1990]).

The queen who fashioned them, Mistress Mami,
Gave twisted words to the human race.
They endowed them in perpetuity with lies and falsehood.[10]

By way of contrast, the aphorism from the Bible is silent with respect to blame, simply stating that the mind is most perverse and twisted. It then inquires: "Who can grasp it?" (Jer. 17:9).[11] The anticipated response is: "No one." Like the proverb about transgenerational sin and retribution ("The parents have eaten sour grapes and the children's teeth have become sensitive," Jer. 31:29 and Ezek. 18:2), this assertion of intellectual malady bore a bountiful harvest, for the idea took many forms, sometimes resembling the well-known Greek example of Diogenes, lantern in hand, searching for a single righteous individual. In the case of Jeremiah 5:1, the aim was to locate someone who could ransom a sin-laden Jerusalem, but in Jeremiah's view neither the lowly nor the nobility possessed sufficient goodness to spare Zion. At other times, the idea shaped Israel's historiography in a manner that became a self-fulfilling prophecy, while providing a rationale for the destruction of Jerusalem at the hands of Babylonian soldiers.

Despite these attenuations to the principle of similarity, the principle eventually shaped theological discourse and undergirded the concept of reward and retribution. Human standards of conduct were extended to the divine realm through an argument from the least to the greatest. If humans were

---

[10] *From Distant Days*, 323. Utnapishtim, the hero of the flood in Mesopotamia, had a similar view of human nature when instructing his wife to devise a scheme to prevent Gilgamesh from lying about falling asleep. "Since to deceive is human," Utnapishtim said, "he will seek to deceive thee" (*ANET*, 95). Receptive to her husband's advice, she baked bread each day Gilgamesh slept, and upon awaking he saw the irrefutable evidence that he had succumbed to sleep, the tell-tale sign that he was a mortal.

[11] The irony of theological claims by humans, who are by nature perverse, is seldom acknowledged (James L. Crenshaw, "Deceitful Minds and Theological Dogma: Jeremiah 17:5–11," 105–121 in *Utopia and Dystopia in Prophetic Literature*, ed. Ehud Ben Zvi (Helsinki: The Finnish Exegetical Society and Göttingen: Vandenhoeck & Ruprecht, 2006), reprinted in Crenshaw, *Prophets, Sages & Poets* (St. Louis: Chalice Press, 2006), pp. 73–82, 222–24. Ignorance, one result of a perverse mind, was widely ceded, as in the following proverb from Mesopotamia.

> ... The will of god cannot be understood,
> The way of god cannot be known:
> Anything divine is [impossible] to find out" (*From Distant Days*, 387).

A prayer to Marduk with an agnostic sentiment strikes a strong note of dismay: "Men, by whatever name, what can they understand of their own sin? Who has not been negligent, which one has committed no sin? Who can understand a god's behavior? (*From Distant Days*, 247). Similarly, a prayer "To Any God" states that "Men are slow-witted and know nothing, no matter how many names they go by, what do they know? They do not know at all if they are doing good or evil!" (*From Distant Days*, 271).

expected to follow a strict code of ethics, surely, it was deduced, the gods should at a minimum live up to these standards of conduct. This kind of reasoning also meant that the gods expressed both pleasure and anger, which became a source of either joy or dismay. It therefore became incumbent on every individual to search for ways to please the deities or, in a monotheistic context, the sole deity. Alternatively, it was imperative to devise various means of dealing with divine anger, the cause of which was often shrouded in mystery.

The most poignant biblical application of the principle that God is subject to the same ethical code as humans involves Abraham. When informed of the deity's intention to destroy the cities of the plain, Sodom and Gomorrah, he is said to have uttered this bold response: "Shall not the Judge of all the earth do what is right?" (Gen. 18:25).[12] The story, which belongs to the category of theodicy, illustrates the narrator's unease over attributing a possible miscarriage of justice to Yahweh. A similar refrain can be heard in the Gilgamesh Epic, where Enkidu pays the price for both his and Gilgamesh's offense and evokes Gilgamesh's plea amounting to: "On the guilty impose the punishment." These ancient thinkers refused to travel the road later taken by Søren Kierkegaard, who posited a teleological suspension of the ethical that allowed him to make sense of God's demand that Abraham sacrifice his beloved son.[13] To them, right was right, whether involving gods or humans. Much later, Immanuel Kant used the same logic to deny that the command to sacrifice Isaac issued from God.

To some degree, the mechanisms for rewarding virtue and punishing evil complicated the principle of similarity, for there is some evidence that the ancients believed that a natural law governed reward and retribution.[14] Woven

---

[12] James L. Crenshaw, "The Sojourner Has Come to Play the Judge: Theodicy on Trial," in *God in the Fray: A Tribute to Walter Brueggemann*, eds. Tod Linafelt and Timothy K Beal (Minneapolis: Fortress Press, 1998), 83–92. Abraham's question to God in this story provides the title for an examination of theodicy by various scholars: *Shall Not the Judge of All the Earth Do What Is Right? Studies on the Nature of God in Tribute to James L. Crenshaw*, eds. David Penchansky and Paul L. Redditt (Winona Lake, IN: Eisenbrauns, 2000). Whereas this volume is thematic, another recent treatment of theodicy combines theme with canon (*Theodicy in the World of the Bible*, eds. Antti Laato and Johannes C. de Moor [Leiden and Boston: Brill], 2003).

[13] *Fear and Trembling* (Garden City, NY: Doubleday, 1941). R. W. L. Moberly gives a theological defense of the divine test in Genesis 22, but he fails to reckon seriously with the theological consequences of mandating such a monstrous test for a faithful servant (*The Bible, Theology, and Faith: A Study of Abraham and Jesus* [Cambridge: Cambridge University Press, 2000]).

[14] John J. Collins, *Encounters with Biblical Theology* (Minneapolis: Fortress, 2005), 126, links natural theology with the upwardly mobile Jews of Alexandria. He also recognizes a flaw in Wisdom of Solomon, namely, tension between particularism, fueled by ethnic survival, and

into the fabric of the universe, this operative principle, they thought, was completely independent of further influence from the gods, except that they may have acted as a kind of midwife to assist the birth of weal or woe. The controversy occasioned by Klaus Koch's application of this hypothesis to the Bible under the formula *Tun-Ergehen Zusammenhang*[15] shows how difficult it is to reconcile the nexus of cause and effect with belief in an interactive deity who knows the very thoughts of every person, according to Psalm 139.

Without a doubt, however, the largest challenge to comparing God to humans was ignorance. An element of mystery surrounded deity, for every revelation was believed to be simultaneously a veiling.[16] The prophet who is known as Deutero-Isaiah minces no words when expressing this idea: "Truly you are a God who hides, God of Israel, Savior!" (Isa. 45:15). Even moments of exceptional disclosure such as Yahweh's revelation of the divine name as "I am That I am" (Exod. 3:14) and the concession to Moses's persistent request to see the deity convey a sense of undisclosed mystery (Exod. 33:1–7).[17] Foreigners also recognized divine mystery, according to the author of the book of Job, which gives a spine-curdling account of a theophany to Eliphaz that left him terrified and unable to recognize the mysterious visitor, who, one may infer, bristled at the thought that Job was more righteous than God (Job 4:12–17). Gilgamesh, too, had three dreams that left him distraught as he pondered both their originating cause and its effect.

Extrabiblical literature from the ancient Near East attests wide awareness of mystery surrounding the gods, despite their anthropomorphism. Egyptian iconography[18] best conveys this sense of the unknown, for the deities are frequently depicted in quasi-human form, with animal parts and features of winged creatures. In Mesopotamian art, the lion, symbolic of royalty, indicates both earthly and heavenly rulers. The solar disc that played such a prominent

---

universalism. Collins finds a precedent for natural theology within wisdom literature, in the linking of act and consequence, and in the idea of personified wisdom (p. 101).

[15] "Is there a Doctrine of Retribution in the Old Testament?" in *Theodicy in the World of the Old Testament*, ed. James L. Crenshaw (IRT 4; Philadelphia: Fortress Press; London: SPCK, 1983), 57–87. Koch's article first appeared as "Gibt es ein Vergeltungsdogma im Alten Testament?" *ZThK* 52 (1955), 1–42. The English translation is an abridged version.

[16] Samuel E. Balentine, *The Hidden God: The Hiding of the Face of God in the Old Testament* (Oxford: Oxford University Press, 1983); Kornelis H. Miskotte, *When the Gods Are Silent* (New York and Evanston: Harper & Row, 1967); and Karl Rahner, *Encounters with Silence* (Westminster, MD: Newman Press, 1965), provide different readings of the same religious experience.

[17] The linguistic possibilities of this disclosure retain its mystery. It can be read to imply divine causation, philosophical being, or a meteorological phenomenon.

[18] Othmar Keel, *The Symbolism of the Biblical World: Ancient Near Eastern Iconography and the Book of Psalms* (Winona Lake, IN: Eisenbrauns, 1997).

role in the ancient world nicely illustrates the combination of visibility and invisibility, for although accessible to all, the sun burns with such intensity that onlookers dare not risk more than a quick glance. Shamash's mystery is thereby protected, and humans are reminded that all knowledge is partial, particularly that concerning Being itself. The appropriation of mythic ideas pertaining to the sun god by the author of Psalm 19 shows how concepts from a different religious context can enrich another one. In this instance, the sun's penetration of everything below is matched by the illuminating power of the Torah, which reaches as far as the human conscience.

To overcome partial knowledge about the heavenly realm, religious thinkers applied analogical reasoning, which by necessity assumed real continuity between what was seen and what could not be seen. In reality, analogies worked only if God thought and acted like humans. In the final analysis, metaphors conveyed truths that could not be stated otherwise: God was father, shepherd, warrior, healer, king, teacher, rock, and so on.[19] Each of these metaphors captured an essential characteristic of deity; taken literally, they were woefully inadequate.

Limited knowledge did not, however, prevent ancient artisans from crafting images of the gods. According to the second-century author of Wisdom of Solomon, the practice originated in one of three ways: (1) a bereaving father carved a likeness of his deceased son; (2) a subject of a distant ruler made an image as a token of loyalty; and (3) a gifted artist created a work of beauty that became an object of supreme devotion. Regardless of its origin, the making of visible images to represent an invisible deity served royal liturgy and personal piety well.

The Babylonian *Mis Pi* ritual that symbolized the opening of the god's mouth and regular feeding is particularly illuminating.[20] The daily exercises to which the gods' statues were subjected testify to their importance in sustaining a positive relationship with the ones to whom the visible objects pointed. Admittedly, the role of the god's statue in prophecy from Neo-Assyrian times may strike moderns as bizarre, but ancient worshippers viewed it as apt.[21] Standing in front of a statue of a god, a prophet functioned as the mouthpiece

---

[19] William P. Brown, *Seeing the Psalms: A Theology of Metaphor* (Louisville, KY: Westminster John Knox, 2002), introduces an innovative way of viewing the book of Psalms from the perspective of its rich use of metaphors.

[20] John F. Kutsko, *Between Heaven and Earth: Divine Presence and Absence in the Book of Ezekiel* (BJS 7; Winona Lake, IN: Eisenbrauns, 2000), 57n109, refers to convenient discussions of the ritual referred to as washing or opening the mouth.

[21] Karel van der Toorn, "From the Oral to the Written: The Case of Old Babylonian Prophecy," 219–34, and Martti Nissinen, "Spoken, Written, Quoted and Invented: Orality and Writtenness in Ancient Near Eastern Prophecy," 235–72, in *Writings and Speech in Israelite and Ancient*

of the deity while pronouncing a divine oracle, which would subsequently
be conveyed to kings Esarhaddon or Aššurbanipal, the two Assyrian kings
during whose reigns prophetic texts have survived.[22] Although biblical orthodoxy forbade the worship of idols, the fervor with which this practice was
denounced suggests that ordinary people were favorably impressed by idols,
so much so that religious leaders found various substitutes, not the least
of which was verbal. The tablets containing the Decalogue and the written
Torah of Moses are the two most notable examples. Nevertheless, biblical
tradents insisted that nothing in heaven or on earth adequately resembled
God. Accordingly, an empty throne in the temple symbolized the presence
of an invisible Yahweh. Worship at the northern sanctuaries of Bethel and
Dan, however, indicates a different view of representations for deity. In these
two cult centers, images of bulls, overlaid with gold, signaled continuity
with the cultic ritual associated with the period of wandering in the wilderness.[23] Traditions from the southern kingdom of Judah took exception to
such aids to worship, as the episode about the "golden calf" in Exodus 32
illustrates.

Because communication with the gods was considered essential to the well-
being of the nation and individuals alike, an elaborate system of detecting the
future was devised. In Mesopotamia, specialists in reading the signs were
highly trained in the art of extispicy, and careful records were kept in archives
for future consultation. Diviners studied the configuration of animals' livers,
the flight of birds, the trajectory of arrows, the fall of lots, and so forth, searching for clues about the intentions of the gods. Visionaries were widely believed
to have seen things concealed from ordinary people, and this extrasensory gift
was understood to have been bestowed on them by deity. Biblical prophecy
was apparently reluctant to stress the auditory over the visual, as the superscription to the book of Amos indicates: "The words of Amos which he saw"
(Amos 1:1).[24] An inscription discovered at Deir 'Alla that mentions the diviner

---

Near Eastern Prophecy, ed. Ehud Ben Zvi and Michael H. Floyd (Symposium 10; Atlanta:
Society of Biblical Literature, 2000).

[22] Simo Parpola, Assyrian Prophecies (SAA 9; Helsinki: Helsinki University Press, 1997), repro-
duces the texts in translation and ventures a controversial synthesis of the religious worldview
they presuppose, one greatly resembling early Christianity.

[23] Patrick D. Miller, The Religion of Ancient Israel (London: SPCK; Louisville, KY: Westminster
John Knox Press, 2000), and Mark S. Smith, The Early History of God: Yahweh and the
Other Deities in Ancient Israel (New York: Harper & Row, 1990), trace both the evolution of
religious thought and its diversity. For Smith, Canaanite influence on Israelite religion was
far-reaching.

[24] The unusual syntax of this verse has been treated by Francis I. Andersen and David Noel
Freedman in Amos (AB 24A; New York: Doubleday, 1989), 188–90. The problem arises from
the twofold use of the relative 'ašer, with no clear antecedent for the second occurrence.

Balaam, otherwise known from Numbers 22–24, shows the popularity of this visual mode of receiving communications from God.[25]

The Mesopotamian world also developed a "science" of omens covering a seemingly endless array of anomalies that were thought to lend insight into the future. Perhaps the most lasting of these endeavors is astronomy, for observation of heavenly bodies was indispensable to ritual accuracy.[26] The many debates within Judaism over the correct calendar demonstrate similar interest in performing the ritual at exactly the right time.

II. QUESTIONING THE PRINCIPLE OF SIMILARITY

Such specialized research and clairvoyance notwithstanding, individuals sometimes experienced an alien God who seemed to lack even rudimentary human goodness. Personal suffering befell them for no apparent reason, and their prayers for relief went unanswered. Perplexed and bewildered, they began to question their knowledge of deity. The distraught sufferer in "I Will Praise the Lord of Wisdom" put the matter this way:

> I wish I knew that these things were pleasing to a god!
> What seems good to one's self could be an offense to a god,
> What in one's own heart seems abominable
> could be good to one's god!
> Who could learn the reasoning of the gods in heaven?
> Who could grasp the intentions of the gods of the depths?
> Where might human beings have learned the way of a god?[27]

Ignorance, that is, prevails among humans where the gods are concerned, and the premise that they are essentially like people flies out the window.

The author of the fictive masterpiece the book of Job has his hero undergo a similar collapse of a previous understanding of God when his erstwhile friend becomes an inveterate foe. Extreme loss and personal misery force Job to view God as a wild beast intent on devouring prey. Then when God finally shows up, Job can no longer recognize the face in the tempest. He has gone from the center of Yahweh's attention, his pride and joy, to the outer edges of thought where humans are no longer the measure of all things, indeed

---

[25] Baruch A. Levine has provided a translation with introduction and notes in volume 2 of *The Context of Scripture: Monumental Inscriptions from the Biblical World*, ed. William W. Hallo (Leiden and Boston: Brill, 2003), 140–45.

[26] J. Edward Wright, *The Early History of Heaven* (Oxford and New York: Oxford University Press, 2000), gives an informative analysis of the origin of astronomy in the biblical world.

[27] Foster, *From Distant Days*, 305.

where Leviathan and Behemoth have replaced Job as objects of Yahweh's boasting.[28]

It is unclear whether the root cause of this loss of confidence in the basic affinities between humans and deity is personal or national. Instances of individual dismay over the contradiction between ancestral belief and actual experience probably lie behind narratives like the one focusing on Gideon's sharp retort to an angel who seemed blissfully unaware that assurance of Yahweh's presence rang hollow after foreign raiders had destroyed Israel's grain fields (Judg. 6:12–13). When such personal questioning of divine governance was fueled by more than empty stomachs, specifically a failed cult, the angst intensified to near-breaking point. That is what happened in the wake of Jerusalem's destruction as depicted in the agonizing cry preserved in the book of Lamentations, one that ends in utter confusion: "[U]nless you have completely rejected us; [you] have raged against us mightily" (Lam. 5:22).

A witness to the vanishing hope associated with the royal sanctuary in Zion has left an even more penetrating analysis of that dark period. If not the actual composer of the "confessions," then at least their primary subject, Jeremiah struggled valiantly with what he perceived to be a scandalous transformation of Yahweh. The one whom the prophet had known previously as a fountain of living water had become in his mind a deceitful rake bent on destroying a loyal spokesman (Jer. 20:7). The lonely journey into disenchantment, presented here as deeply personal, is universalized in the book of Job. In general, despite Job's foreign ancestry according to the biblical text, Jewish interpreters have viewed him as a cipher for the nation Israel, whereas Christians often have seen him as a single individual. Both groups of interpreters have been troubled by some aspects of his character, which they have managed to explain away by adopting an allegorical approach. Many modern readers admire Job's rebellious spirit rather than viewing it as a flaw in his character.

Among religious leaders, the initial shock occasioned by cognitive dissonance eventually brought adjustments to the basic understanding of God. The most notable change concerned the way Yahweh was thought to interact with humans. The idea of the deity's intimate involvement by appointing leaders and by controlling the course of history to benefit a chosen people was replaced by the concept of a distant, silent creator. Revelation, once believed to have been immediate and episodic, became looked upon as derivative, with

---

[28] No individual can adequately describe the vast literature on the book of Job, although James L. Crenshaw, "Job, Book of," in volume 3 of *The Anchor Bible Dictionary*, ed. David Noel Freedman (New York: Doubleday, 1992), 858–68; Samuel E. Balentine, *Job* (Macon, Ga.: Smyth and Helwys, 2006); and Carol Newsom, "The Book of Job," in *The New Interpreter's Bible*, vol. 4 (Nashville: Abingdon Press, 1996), 317–637, indicate its general character.

written texts identified as the font of knowledge. In some circles, however, divine pedagogy that included hunger and thirst was not understood as signaling Yahweh's absence but rather an intimacy involving whispered guidance about where to walk on dangerous paths (Isa. 30:20–21). Rare individuals have always managed to interpret adversity as confirmation of profound trust or, as in the case of the author of Psalm 73, to look beyond calamity or injustice to buttress traditional belief.

In this confusing spiritual environment, even prophets who stood in a long tradition of boldly announcing Yahweh's words abandoned that confident mien and began to interpret the fuller ramifications of what others had said rather than delivering a new oracle from God.[29] In such fallow ground apocalyptic easily took root,[30] pushing divine activity into the foreseeable future and introducing angels with names like Gabriel and Uriel who assisted God in disclosing the secrets of the hidden realm to special individuals like Enoch and Ezra. More importantly, this sea change brought mainstream intellectualism into line with sapiential thought, until now something of a maverick because of its emphasis on human achievement rather than on God's control of history.[31]

These adjustments to religious thinking were necessitated by a combination of other factors as well. First, it became apparent that the claim to speak in the name of Yahweh was in essence *testimony* to a perceived encounter with transcendence. Moreover, that *testimony* was by its very nature broken, for it involved fallible humans – intellectually, ethically, and culturally. As conflict among prophets demonstrated, the audacious claim to be a mouthpiece for Yahweh did not assure authenticity.[32] Second, every attempt to speak theologically brought one face to face with personal limitations, ultimately issuing in little more than stammering. The indescribable and unutterable did not lend

---

[29] John Barton, *Oracles of God: Perceptions of Ancient Prophecy in Israel after the Exile* (New York: Oxford University Press, 1986).

[30] A perceptive introduction to apocalyptic thinking can be found in the various publications of John J. Collins, particularly *The Apocalyptic Imagination: An Introduction to the Jewish Matrix of Christianity* (New York: Crossroad, 1984); "Early Jewish Apocalypticism," in *The Anchor Bible Dictionary*, vol. 1 (New York: Doubleday, 1992), 282–8, and "The Reinterpretation of Apocalyptic Traditions in The Wisdom of Solomon," in *Deuterocanonical and Cognate Literature Yearbook 2005* (*The Book of Wisdom in Modern Research: Studies on Tradition, Redaction, and Theology*, eds. Angelo Passaro and Geirceppe Bellia [Berlin/New York: Walter de Gruyter] 2005), 143–55.

[31] James L. Crenshaw, *Old Testament Wisdom: An Introduction* (Louisville: Westminster John Knox, 1998), and Gerhard von Rad, *Wisdom in Israel* (Nashville: Abingdon Press, 1972).

[32] James L. Crenshaw, *Prophetic Conflict: Its Effect Upon Israelite Religion* (BZAW 124; Berlin and New York: Walter de Gruyter, 1971), discusses the futile effort to formulate adequate criteria by which people could determine which prophets to heed and whom to ignore.

itself to articulate speech, as religious mystics have long recognized. Third, visual acuity was severely hampered when gazing into eternity. The best one could hope to do was catch a glimpse of holiness, as if through stained-glass windows, hardly more reliable than observing shadows on the wall of a cave.

The effect of the religious crisis on the point at which faith and daily experience came together was enormous. The central assumption that reward and retribution corresponded exactly with one's deeds gave way to belief in random distribution of both the benefits of virtue and punishment for evil deeds without regard to either merit or blame. Admittedly, that association of deed and consequence had no thorough grounding to start with, for exceptions like Abel and Josiah were well known. Still, hardened dogma alone explains comments like that expressed in Psalm 37:25 denying want on the part of righteous people, the jaundiced reasoning by Job's three friends, and the near certitude in the book of Proverbs that virtue was rewarded and vice punished. Against such a dogmatic background, the radical dismissal of orthodoxy with a rhetorical flick of the wrist ("Who knows?") by Qoheleth, the speaker in Ecclesiastes, makes sense. For him, the firm belief that one could control destiny by rational means had become fatally flawed, for time and chance governed all things. Subjection to fate's cruel mockery of both good and evil was a far cry from shaping one's own future by applying ancestral knowledge to daily experience.

The removal of Yahweh from ordinary affairs created a void that was soon filled by a mediating figure. At emotionally charged moments, Job gave voice to the possibility that someone would bridge the chasm between him and God. Variously referred to as a conciliator (Job 9:33), a heavenly witness (Job 16:19), and a vindicator (Job 19:25), this figment of Job's imagination who, Job hoped, would bring about a change in Yahweh's treatment of him never materialized. A mediating figure did come to play a significant role in the sapiential pedagogy of the unknown author of Proverbs 1–9 and in Ben Sira's instruction of aspiring scribes of second-century Judaism. This female persona, *hokmâ*, developed from metaphorical beginnings (cf. the four metaphors for divine attributes that are mentioned in Ps. 85:10) into a hypostasis, an earthly manifestation of the invisible God.[33]

---

[33] Alice M. Sinnott, *The Personification of Wisdom* (SOTSM; Aldershot: Ashgate, 2005); Judith E. McKinlay, *Gendering Wisdom the Host: Biblical Invitations to Eat and Drink* (JSOT SS216; Sheffield: Sheffield Academic Press, 1996); Gerlinde Baumann, *Die Weisheitsgestalt in Proverbien 1–9* (FAT 16; Tübingen: J. C. B. Mohr [Paul Siebeck], 1996); and Silvia Schroer, *Wisdom Has Built Her House: Studies on the Figure of Sophia in the Bible* (Collegeville, MN: The Liturgical Press, 2000).

To strengthen her mediating function, she was given an extraordinary pedigree, one originating in heaven and antedating the created world (Prov. 8:22–31). In addition, she was linked with primordial sages of Mesopotamian lore (Prov. 9:1) and later identified as the visible expression of the divine Torah revealed to Moses. In short, she was God's universal will that reached all the way back to the Garden of Eden and also the covenantal presence at Zion (Sir. 24:1–23). Above all, however, she was thought to possess divine attributes and to be an extension of God similar to the relationship between the sun and its rays (Wis. Sol. 7:22–26). As such, she took on herself a soteriological role that had previously belonged to the spirit, thereby rewriting religious history.

III. A CLOUD OF UNKNOWING

Much has been made in scholarly literature of a crisis among biblical sages brought on by a collapse of belief in divine order regulating the universe. The basic thesis, presented cogently by Hartmut Gese and Hans Heinrich Schmid,[34] seems to correspond to what transpired in the ancient Near East, first in Egypt and later in Mesopotamia and Israel. Dogma tends to harden over time, bending with each perceived counterargument until finally breaking under the weight of reality. The books of Job and Ecclesiastes, together with comparable literature from Egypt and Mesopotamia, attest to a temporary breakdown of a worldview.

At the same time, however, this testimony to the inadequacy of religious consensus reveals the extraordinary resilience of the human mind, its creative capacity when old views are shown to be bankrupt. Crisis therefore becomes an occasion for a religious breakthrough.[35] That is precisely what happens

---

[34] "Die Krisis der Weisheit bei Kohelet," in *Les Sagesses du proche-Orient ancient: Colloque de Strasbourg 17–19 Mai 1962* (Paris: Presses Universitaires de France, 1963), 139–52, and *Wesen und Geschichte der Weisheit* (BZAW 101; Berlin: Töpelmann, 1966), respectively. Martin Rose, "De la Crise de la Sagesse à la Sagesse de la Crise," *RThPh* 131 (1999), 115–34, stresses the creative potential in a crisis of belief. One may compare the positive correlation between evil and the creative in literature and art.

[35] Eric Weil, "What Is a Breakthrough in History?" *Daedalus* (Spring 1975), 21–36 (*Wisdom, Revelation and Doubt: Perspectives on the First Millennium B.C.*). In my view, two remarkable intellectual revolutions occurred in ancient Israel. The first was the transition from polytheism to monotheism, recorded in Psalm 82. The sentence of death, imposed by Elohim on the gods for failing to maintain justice, signals this radical shift in worldview. The second revolution was the belief that humans might transcend death through faithful service of God, as indicated in Psalm 73 (James L. Crenshaw, "Love Is Stronger Than Death: Intimations of Life beyond the Grave," in *Resurrection: The Origin and Future of a Biblical Doctrine*, ed. James H. Charlesworth [New York and London: T&T Clark, 2006], 53–78).

when the author of the book of Job replaces retributive justice with the concept of gratuitous love. The centrality of the Hebrew word *hinnam* in the prologue signals this remarkable change in perspective. The fact that it is placed in the mouths of both the Adversary and Yahweh indicates agreement on the issue underlying all that follows (Job 1:9, 2:3). As the ensuing poetic dialogue demonstrates with increasing exactitude, dogma is seldom surrendered without a fight. For what seems an eternity, the argument moves within the realm of discourse established by the old belief in reward and retribution. Remarkably, Job is caught in this treacherous web even when challenging it, for apart from the principle of retributive justice he has no basis for complaint. Only the divine speeches fall outside this restrictive box; in the end, ambiguous syntax and grammar make it impossible to determine whether or not Job finally embraced the radical understanding of relating to Yahweh without cause (Job 42:6).[36] The ironic epilogue dramatically underscores the unpredictable nature of *hinnam*, while also demonstrating divine freedom.[37]

Now if the book of Job explored a radically new principle that destroyed every vestige of a calculating morality, Ecclesiastes began to flirt with philosophical issues beyond the question: "What is true virtue?" For Qoheleth, the only topic worthy of serious consideration was that of meaning. His approach was unabashedly anthropocentric: "What is good for mortals?" Moreover,

---

[36] Newsom, "The Book of Job," 629, discusses five possible translations of Job 42:6. They are as follows:
  1. "Therefore I despise myself and repent upon dust and ashes" (i.e., in humiliation);
  2. "Therefore I retract my words and repent of dust and ashes" (i.e. the symbols of mourning);
  3. "Therefore I reject and forswear dust and ashes" (i.e., the symbols of mourning);
  4. "Therefore I retract my words and have changed my mind concerning dust and ashes" (i.e., the human condition); and
  5. "Therefore I retract my words, and I am comforted concerning dust and ashes" (i.e., the human condition).

[37] Aversion to unresolved endings is widespread. It dictates the practice in synagogues of ending the scripture reading on a positive note. Similarly, it has produced wholly unanticipated endings in literature and film, for example, Goethe's *Faust* and the movie *Fatal Attraction*. The epilogue to the book of Job overlooks Job's ten children and his servants, whose deaths seem to matter little more than extras in a movie. This feature of the biblical book presents a serious challenge to the method that governs the stimulating analysis of the epilogue by Kenneth Numfor Ngwa, *The Hermeneutic of the "Happy" Ending in Job 42:7–17* (BZAW 354; New York and Berlin: Walter de Gruyter, 2005). He employs a threefold dynamic: inward toward the center in search of unity, outward toward other experiences in search of diversity, and forward toward the transcendent search of meaning. In Ngwa's view, the epilogue transcends any strict concept of retribution, but as I read the text, an ironic wink lingers despite every attempt to resolve the tension between the prose and poetry. God's action is still outrageous, even if construed as outside the norms of a human concept of reward and retribution. The epilogue sabotages the message of the poetic dialogue.

he set himself up as supreme judge about everything under the sun, giving pride of place to experience but also accepting much conventional wisdom, especially concerning creation.

Qoheleth's view of all things as *hebel* closely resembles that of the Greek philosopher Monimus, for whom mist was the best term to indicate everything. Appropriately, *hebel* was nearly as elusive as vapor, for it had various nuances: breath, transience, idol, stench.[38] Qoheleth took advantage of this richness, although the majority of his uses convey something like absurdity or futility. His assessment of things as *hebel* was all-encompassing, so much so that it elicited hatred of life. For him, religion brought no comfort, for a distant and silent Elohim dispensed favors and calamities gratuitously, without rhyme or reason. Death was certain; anything beyond that moment was a mystery. Nothing therefore carried enduring worth: not work, not fame, not life itself. There was simply no profit, nothing in excess, despite all human striving.

The macrostructure of Ecclesiastes emphasizes Qoheleth's disenchantment with human existence. After initial superscription, motto, and thematic statement, the book has an exquisite poem about nature's ceaseless rhythm (Eccl. 1:4–11). It closes with a poignant description of human aging and demise in a context of nature's extraordinary rejuvenation (Eccl. 11:8–12:7). The prominence of earth, air, fire, and water in the first poem is hardly accidental, for Qoheleth was attempting to juxtapose what he took to be the essential substances of the universe with transient mortals.[39] The closing poem sets death in an ambiguous context suggesting an apocalyptic cataclysm and perdurance, as if Qoheleth could not choose between competing philosophical views about the future of the universe.

This fascination with philosophy extends beyond the two poems mentioned earlier. Qoheleth reflected on his own intellectual process in a way that resembles second-order thinking. Peter Machinist has pointed to Qoheleth's choice of vocabulary, specifically *hešbon*, *ma'aśeh*, *miqreh*, and *'olam* as proof that he had made a rudimentary breakthrough with respect to thinking about

---

[38] Ethan Dor-Shav, "Ecclesiastes, Fleeting and Timeless," *Azure* 18 (2004), 67–87, reflects continuing interest in a topic that was widely researched in the last half of the twentieth century; witness two recent commentaries by Thomas Krüger and Ludger Schwienhorst-Schönberger, namely, *Kohelet* (*Prediger*) (BKAT XIX; Neukirchen Vluyn: Neukirchener Verlag, 2000), and *Kohelet* (HThKAT; Freiburg: Herder, 2004).

[39] Norbert Lohfink, "Die Wiederkehr des immer Gleichen. Eine frühe Synthese zwischen griechischen und jüdischen Weltgefuhl in Kohelet 1, 4–11," in *Studien zu Kohelet* (SBA 26; Stuttgart: Verlag Katholisches Bibelwerk GmbH, 1998), 95–124.

thought itself.[40] Qoheleth was fully aware that he had to connect vital pieces of cognition in additive fashion in order to arrive at the larger picture (Eccl. 7:27).[41]

The case for viewing Qoheleth as a pioneer in the attempt to think philosophically in a language that hardly encouraged such an enterprise can be strengthened further by recognizing the manner in which he used the particle *kōl* ("everything"). Qoheleth's use of the word "everything" coincided with universalist tendencies in some late biblical literature.[42] The similarities with Greek philosophical explorations of concepts for totality need not indicate dependence, although Qoheleth may well have been familiar with popular philosophy of his day. In Ben Sira's case, the use of the expression "He is the all" (Sir. 43:27) must surely imply acquaintance with the Stoic notion *tó ôn*.

Joseph Blenkinsopp has advanced the hypothesis of a Stoic source for the well-known poem about a time for everything in Eccl 3:1–8.[43] The philosophical presupposition of these fourteen opposites is, in his view, the Stoic concept of the principle governing the universe itself. Whether in the end Blenkinsopp's view will ring true remains to be seen, but his readiness to interpret Ecclesiastes in the light of Greek philosophy is not off the mark. In my view, the fairly mundane nature of the opposites in Qoheleth's list, except for the first and last (birth/death; war/peace) makes this text less akin to Stoic teaching than Ben Sira's use of comprehensive concepts such as good and evil in the service of theodicy (Sir. 39:17–40:11).

The cumulative weight of thinking about God's relationship with humans as gratuitous and denying both meaning and permanence to anything under the sun pushed toward acceptance of epistemological agnosticism. The result was increasing emphasis on mystery, for the authors of both Job and Ecclesiastes agreed that the true nature of God was veiled. By necessity revelation implied divine inscrutability, as well as esotericism. The latter idea became full-blown in apocalyptic literature and in sectarian Judaism.

---

[40] "Fate, *miqreh*, and Reason: Some Reflections on Qohelet and Biblical Thought," in *Solving Riddles and Untying Knots: Biblical, Epigraphic and Semitic Studies in Honor of Jonas G. Greenfield*, ed. Ziony Zevit et al. (Winona Lake, IN: Eisenbrauns, 1995), 159–75.

[41] James L. Crenshaw, "Qohelet's Quantitative Language," in *Prophets, Sages & Poets*, 83–94, 224–30, also appearing in *The Language of Qohelet in Context: Festschrift Antoon Schoors* (Leuven: Peeters). This article discusses incipient philosophy in the heavy use of quantitative terminology by Qoheleth and offers a rationale for such language among sages in the second century.

[42] Norbert Lohfink, "Koh 1, 2: Alles ist Windhauch – universale oder anthropologische Aussage," in *Studien zu Kohelet*, 125–42.

[43] "Ecclesiastes 3.1–15: Another Interpretation," *JSOT* 66 (1995), 55–64.

The covenanters from Qumran pondered the *raz nihyeh*, mystery that is to be,[44] while considering themselves and their righteous teacher to be keepers of heavenly secrets. That sense of chosenness flourished in various apocalyptic accounts of special people who were escorted into heaven, given divine mysteries of creation, and allowed to return to earth with secret knowledge. This speculation occurred, it should be noted, simultaneously with flourishing mystery religions in the Greco-Roman world. Precisely when knowledge of deity was strongly questioned in favor of *theos agnostos*, teachers sought to fill the void with Gnostic responses: knowledge comes via special revelation and conveys elite status on those "in the know." In 2 Corinthians 12:2–4 the apostle Paul debunked such elitist attitudes that grew out of special revelation, suggesting instead that personal weakness made strong by God was the only cause for boasting. In this context, he managed to report on his own mystical experience while also allowing the experience to retain its basic secrecy.

In Jewish circles, the expression *'en mispar* arose to express the vast gulf between what could be known about deity and what remained hidden. Ben Sira conveyed the same idea differently: "although we speak much, we cannot reach the end" (Sir. 43:27a). In a word, beginnings and endings stand outside human purview-like divinity.

Religious breakthroughs like *hinnam* and *hebel* do not take place without resistance, even when traditional views have become obsolete because of changing times. The astonishing thing is that the two canonical works of wisdom literature after Job and Ecclesiastes resumed older thinking as if the radical insights *hinnam* and *hebel* never existed. There is a difference, however, for both Ben Sira and the unknown author of the strongly Hellenized Wisdom of Solomon[45] consciously sought to provide rational theodicies grounded in psychology and philosophy.[46] So much for *hinnam* thinking about the relationship between God and humans or for *hebel* as the descriptor of all existence. Reaching back into sacred history, Ben Sira identified the Mosaic legislation as Israel's wisdom before the court of international inquiry. By introducing the idea of proportional punishment at the hands of an infinitely patient deity, Wisdom of Solomon tried to exonerate Yahweh from the charge of cruelly exterminating Egyptians and Canaanites.[47] Traditional theology

---

[44] Daniel J. Harrington, *Wisdom Texts from Qumran* (London and New York: Routledge, 1996).

[45] John J. Collins, *Jewish Wisdom in the Hellenistic Age* (OTL; Louisville, KY: Westminster John Knox, 1997).

[46] James L. Crenshaw, "The Problem of Theodicy in Sirach: On Human Bondage," *JBL* 94 (1975), 49–65, reprinted in *Urgent Advice and Probing Questions*, 155–74.

[47] Moyna McGlymn, *Divine Judgment and Divine Benevolence in the Book of Wisdom* (WUNT, 139; Tübingen: Mohr Siebeck, 2001), 25–53, and Giuseppe Bellia-Angelo Passare, "Infinite

flourished once more: God could be known and was just, according to Ben Sira and Wisdom of Solomon. Furthermore, the prospect of death, so troubling to Qoheleth, seems not to have disturbed Ben Sira unduly, and the Neoplatonic idea of an immortal soul eased its burden for the author of Wisdom of Solomon.[48]

IV. SIMILARITY RESTORED?

The penultimate chapter in Wisdom of Solomon introduces a parallel notion to *hokmâ*. It states that the divine word leaped from the royal throne in heaven and stood on earth, touching heaven at the same time, and brought death to inhospitable Egyptians who worshipped created things instead of their maker (Wis. Sol. 18:14–19). Such fearsome figures of gigantic proportions were familiar lore in the ancient world, perhaps the most memorable being Sheol, whose insatiable appetite was symbolized by lips that touched both heaven and earth. The personification of the divine word is anticipated in poetic lyrical texts in Deutero-Isaiah (Isa. 55:10–11), but this type of rhetoric was widespread.

The author of Wisdom of Solomon could never have imagined the future role of this particular personification. Incarnational theology was clearly aided by the equation of the Hebrew concept of *hokmâ* with two Greek words, *sophia* and *logos*. The natural translation of *hokmâ* by *sophia* in the Septuagint was the first step toward such theology, and Stoic teaching about a universal rational substance that resided to a lesser degree in the human intellect was the second. Notwithstanding the discrepancy in gender, the identification of *sophia* with *logos* made it possible to think of a single individual as both *hokma/sophia* and *logos*. When Christians began to view Jesus as God's eternal wisdom, it was but a small step to see him as the incarnation of the divine word. The result was the restoration of the principle of similarity, now applied absolutely with reference to Jesus. Here in the person of Jesus was a second Adam, truly God and truly man, according to later Christian orthodoxy.

What, then, did the theologians responsible for the Synoptics and the Gospel of John think he believed about *hinnam* and *hebel* as the most

---

Passion for Justice," in *Deuterocanonical and Cognate Literature Yearbook, 2005: The Book of Wisdom in Modern Research*, 307–28. The articles from a Conference of Biblical Studies organized by the Theological Faculty of Sicily, "St. John the Evangelist," and held March 22–23 in 2002 reveal the extraordinary vitality of current Italian scholarship on the Book of Wisdom, along with notable contributions by David Winston, John J. Collins, Emile Puech, and Maurice Gilbert.

[48] Michael Kolarcik, *The Ambiguity of Death in Wisdom Chapters 1–6: A Study of Literary Structure and Interpretation* (Rome: Editrice Pontificio Instituto Biblico, 1991).

accurate descriptions of the human dilemma? They have preserved just enough information to indicate an awareness of gratuitous love, specifically the allusion to innocent Galileans who were killed by Pilate or eighteen unfortunate persons on whom a tower fell (Lk. 13:2–5) and Jesus's refusal to attach blame either to a blind man or to his parents (Jn. 9:1–3). The recognition that the sun shines on individuals irrespective of their conduct (Matt. 5:45) and the emphasis on the heavenly Father's readiness to forgive fit within *hinnam* thinking just like the stories about victims of special circumstances.

This limited acceptance of *hinnam* theology is only half the story, for it is dwarfed by another theme, the retributional, which clashes with the belief that God freely dispenses good things to all without regard to worth. Even the observation about sun and rain falling on one and all is set within a context of reward and retribution. The many exhortations to earn divine favor by means of exceptional virtue within the Gospels give a wholly different impression from the reminder of God's providential care. So do the frequent threats of hell fire awaiting all who fail to respond obediently to Jesus's teachings. The tradents who transmitted the Gospels depict a Jesus who leaned more heavily in the direction of a dogmatic position that had been found wanting by at least two representatives of the sapiential enterprise than toward disinterested righteousness.

How did *hebel* thinking fare in their recollection of the tradition associated with Jesus? Less well than *hinnam* theology. Qoheleth's sense of the grand absurdity left no place for manipulative behavior by humans, however selfless the act. In his view, Elohim did not respond in a predictable manner, regardless of how virtuous an individual became. Such a dark assessment of reality would seem to have been attractive to Jesus's followers, who were trying to make sense of his death on the cross, the supreme scandal facing any theodicy. The marvel is that the Gospel writers refused to cast their eyes "under the sun" but appealed to apocalyptic hopes that, in the language of Jonathan Z. Smith,[49] abandoned locative spirituality for the utopian.

For all they knew, Jesus was caught up in the same web that had entangled the sages who preceded him. Like them, he tried to unite justice and mercy in his understanding of God. Like them, too, he found the task impossible. However sublime the concept of gratuitous love may have been, it had an unwelcome corollary: the total loss of a bargaining chip when finally ushered into divine presence. And however true *hebel* thinking rang in the shadow of death, it left individuals without hope. Because the Gospel writers believed that the God who had raised Jesus from the grave could be trusted to make

---

[49] *Map Is Not Territory: Studies in the History of Religions* (Leiden: Brill, 1978).

all things new, they grounded this conviction in a worldview burdened by retributive morality and a utopian escape from reality itself. In doing so, they cast their vote for the principle of similarity and remained oblivious to the epistemological revolution ushered in by the unknown authors of the books of Job and Ecclesiastes.

3

∞

The Jesus of the Gospels and Philosophy

Luke Timothy Johnson

This essay considers four ways in which the figure of Jesus as found in the canonical Gospels (Matthew, Mark, Luke, and John) gives rise to the sort of thinking that can properly be called philosophical. I do not want to argue that one way is better than another; each has its merit and each has its limits. I do want to argue that the ways are sufficiently discrete as to demand clarity concerning choices made with respect to the Gospel narratives and how they are being read. I further argue that each approach also carries with it different understandings of what is meant by "philosophy."

THE HISTORICAL JESUS AS SAGE

The first approach is to consider Jesus not as a character in the Gospel narratives but as a historical figure whose words can be abstracted from those narratives and provide the basis for consideration of Jesus as an ancient Jewish sage. The antecedents of the approach are impressive: the Manichaean teacher Faustus dismissed the Gospel narratives as inventions of the apostles and considered only Jesus's words to be authentic and trustworthy.[1] From Thomas Jefferson to Robert Funk, certain searchers after the "historical Jesus" have also focused on the sayings of Jesus as distinctively providing access to his human identity and mission.[2]

The difficulties of determining the *ipsissima verba* – or even the *ipsissima vox* – of Jesus are notorious, as are the diverse motivations of those seeking to discover the "real Jesus" through his speech alone.[3] The uncertain attribution

---

[1] Augustine, *Reply to Faustus*, II, 1; V, 1.
[2] See T. Jefferson, *The Life and Morals of Jesus of Nazareth* (Washington, DC: USPGO, 1904; New York: Henry Holt, 1995); R. Funk and R. Hoover, *The Five Gospels: The Search for the Authentic Words of Jesus* (New York: Macmillan, 1993).
[3] See L. T. Johnson, *The Real Jesus: The Misguided Quest for the Historical Jesus and the Truth of the Traditional Gospels* (San Francisco: HarperSanFrancisco, 1996).

and shape of specific sayings, whether *logia, chreia,* or parable, makes the determination "Jesus said X" hazardous.[4] And the effort to displace Christian belief in Jesus as the resurrected Son of God on the basis of "what he said" lacks both philosophical detachment and religious sensibility.[5] Even if such difficulties could be surmounted, there remains the greatest obstacle: the very premise that a collection of sayings, removed from narrative context, provides sure access to anyone's "identity and mission."[6]

Preoccupation with fixing Jesus's historical words or voice, moreover, is more fundamentally suited to a biographical rather than a philosophical inquiry; in the same fashion, one could seek the "genuine words of Socrates" in the writings of his contemporary Aristophanes or his students Xenophon and Plato, without ever having those words "give rise to thought" in the form of philosophy.[7] Jesus in this sort of quest might appear as one of the sages whose words are reported by Diogenes Laertius, a figure of the past whose opinions are worth noting because they had influence on some followers, but not as one of the significant shapers of thought.[8] Thus, if it is possible to determine that Jesus actually said, "The kingdom of God has arrived; repent and believe the good news" (Mk. 1:15), the statement might have great significance for describing Jesus's self-conception and sense of mission, might also make an important (if difficult to verify) claim to truth, but still fall outside the interests of philosophy.

Some of the words of Jesus in the Gospels are of interest to philosophy understood in the ancient sense as the love of wisdom, namely, those statements that construct an imaginary narrative world (as do the parables) or statements that affirm a truth about humans, or statements that exhort to a certain kind of moral behavior. Such statements give rise to thought in the

---

[4] The elaborately devised "criteria" for determining authentic sayings serve, even when appropriately employed, to identify only the earliest available and verifiable form of a saying in the data pool; the fact that even the earliest versions derive not directly from Jesus but from some stage of tradition is seldom taken seriously by the searchers.

[5] The desire to use a reconstituted Jesus as normative for contemporaries is implicit in virtually all historical Jesus research, but is most obvious in R. Funk, *Honest to Jesus: Jesus for a New Millennium* (San Francisco: HarperSanFrancisco, 1996).

[6] See L. T. Johnson, "The Humanity of Jesus: What's at Stake in the Quest for the Historical Jesus?" in *The Jesus Controversy* (Rockwell Lecture Series; Harrisburg, PA: Trinity Press International, 1999), 48–74, and now, W. A. Meeks, *Christ Is the Question* (Louisville: Westminster John Knox Press, 2006).

[7] Socrates is given distinct representations by his critic Aristophanes, *The Clouds,* and by each of the students who memorialized him: see Xenopohon, *Apology, Memorabilia;* Plato, *Dialogues.* In the first, Socrates is a charlatan; in the second, a simple moral teacher; and in the third, a dialectician and metaphysician.

[8] See especially the treatment of the pre-Socratic sages in Diogenes Laertius, *Lives of Eminent Philosophers.*

philosophical sense when they are considered not as avenues to the mind of Jesus but as declarations to be weighed in light of human experience past and present: thus, we might ask of each of them, Do they, in fact, contain wisdom or provide an avenue along which wisdom can be discovered?

The parables have been particularly favored by historical-Jesus questers, because they are thought to give privileged access to Jesus's worldview.[9] Certainly, the parables ascribed to Jesus in the Synoptic Gospels are distinctive. Although some Jews used *mashalim* to explicate Torah, and some Greeks used fables to teach morals,[10] ancient literature has no parallel to the remarkably compressed and vivid stories ascribed to Jesus.[11] When read within the Gospel narratives, the parables appear as elements within the rhetorical constructions of those compositions, serving among other things to interpret the larger narrative.[12] When detached from the Gospels and read in isolation, however, the parables are polyvalent, inviting a variety of interpretations and fitting into any number of hermeneutical frameworks.[13] The parables of Jesus abstracted from the Gospel narratives are appreciated for their elements of paradox, reversal, and surprise; they are regarded as stories that subvert rather than confirm conventional expectations.[14] As discreet narratives, they can even be put into conversation with other provocative literary voices such as Kafka and Borges.[15] The literary quality of the parables is patent; less clear is how they give rise to thought, unless it is through inducing that sense of surprise and wonder and uncertainty that ought to accompany serious reflection on the world.

Other discrete statements by Jesus take the form of aphorisms (*logia*). They may be organized by the evangelists into sermonlike collections, but probably

---

[9] See J. D. Crossan, *Parables: The Challenge of the Historical Jesus* (New York: Harper and Row, 1973); Crossan builds on the premises and procedures of J. Jeremias, *The Parables of Jesus*, translated from the 6th edition by S. H. Hooke (New York: Scribner's, 1963).

[10] For examples of each, see D. R. Cartlidge and D. L. Dungan, *Documents for the Study of the Gospels* (Philadelphia: Fortress Press, 1980), 137–41.

[11] Crossan memorably characterizes Jesus's parables in terms of brevity, narrativity, and metaphoricity; see J. D. Crossan, *Cliffs of Fall: Paradox and Polyvalence in the Parables of Jesus* (New York: Seabury Press, 1980).

[12] See M. Boucher, *The Mysterious Parable: A Literary Study* (Catholic Biblical Quarterly Monograph Series 6; Washington, DC: Catholic Biblical Association of America, 1977), and L. T. Johnson, "The Lukan Kingship Parable (Luke 19:11–27)," *Novum Testamentum* 24 (1982), 139–59.

[13] See M. A. Tolbert, *Perspectives on the Parables: An Approach to Multiple Interpretations* (Philadelphia: Fortress Press, 1979).

[14] See J. D. Crossan, *The Dark Interval: Towards a Theology of Story* (Niles, IL: Argus Communications, 1975).

[15] J. D. Crossan, *Raid on the Articulate: Comic Eschatology in Jesus and Borges* (New York: Harper and Row, 1976).

circulated originally in the form of isolated declarations. They resemble the short snappy observations that also find parallel in Jewish proverbs and Greco-Roman *apophthegmata*. When found in the form of a *chreia* (whether simple or developed), such declarations tend toward biographical enmeshment, finding their significance in the narrative context provided. An example is the statement in Luke 12:15, "No one's life is based on an abundance of riches." It is found with a preliminary warning, "Watch out! Protect yourself from every form of greed," and is part of a developed *chreia*,[16] yet when taken in isolation can stand as an observation concerning human existence that gives rise to serious thought concerning the connection and lack of connection between being and having.[17]

More obviously akin to proverbial wisdom are such statements as "Can a blind person be a guide for another blind person? Won't they both fall in a ditch?" (Lk. 6:39), and "A sound tree does not produce rotten fruit, nor does a rotten tree produce good fruit. For each tree is known by its own fruit" (Lk. 6:43–44). They appear now in a collection conventionally called "Luke's Sermon on the Plain" (6:17–49), but can each stand alone as an invitation to reflection on life. Both state succinctly and indirectly (through the image of unsighted people leading each other into a ditch and through the image of trees bearing fruits) something of larger significance concerning human existence: leadership requires greater capacities of people; human actions reveal human internal dispositions. Such statements may be trivial or profound. They may also be both deeply provocative and counterintuitive, as when Luke's Jesus declares, "Blessed are the poor" (6:20). The evangelists clearly considered them to have greater authority because they were spoken by Jesus. But as statements about life, they can be considered by thinkers in the same way that the wise sayings of Solomon or Solon or Confucius. Origen states the principle clearly:

> If the doctrine be sound and the effect of it good, whether it was made known to the Greeks by Plato or any of the wise men of Greece, or whether it was delivered to the Jews by Moses or any of the prophets, or whether it was given to the Christians in the recorded teachings of Jesus Christ, or in

---

[16] For the translation, see L. T. Johnson, *The Gospel of Luke* (Sacra Pagina 3; Collegeville, MN: Liturgical Press, 1991), 197; for analysis from the perspective of Greco-Roman rhetoric, see A. J. Malherbe, "The Christianization of a *Topos* (Luke 12:13–34)," *Novum Testamentum* 38 (1996), 123–35, and T. D. Stegman, "Reading Luke 12:13–34 as an Elaboration of a Chreia: How Hermogenes of Tarsus Sheds Light on Luke's Gospel," *Novum Testamentum* 49 (2006), 1–25.

[17] Such as can be found in G. Marcel, *Being and Having*, trans. K. Farrer (Westminster: Dacre Press, 1949), and *The Mystery of Being*, trans. R. Hague (London: Harvill Press, 1951).

the instructions of his apostles, that does not affect the value of the truth communicated.[18]

Finally, there are those statements of Jesus that take the form of direct exhortation to his followers concerning their manner of life. Such instructions most resemble those found in Greco-Roman philosophical schools for the training of students within a specific tradition; perhaps the most obvious analogy would be the *Sovereign Maxims*, ascribed to Epicurus.[19] It must be remembered that, especially in the early empire, philosophy was considered above all to be a manner of life, less a matter of wisdom in the sense of theory as wisdom in the sense of virtue.[20] Protreptic discourses that exhorted would-be philosophers to match their profession with practice are widely attested.[21] In this set of sayings, Jesus's words provide neither an imaginative construal of the world (as in parable) nor a general truth about the world (as in an aphorism), but specific requirements of a follower. Once more, Luke's Sermon on the Plain provides a good example. Immediately after having Jesus pronounce the blessings and woes (6:17–26), Luke continues,

> But I declare to you who are listening: love your enemies. Act well toward those who hate you. Bless those who curse you. Pray for those who abuse you. To the one who strikes you on the cheek, offer your other cheek as well. Do not hold back even your shirt from the one who takes your coat. Give to everyone who asks you, and do not demand restitution from one who takes what is your own. Just as you want people to act toward you, act in the same way toward them.

Such moral instructions are impressively rigorous, especially in combination, although specific commands find parallels in the statements of Greco-Roman and Jewish moralists. The "Golden Rule" is fairly well attested in antiquity,[22] and the offering of the body in service appears as an ideal for the Cynic philosopher.[23] Such parallels confirm that these statements fit within an

---

[18] Origen, *Against Celsus*, 7.59.

[19] For the role of philosophical maxims as guides to behavior, see A. J. Malherbe, *Moral Exhortation: A Greco-Roman Sourcebook* (Philadelphia: Westminster Press, 1986), esp. 68–120.

[20] See the classic discussion in S. Dill, *Roman Society from Nero to Marcus Aurelius* (New York: World Publishing Company, 1956 [1904]), and the more recent treatment in M. C. Nussbaum, *The Therapy of Desire: Theory and Practice in Hellenistic Ethics* (Princeton: Princeton University Press, 1994).

[21] For protreptic discourse, see Malherbe, *Moral Exhortation*, 122–3; for a reading of a NT composition as protreptic, see L. T. Johnson, *The Letter of James* (Anchor Bible 37A; New York: Doubleday, 1995).

[22] The negative form is found in *Tobit* 4:15 and is ascribed to Hillel in *bTShab* 31a; the positive form is attested by Pseudo-Isocrates, *Demonicus* 14; *Nicocles* 61.

[23] Epictetus, *Discourse* III. 22. 21–22, 69–70, 88–89; Dio Chrysostom, *Oration* 77/78. 40–45.

understanding of philosophy as a way of life, in which the point of language is less to describe reality than to change character.

This first approach concentrates on the historical Jesus's speech as giving rise to thought. The fact that Jesus's words are found in narrative Gospels is immaterial; indeed, the forms of those sayings in apocryphal Gospels– most intriguingly, the Coptic *Gospel of Thomas* – are legitimately, even necessarily, included in the data base.[24] Jesus's parables subvert conventional ways of viewing the world, his aphorisms invite consideration of human existence, and his exhortations lead to a certain way of living. However distinctive his sayings might be in content, this approach places Jesus firmly in the context of the sort of moral teaching found among ancient Greco-Roman and Jewish philosophers.

THE NARRATIVE JESUS AS MORAL EXEMPLAR

A second philosophical approach to Jesus is equally consonant with the ancient conviction that philosophy was not only about thoughts but about practice. Some aspects of this moral philosophy were touched on in the previous section, in the consideration of Jesus's exhortations to a manner of life. Concern for virtue and vice was not merely a matter of accurate analysis,[25] but had the practical aim of shaping consistent habits of disposition and behavior. Aristotle is the main source of the sort of "character ethic" that persisted among the Greco-Roman and Jewish moralists of the early empire.[26] The emphasis on character makes intelligible the insistence among such philosophers that students not only learn wise maxims but learn through the close observance and imitation (and memory) of models.[27] Models or exemplars are important because they demonstrate virtue in action.[28] The best models

---

[24] See, e.g., S. J. Patterson, *The Gospel of Thomas and Jesus* (Sonoma, CA: Polebridge Press, 1993) and M. Franzmann, *Jesus in the Nag Hammadi Writings* (Edinburgh: T&T Clark, 1996). Use of the full spectrum of sayings material is found especially in J. D. Crossan, *The Historical Jesus: The Life of a Mediterranean Jewish Peasant* (San Francisco: HarperSanFrancisco, 1991).

[25] For a sample of the exquisite dissection of virtues and vices, see Plutarch, *On Envy and Anger* (Mor. 536–538), *On Control of Anger* (Mor. 452–464), and *On Brotherly Love* (Mor. 478–492).

[26] See Aristotle's *Eudaimonian Ethics* and *Nicomachean Ethics*, as well as the analyses of dispositions in his *Rhetoric*.

[27] For a discussion of this combination of elements and their application to a NT text, see L. T. Johnson, "The Mirror of Remembrance (James 1:22–25)," *Catholic Biblical Quarterly* 50 (1988), 632–45.

[28] In the same way, vices are demonstrated in the behavior of those who betray the philosophical ideal; thus, protreptic discourses often contain slander against "false philosophers"; see L. T. Johnson, "II Timothy and the Polemic against False Teachers," *Journal of Religious Studies* 6/7 (1978–79), 1–26, and "The New Testament's Anti-Jewish Slander and the Conventions of Ancient Polemic," *Journal of Biblical Literature* 108 (1989), 419–41.

to imitate were living persons, whether a parent or a leader, or a philosoph-ical mentor.[29] But the literary representation of exemplars can also serve to instruct in the moral life. There is in antiquity a direct connection between the construction of moral exemplars and the writing of biographies, as seen most vividly in the *Moralia* and the *Parallel Lives* of Plutarch; what is rendered analytically – with many small examples – in the essays is displayed narratively in his biographies of eminent figures.

Approaching Jesus in the Gospels from such a philosophical perspective involves a very different evaluation of the Gospels themselves. Now the point of reading is not the abstracting of some golden sayings of "Jesus the historical sage" from the dross of unworthy narratives, but rather of focusing on how the Gospel narratives render the character of Jesus, not least in the ways in which what he proclaims is embodied in what he does, so that the *bios* of the human Jesus becomes an example to readers. The narratives as such are valorized as vehicles of character ethics. In contrast to the quest for Jesus as a historical sage, furthermore, analysis here must restrict itself primarily to the four canonical Gospels.[30]

That reading the Gospels as exemplary narratives came naturally to early Christian readers is easy to demonstrate, perhaps nowhere more magnificently than in the sermons of Leo the Great. After speaking about Jesus humility and ministry of service, Leo concludes his sermon with these words:

> These words of our Lord, dearly beloved, are useful to us, not only for the communication of grace, but as an example for our imitation also – if only these remedies would be turned into instruction, and what has been bestowed by the mysteries would benefit the way people live. Let us remember that we must live in the "humility and meekness" of our Redeemer, since, as the Apostle says, "If we suffer with him, we shall also reign with him." In vain we are called Christians if we do not imitate Christ. For this reason did he refer to himself as the Way, that the teacher's manner of life might be the exemplar for his disciples, and that the servant might choose the humility which had been practiced by the master, who lives and reigns forever and ever. Amen.[31]

---

[29] In Pseudo-Isocrates' *Demonicus*, the young man's father is presented as the ideal example for imitation; in Lucian of Samosata's *Demonax* and *Nigrinus*, the philosophical teacher is a model for students to emulate.

[30] See the comments on the narrative character of the canonical Gospels in contrast to the "Gnostic Gospels" found at Nag-Hammadi in L. T. Johnson, "Does a Theology of the Canon-ical Gospels Make Sense?" in *The Nature of New Testament Theology: Essays in Honor of Robert Morgan*, ed. C. Rowland and C. Tuckett (Oxford: Blackwell, 2006), 93–108.

[31] Leo the Great, *Sermon* 25:5–6 (25 December 444); citation from St. Leo the Great, *Sermons*, trans. J. P. Freeland and A. J. Conway (The Fathers of the Church 93; Washington, DC:

Contemporary historical critics who have recovered an appreciation for ancient literary conventions have also recognized this dimension of the narrative Gospels, seeing them (correctly) as a species of philosophical *Bios*.[32] To date, however, attention has tended to focus on the question of genre, rather than on the specific ways in which the diverse Gospels shape the character of the human Jesus. For the purposes of the present, largely descriptive essay, I can touch on only three broad aspects of the canonical Gospels' rendering of Jesus's character.

1. The Gospel narratives diverge in their rendering of Jesus's character. Beyond the multiple differences among the Gospels that befuddle historical questers – differences in sequence, location, wording, and the like – are the distinct portrayals of Jesus that are found in the narratives precisely as narratives, effects accomplished through a variety of literary techniques, including direct characterization (of Jesus, of the Jewish populace, of his followers, and of his opponents), employment of symbols and metaphors, authorial commentary, scriptural citation, and allusion. The cumulative result of these many small touches are internally consistent and distinct portraits, so that the reader truly comes to know a different literary "Jesus" in each of the Gospel narratives. The point can be made quickly by looking at the portrayal of Jesus in Matthew and Luke.

In Greco-Roman moral philosophy, the authenticity of teaching was demonstrated by behavior consistent with the teaching. Seneca's states the principle succinctly: *verba rebus proba* ("prove the words by deeds").[33] Both Matthew and Luke show Jesus enacting that principle. Written in the context of competition between formative Judaism and the messianic movement associated with Jesus, Matthew's Gospel portrays Jesus as a teacher of the church who is clothed with the symbols of Torah so central to the form of Judaism that his community engages: in his Gospel, Jesus is the interpreter of Torah, the fulfiller of Torah, and even the personification of Torah.[34] Written in the context of Paul's mission to the Gentiles, Luke's Gospel portrays Jesus as a public philosopher and prophet who carries God's good news to

---

Catholic University of America Press, 1996), 103–4; see also *Sermon* 37:3–4; 46:2–3; 59:4–5; see also Origen, *Homilies on Luke* 20:5; 29:5–7; 34; 38:1–3.

[32] The pioneering work by C. W. Votaw, *The Gospels and Contemporary Biographies in the Greco-Roman World* (Philadelphia: Fortress Press, 1970; original essays in 1915), was taken up by C. H. Talbert, *What Is a Gospel? The Genre of the Canonical Gospels* (Philadelphia: Fortress Press, 1977), and developed still further by others.

[33] Seneca, *Moral Epistles* 20.1.

[34] For a fuller characterization, see L. T. Johnson, *The Writings of the New Testament: An Interpretation*, revised, enlarged edition, with T. Penner (Minneapolis: Fortress Press, 1999), 187–212.

the outcast among Jews and whose disciples carry it to the ends of the earth (Acts 1:8).[35]

Matthew's Gospel illustrates Seneca's principle by showing through narrative how Jesus acts in a manner consistent with his own teachings. In Matthew's version of the beatitudes, Jesus declares, "Blessed are the poor in spirit (*ptochoi to pneumati*) for theirs is the kingdom of heaven" (Matt. 5:3), "Blessed are the meek (*praeis*) for they shall inherit the land" (Matt. 5:5), and "Blessed are the merciful (*eleemones*) for they shall receive mercy" (Matt. 5:7). The first two characteristics are ascribed to Jesus directly in the declaration of Matthew 11:27, "Take my yoke upon you and learn from me, for I am meek (*praus*) and humble of heart (*tapeinos te kardia*)."

The characteristic of meekness is further confirmed by the citation of Zechariah 9:9 at Jesus entry into Jerusalem, "Behold your king comes to you, meek (*praus*) and riding on an ass" (Matt. 21:5), while the characteristic of lowliness is affirmed by the application to Jesus of the suffering servant song from Isaiah 42:1–4 (Matt. 12:18–21), and the quality of mercy is affirmed by the application of Hosea 6:6 to Jesus's call of sinners, "I desire mercy (*eleos*) and not sacrifice" (Matt. 9:13). That such narrative characterization is not accidental is shown by the negative portrayal of Peter. In his opening sermon, Jesus expressly forbids taking oaths, declaring that anything more than a simple yes or no is "from the evil one" (Matt. 5:33–37). The declaration is given narrative expression when Peter's resistance to Jesus's passion takes the form of an oath ("God forbid, Lord!"), leading to Jesus calling Peter "Satan" (Matt. 16:22:23), and when Peter twice is said to swear an oath when he denies Jesus (Matt. 26:72–74).[36]

Luke's two-volume narrative of the good news (Luke-Acts) gives a distinctive characterization to Jesus and his disciples, but equally connects their actions to Jesus's words. In Luke's case, Jesus (and his mother Mary [Lk. 1:46–55]) give expression to a prophetic vision that expresses God's will for humans: God's visitation accomplishes a reversal of human expectations and measurements that is most succinctly stated by Jesus's statement, "Blessed are you poor" and "Woe to you who are rich" (Lk. 6:20, 24). The spirit-anointed Messiah proclaims as fulfilled in himself Isaiah's prophetic vision of a mission to the outcast and the oppressed as "a year acceptable to the Lord" (Isa. 61:1–2, 58:6; Lk. 4:16–21).

The Lukan narrative shows Jesus enacting this vision. He heals those who are oppressed by Satan (Lk. 6:31–37), he calls into God's people those who

---

[35] Johnson, *Writings*, 213–58.
[36] Johnson, *Writings*, 205–6.

for one reason or another were marginal to full participation: the lame, the blind, the poor (7:22), and women (8:1–3) and children (9:46–48). His status-reversing message is in turn rejected by the rich and the powerful and the religiously established (16:14, 18:18–23). In Acts, Luke shows Jesus's prophetic successors continuing to enact the prophet's vision of God's rule, by healings (Acts 3:1–10, 8:32–35) and exorcisms (16:16–18), by embracing the outcast of Israel (Samaritans [8:4–8], Eunuchs [8:26–40]), and by extending Jesus's ministry of open table fellowship even to the despised Gentiles (10–15). Even more impressive, from the perspective of ancient character ethics is the way in which Jesus and his followers embody the radical lifestyle consonant with the prophetic vision of the reversal of values: Jesus and his followers are poor (Lk. 9:58; Acts 3:6), are itinerant (Lk. 9–19; Acts 13–28), are dependent on God in prayer (Lk. 9:28–29; Acts 4:23–31), exercise leadership in the mode of servants (Lk. 22:25–30; Acts 4:32–37), and speak truth boldly to religious and political authorities (Lk. 11:39–52; Acts 5:27–32).[37]

2. If they diverge in tone and nuance, the Gospel narratives also converge concerning the essential character of Jesus. The distinctive portraits of Jesus by Matthew and Luke are matched by those found in the narratives constructed by Mark and John. The literary character "Jesus" is distinct in each narrative: Mark's Suffering Son of Man, Matthew's Teacher of the Church, Luke's Prophet of God's Visitation, and John's Man from Heaven are impossible to harmonize fully. Similarly, the portrayal of the disciples in each Gospel is distinct: In Mark, Jesus's chosen followers are both stupid and faithless; in Matthew, morally inadequate but intelligent; in Luke, prophetic successors trained to continue Jesus's mission; in John, the friends who will experience from the world the same hatred shown Jesus. The narrative Gospels bear witness to Jesus by the way in which they interpret him so diversely. Precisely the diversity of this witness, however, makes all the more startling the fact that these narratives converge on the heart of Jesus's character and, for that matter, on the character of discipleship.

I speak here of the fundamental and defining dispositions of Jesus, in contrast to the diverse roles – wonderworker, teacher, prophet, revealer – emphasized by the respective narratives. These fundamental dispositions are utterly simple. In all the Gospels, Jesus is a human being totally defined by his relationship with God, a relationship expressed by faithful obedience to God's will. Jesus is not defined by human expectations or perceptions, his own or others, but by a radical stance of hearing and responsiveness to his Father.

---

[37] See L. T. Johnson, *The Gospel of Luke* (Sacra Pagina 3; Collegeville, MN: Liturgical Press, 1990), and *The Acts of the Apostles* (Sacra Pagina 5; Collegeville, MN: Liturgical Press, 1992).

This "vertical" relationship of faithful obedience is expressed by an equally fundamental "horizontal" disposition toward other humans, a disposition of loving service. The narratives of the canonical Gospels – in this respect fully in agreement with the other canonical witnesses – see Jesus as "the man for others" precisely because he is also a completely "God-defined man."

Similarly, for all their disparate ways of describing Jesus's actual disciples, the four canonical Gospels agree completely on the fundamental character of discipleship. It has nothing to do with self-seeking or self-aggrandizement, with success or prosperity. Rather, authentic discipleship means having the same "character" as Jesus, following in the path that he walked ahead of them. True "students" (*mathetai*) of this teacher will show the same faithful obedience toward God that he did and will imitate the life of service toward others that he exemplified. Readers of these narratives, in turn, learn from the diversity of the Gospels' portrait of Jesus how complex and diverse the expressions of this basic character can be, and yet how simple and profound in its essence. Likewise, they learn from the actual performance of Jesus's followers how not to be disciples, but from Jesus's words concerning discipleship they learn how it means an imitation of his example.[38]

In short, despite their literary diversity and the distinctiveness of their portraits of Jesus, the canonical Gospel narratives render "the identity of Jesus Christ" in a clear and unequivocal form.[39] The character of Jesus in the Gospels is so distinct than it cannot be mistaken for any other religious or political leader. The "Christ Image" of the Gospels represents a certain way of being human – the way of God's servant and servant of other humans – that is so unmistakable that literary critics can speak confidently of other narrative renderings of innocent sufferers in terms of this image.[40] The character of Jesus as depicted in the narrative Gospels was meant to be imitated, and in fact the history of Christianity has shown that movements of radical discipleship in the church – think of Francis of Assisi, Martin Luther, Dorothy Day, Martin Luther King, Mother Teresa – have most often been stimulated by those challenged to imitate his character in their own historical circumstances.

3. The character of Jesus (and of discipleship) in the narrative Gospels of the New Testament challenges (or should challenge) the philosophical understandings of the self in the contemporary world. Not only does the Christ image in the Gospels stand in opposition to classical construals of the

---

[38] This argument is made more fully in L. T. Johnson, *Living Jesus: Learning the Heart of the Gospel* (San Francisco: HarperSanFrancisco, 1999).

[39] See Hans Frei, *The Identity of Jesus Christ: The Hermeneutical Basis of Dogmatic Theology* (Philadelphia: Fortress Press, 1975).

[40] For example, Dostoyevsky's *The Idiot*, or Melville's *Billy Budd*.

noble person – obedience, service, meekness, and humility are all associated with the slave class, not the aristocracy – but it also stands in opposition to the sovereign self cultivated since the Enlightenment. Friedrich Nietzsche made the challenge explicit when he appealed to the older Greek sense of nobility and scorned the "slave mentality" of Christians.[41] Even within some forms of Christian theology, the character of Jesus and of discipleship as portrayed by the Gospels – and the other NT writings – is criticized as dangerous to the self-esteem and self-worth of some people: humility, obedience, and service are considered contrary to the flourishing of humans within just social structures.[42]

Insofar as philosophy has to do with thinking about the proper way of being human, the character of Jesus in the narrative Gospels ought to give rise to the most serious sort of thinking. Is the Gospels' depiction of Jesus's character and the character of discipleship good for humans or not? Can a serious politics be based on such a construal of the person? Or is this way of human essentially pathological, leaving those shaped by it wounded, weak, and incapable of robust action in the world? Or is it, in fact, a way of living that reveals the deepest truth within humans and paradoxically elevates them to their highest excellence?

THE NARRATIVE JESUS AS REVEALING GOD

The two previous approaches to the Jesus of the Gospels focus entirely on his humanity: in the first instance, attention is given to his words apart from the narrative, and in the second, to the depiction of his human character through the respective Gospel narratives. Both approaches are available to the philosophically inclined whether they share Christian faith or not. A third approach leads us into the realm of what is properly called "Christian philosophy." It reads the Gospel narratives from the perspective of early Christian experiences and convictions concerning Jesus that transcend ordinary humanity, expressed by the creed respectively as "descended from heaven" and "ascended into heaven." The conviction that Jesus after his death was exalted to the right hand of God and shares fully in God's life and power (at one end of his human story) corresponds (at the other end) to the conviction that he was the

---

[41] See, in particular, *On the Genealogy of Morality*, trans. C. Diethe (Cambridge: Cambridge University Press, 1994), and *Twilight of the Idols* and *The Anti-Christ*, trans. R. J. Hollingdale (London: Penguin Books, 2003).

[42] Delores Williams, for example, argues that the cross is no longer a viable Christian symbol for women of color who have experienced oppression, in *Sisters in the Wilderness: The Challenge of Womanist God-Talk* (Maryknoll, NY: Orbis Books, 1993).

incarnate word of God. This approach, in short, takes seriously the larger "mythic" story that is mostly only implied within the Gospel narratives themselves – with the notable exceptions of John and Acts – but that is made explicit by Christian confession.

In this approach, the Jesus of the Gospels is not simply a sage of first-century Palestine or a moral exemplar, but the revelation of God in a human person. What gives rise to thought concerning Jesus, therefore, is not what he says or what he did, but above all who he is; what gives rise to thought concerning discipleship is not living by his words or following his example, but rather being transformed through participation in his being.

Such a perspective, it should be emphasized, is not imposed violently on the Gospels. They were, after all, composed by followers who had strong experiences and convictions concerning Jesus's exalted status as Lord and were written after – and undoubtedly in light of – the very "high" Christology found in Paul and Hebrews (see only 1 Cor. 8:6–8; Gal. 4:3–7; Heb. 1:1–13). The understanding of Jesus as the one who by his very being reveals God is, to be sure, most explicit in the narrative of John's Gospel. In the Prologue, Jesus is identified with the preexistent word that became flesh and revealed God's glory (Jn. 1:1–18). John similarly introduces Jesus's last meal with his followers with the solemn declaration that "Jesus knew that his hour had come to pass from this world to the Father" (13:1), and that Jesus was "fully aware that the Father had put everything into his power and that he had come from God and was returning to God" (13:3). In John's Gospel, Jesus reveals the God no one has ever seen (1:18); though a man, he "makes himself God" (10:33) and is declared by Thomas to be "Lord and God" (20:28). But the second part of Luke's Gospel narrative – the Acts of the Apostles – is equally emphatic in its assertion of the "mythic" dimensions of the Jesus story: he is "taken up into heaven" (Lk. 24:51; Acts 1:10) and "will return again in the same way" (Acts 9:11); elevated to the Father's right hand, he pours out the Holy Spirit on all flesh (Acts 2:17–34); as risen Lord, he will "judge the world with justice" (Acts 17:31).

Readers with such convictions concerning Jesus can find them confirmed as well by the less explicit statements found in the Synoptic Gospels. In Matthew and Luke, Jesus's birth is ascribed to the Holy Spirit, making him "God with us" (Matt. 1:20–23) and "Son of the Most High," indeed, "Son of God" (Lk. 1:31–35). Jesus makes declarations, even in these more realistic narratives, such as "for this purpose I have come" (Mk. 1:38), and "I have come not to call the righteous to repentance but sinners" (Lk. 5:32). Jesus works powerful deeds that make unclean spirits recognize him as "Son of the Most High God" (Mk. 5:20) and make his disciples ask, "Who is this whom even wind and sea obey?"

(Mk. 4:41). He shows himself transfigured in the radiance of God's glory, and his closest followers hear him declared from heaven as God's "beloved son" (Mk. 8:2–8; Matt. 17:1–8; Lk. 9:28–35). And after his resurrection he will show himself among his disciples, commissioning them with "all authority in heaven and earth" (Matt. 20:18–10; Lk. 24:46–49; Mk.16:15).

The mythic dimension of the Gospel narratives provided no shock to the common religious sensibilities of the Greco-Roman world, where the membrane between gods and humans was a permeable one, with noble heroes being elevated to divine status and gods visiting the world in human form.[43] But it did shock the religious sensibilities of pious Jews, who regarded claims made for the divinity of Jesus as a form of idolatry.[44] And it challenged the more sophisticated Christians who shared with other Greco-Roman philosophers abhorrence for crude anthropomorphism in language about the divine and regarded thinking wrongly about the divine (superstition) as more evil than denying the divine altogether.[45]

The Middle Platonism of Philo of Alexandria (together with Aristobolos and others) showed the mental struggle involved in thinking philosophically with the dualistic categories of Plato in response to the cosmology and psychology expressed by the intensely material and realistic biblical narratives. In some cases, thinking well about God demanded recourse to a spiritualization of the biblical text through allegory, precisely to avoid the sort of superstition that mythic language could encourage.[46] The historical human character of Jesus is never evaporated in the developing Christian myth, outside some forms of Gnosticism. But the conviction that in Jesus of Nazareth the God of creation and covenant entered into the frame of human existence made the apparent dissonance between the myth and good thinking about God even greater. Nowhere is the potential for philosophical revolution more apparent than in the anonymous composition *To the Hebrews*, which simultaneously affirms in the strongest possible terms the divine origin and nature of Jesus, and his complete immersion in the lot of suffering humanity, and which, by reading both Platonic and biblical cosmologies through the incarnation,

---

[43] See, above all, Ovid's *Metamorphoses*; for other texts, see Cartlidge and Dungan, *Documents for the Study of the Gospels*, 129–36, 187–202.

[44] See A. F. Segal, *Two Powers in Heaven: Early Rabbinic Reports about Christianity and Gnosticism* (Studies in Judaism in Late Antiquity; Leiden: Brill, 1977).

[45] The point is made repeatedly and emphatically by Plutarch, *On Superstition* (Mor. 164–171), and *Isis and Osiris* 11 (Mor. 355D).

[46] For the way Philo's two worlds came together, see A. Mendelson, *Secular Education in Philo of Alexandria* (Cincinnati: Hebrew Union Press, 1982), and *Philo's Jewish Identity* (Atlanta: Scholars Press, 1988); see also C. R. Holladay, "Jewish Responses to Hellenistic Culture," in *Ethnicity in Hellenistic Egypt*, ed. P. Bilde et al. (Aarhus: Aarhus University Press, 1992), 139–63.

obedient suffering, sacrificial death, and royal exaltation of Jesus, bends both to the point of shattering.

The mythic dimension of the Gospels – and other early Christian compositions – gives rise to thought by challenging the basic categories of existence. If God has entered into humanity (not only Jesus but also those who are "in Christ"), then the nature both of humanity and of divinity need to be rethought, time and eternity require new assessment, and the infinite and the finite demand an accounting. If God has entered into a human body and that body has subsequently entered the life of God, then the very nature of "body" must be rethought, and if "God's Holy Spirit" can enter the bodies of other humans as "the body of Christ," then both body and spirit need to be assessed in terms of what Paul calls the "spiritual body" (*soma pneumatikon*, 1 Cor. 15:44).

If the impassible, all-powerful God can enter so fully into the tangle of human existence as to suffer and die, then both the meaning of the divine and the meaning of suffering require new examination. And if by resurrection, Jesus has become "Lord," then most serious consideration must be given by those considering themselves monotheists to resolving the problem of "two powers in heaven." In short, this dimension of the Gospels gives rise to ontology, to thinking about the meaning of being and existence in light of the shared conviction "[I]f anyone is in Christ, there is a new creation" (2 Cor. 5:17).

Christian theology of the Patristic period can be understood as a philosophical effort to take with equal seriousness the mythic dimension of the biblical idiom ("the truth of the Gospel"), and the requirement to think well and righteously about God, avoiding the superstition that is worse than atheism (the truth of philosophy). The Trinitarian and Christological debates that spanned the third to fifth centuries were spurred by a spirit of philosophical inquiry among teachers who (like Arius and Eunomius) sought to fit the paradoxical claims of the Gospels into the neat categories of classical metaphysics and were answered by thinkers (like Athanasius and the Cappadocians) who had equal facility in those categories but also had a deeper commitment to the mythic language of scripture as the source of the knowledge of salvation.[47] Seen in this light, the appearance of the *homoousios* in the Nicene Creed or of *duo physeis mia prosopon* in the Formula of Chalcedon appears less as an

---

[47] For a sense of the interaction of biblical and philosophical impulses in Patristic thought, see L. Ayres, *Nicaea and Its Legacy: An Approach to Fourth-Century Trinitarian Theology* (Oxford: Oxford University Press, 2004), and R. L. Wilken, *The Spirit of Early Christian Thought: Seeking the Face of God* (New Haven: Yale University Press, 2003).

inappropriate distortion of the Gospel narratives than a bold insistence that they be read faithfully in their mythic dimension.

Such a difficult, and in many ways fruitful, struggle could only be sustained so long as the two partners in the conversation remained alive. Sadly, one of the notable exiles from the contemporary house of philosophy is ontology.[48] Perhaps not coincidentally, the same spirit of Enlightenment that banished metaphysics as a form of nonsense (because nonverifiable) also impelled the quest for the historical Jesus as a new norm for right-thinking Christians – that is, Christians who kept their religion within the bounds of reason (defined in terms of empiricism). That quest memorably began to be "scientific," it will be recalled, when David Friedrich Strauss relegated the mythic dimension of the Gospels to what is nonhistorical and, by the canons of reason then employed, not to be taken seriously in its truth claims. Kierkegaard stands as a notable and heroic example of a genuine philosophical mind continuing to struggle with the challenge posed by the Gospels' mythic language about Jesus.[49]

The present state of affairs generally is perhaps best communicated by the collection of essays that appeared in 1976 under the title *The Myth of the Incarnate God*; each essay, in its fashion, considered the "myth" as something disposable for thoughtful Christians, not in the least worth considering as a claim that should give rise to serious thought.[50] The present situation is further illuminated by the realization that Christian thinkers calling themselves systematic theologians have concluded that Christology should begin with a reconstruction of the "historical Jesus."[51]

The loss of the conversation between philosophy and the mythic dimension of the Gospels is sad on several counts. First, the alternative Jesus offered by a multitude of historical questers is, even when plausible, lacking in any significant depth. He may be an interesting or even important figure of the past, but that is all he is, and it is unclear why (as a sage) he should command our attention more than, say, Epictetus does. Second, the desire for a historically verifiable Jesus means – and Strauss was right on the methodological point –

---

[48] Such banishments are never immediate and seldom absolute. Particularly in continental philosophy, from Hegel to Heidegger there were (and are) those who continued (and continue) to engage metaphysics. But the conversation is not set by them: the retreat from ontology to epistemology and from epistemology to language has been steady and most influential.

[49] See S. Kierkegaard, *Philosophical Fragments or a Fragment of Philosophy by Johannes Climacus*, trans. D. Swenson (Princeton: Princeton University Press, 1936), and *Concluding Unscientific Postscript*, trans. D. Swenson and W. Lowrie (Princeton: Princeton University Press, 1968).

[50] J. Hick, ed., *The Myth of God Incarnate* (Philadelphia: Westminster Press, 1977).

[51] E. Schillebeeckx, *Jesus* (New York: Crossroad, 1979); R. Haight, *Jesus, Symbol of God* (Maryknoll, NY: Orbis Books, 1999).

excluding all those mythic dimensions that give the Gospels, and the figure of Jesus, such compelling depth. Third, as a result, contemporary readers find themselves cut off from centuries of serious engagement with the Jesus of the Gospels found in the sea of literature that addressed this mythic dimension with philosophical acuity.

Fourth, as a further consequence, the language of the Christian faith becomes increasingly unintelligible, even to believers, precisely because so much of this language is grounded in the mythic dimension of the Gospels and other NT literature. Without a phenomenology of body or of spirit (or with only a definition of body and mind that depend on Cartesian dualism), it is impossible to speak meaningfully of the resurrection of Jesus in terms of a *soma pneumatikon*. As a result, even Christians tend to speak of the resurrection either in terms of a resuscitation of Jesus (in order to save historicity) or in terms of a psychological adjustment among his followers (in order to save Enlightenment reasonability) and, in either case, miss the truth of the Gospels.

Finally, the loss of the mythic language of the Gospels and the mode of philosophy that thinks about being and existence means that – as in some forms of "liberation theology" – a more than legitimate passion for social justice among the poor and oppressed is expressed by the rejection of any transcendental understanding of sin and salvation. Sin is defined in terms of evil social structures and the dispositions that support them, and salvation is defined in terms of the dispositions and actions of humans through whom God brings justice to the earth. Once more, this passion is usually linked to an understanding of the prophetic ministry of the historical Jesus. The loss here is extraordinary, no less than the truth of the incarnation expressed in mythic terms: God entered into human existence not so that human social arrangements might be altered, but so that the very frame of human existence might be transformed; the goal that we call salvation is not a utopian society, but a participation in God's glory.

JESUS AND NARRATIVE ONTOLOGY

A final way in which the Jesus of the Gospels gives rise to thought is through reflection on the nature of narrative itself and its way of bringing into existence what previously did not exist, and the peculiar sort of presence it thereby establishes in the world. The third approach, sketched earlier, took the mythic language of the Gospels as referring to the actual figure of Jesus in both human and divine dimension; ontology, therefore, meant inquiry into the implications of the incarnate Word. Now the object of inquiry is the Gospel

narrative as narrative, and the ontological implications of reading. In contrast
to the other approaches described in this essay, the roots of this approach lie
not in an earlier mode of interpretation but in the nature of narrative and in
the practices of the early church with respect to the Gospels. My remarks here
are only suggestive, because I am only at an early stage of thinking about this
perspective. As I seek to find a way toward a kind of ontology that does not
require a misapplication or even a repristination of classical categories, I can
only touch on some of the elements such thinking would require.

The first step is to consider the distinctive way in which stories – above all
personal narratives – create a space in the world. When you tell me the story of
your experience, a complex sort of presence comes into being. The story you
tell is not identical with your empirical self – the story selects elements from the
experience of the past and shapes them – but is nevertheless connected to your
empirical self as source: it is not only about you, it somehow communicates
you. Once the story is spoken, and heard, furthermore, it stands between us
as something both you and I can refer to. Your "storied self" takes its place
in our thoughts and reflections. In our further conversations, both of us can
refer to "your story" as something real, even if it does not correspond, for
example, to your present experience or situation. It is so real that we can both
poke and pull at it interpretively without destroying it. The story is neither
yours nor mine, even though it comes from you and is accepted by me. It
stands between us as a common point of reference. Even when the empirical
you departs, the storied you can continue its presence, and its influence, in
my life. The philosophical question concerns the nature of this presence.

The shared personal story is perhaps only the smallest and most accessible
example of a wide range of phenomena – things about whose "appearance" we
can all agree – concerning which the question of "being" (that is, of ontology)
properly can be asked. Very often, the phenomena are connected to human
imagination, the most creative dimension of human cognition. Psychologists
recognize, for example, that fantasy is somehow something real and that it
has presence and exercises power, even if (or especially) when it fails to be
"realized" physically. Fantasy, moreover, can be both private ("my wife loves
me") and communal ("we are the chosen people"). Lives of individuals and
of populations are more often and more powerfully directed by fantasy than
by fact.[52] But how can we think about the sort of "being" found in fantasy?

Similarly, it is commonly recognized that the performance of music or
drama "brings into being" the notes on a page or the words in a script
with a presence and power that is epiphanic. The ringing tones of an aria

---

[52] See E. S. Person, *By Force of Fantasy: How We Make our Lives* (New York: HarperCollins, 1995).

somehow "fill" the hall and the hearts of the audience, forcing recognition of insistent existence not measurable by the printed notes and lyrics. The sound is evanescent. Yet, Mirella Freni's Mimi remains "real" to all who heard her in that performance of *La Bohème*. Falstaff (whoever plays him) likewise notoriously transcends the plots and plays into which Shakespeare wrote the character, and forces recognition of him as a shared cultural presence the moment his name is mentioned.[53] These performances of texts create a presence that exercises power over others than the performers; the presence is often transitory, but the effects of the power often linger. But what sort of thought concerning "being" does this realm demand and enable?

The second step is to consider the sort of presence and power, what I have earlier called "space in the world" that is created by the performance, through public reading, of a narrative with a central character far more compelling than Falstaff. The Gospel narratives of the New Testament can rightly be considered "personal stories" in two ways. First, they arise from the many smaller stories told about Jesus among his followers during an extended period of oral tradition following the resurrection experience. Such testimonies are ineluctably personal in their selectivity and their subjective shaping. Second, the Gospel narratives are expressly shaped to communicate the person of Jesus (see Lk. 1:4; Jn. 20:31) and are themselves both selective and subjective in their literary shaping. They are narratives, moreover, that were meant to be read aloud in the assembly, that is, "performed" by a reader. That this was the case follows from ancient practice: reading generally was an oral/aural rather than a merely visual experience; the Gospels existed (at first) only in singular manuscripts and (until printing) only in limited numbers of manuscripts, and they were read in the context of the liturgical assembly.

When the Gospel narratives were first read to their intended audiences, the character of Jesus (as well as of the disciples and crowds and opponents) progressively "came into existence" in the real space and time of the hearers. Jesus took on his character among them through the process of reading. It was not there all at once, but emerged. And as it emerged, came into existence through the reading-construction of the hearers, it reshaped or gave more definite shape to the various partial stories about Jesus and to partial apprehensions of his character already present among the listeners. The literary character of Jesus thus came into an extratextual existence among the hearers of the Gospel as the narrative was performed in public. All those

---

[53] So, extravagantly, H. Bloom, *Shakespeare: The Invention of the Human* (New York: Riverhead Books, 1998), and more critically, R. Rosenbaum, *Shakespeare Wars: Clashing Scholars, Public Fiascoes, Palace Coups* (New York: Random House, 2006).

who heard this performance could then refer to a "Jesus" who had come to be among them and who had not existed before.

The process becomes more complicated, however, as the narrative undoubtedly was read repeatedly in the assembly; now, the scattered partial stories as well as the prior hearings of the extended narrative gain greater coherence and greater depth through re-hearing. As we know, the practice of liturgical reading eventually involved far more than the recitation of a single Gospel. All four canonical Gospels were recited in the assembly not in complete sequence but in segments determined by lectionaries, in combination with other fragmentary sections of text from the Old and the New Testament. Such oral performances – which early on included interpretations and applications through homilies – were located within cultic performances of an ever more complex liturgy of the Eucharist, which put into ritual action segments of the Jesus story (above all the Last Supper). If the philosophical question concerning being is asked concerning the narratives that make the literary character of Jesus present among hearers, that question itself must respond to the complications involved in these diverse forms of "presentation" and the "Jesus" being presented: the character of Jesus found in one Gospel, the character of Jesus constructed and presented by multiple Gospels, and the character of Jesus constructed by the diverse forms of liturgical practice.

The "story of Jesus" existing among believers across the centuries of Christian faith has a real existence through such multiple liturgical performances, as well as other, less verbal representations, such as multiple sacramental and paraliturgical rituals and the example of the saints. I am not suggesting that this presence is of the order as that claimed for the presence of the resurrected Jesus in the Body of Christ that is the church or for the sacramental presence of the Lord Jesus in the Eucharistic meal, but I do suggest that it is a distinctive sort of presence that has its own character and its own reality. It both transcends the specific narratives of the Gospels, yet remains always anchored in and dependent on those narratives, so that with renewed reading of the narratives, specific dimensions of his presence come once more into more powerful existence among readers.

CONCLUSION

My essay has not advanced a constructive position concerning Jesus and philosophy, but has instead performed the modest task of describing four ways in which the Jesus of the Gospels has or might give rise to the serious and disciplined thought worthy of the name philosophy. I have suggested that each approach demands certain decisions concerning how the Gospels are to be read: as sources for the sayings of the historical Jesus, as narratives that display a certain moral character, as myths that reveal the presence of God in a human being, and as narratives that through the process of public reading bring a character into existence among readers. Each approach also yields a different kind of philosophy: the historical Jesus is an ancient sage whose words form part of the history of philosophy, the Jesus who is moral exemplar fits within character ethics, the mythic Jesus gives rise to classical ontology, and the narratively recited Jesus enables thought about the reality of existence in the shared universe of literary, artistic, and literary performance. I consider each approach to have value, but am certain that the collapse of the second and third modes is a sad loss and that the rise of the fourth as a possibility only a meager replacement.

4

∾

Paul, the Mind of Christ, and Philosophy

Paul W. Gooch

I. JESUS, PAUL, PHILOSOPHY

What difference does Jesus make to Paul? And what implications are there, in that difference, for the practice of philosophy?

To answer these questions, we must negotiate difficult territory. The pitfalls include Paul's stance toward philosophy, his relationship to Jesus, and the sources we should trust – not to speak of the conflicting opinions that scholars, skeptics, and true believers have voiced on every detail of such a journey, including the nature of philosophy itself.

The most obvious obstacle for many is the very juxtaposition of Paul and philosophy. Did he not write in Colossians 2:8, "Take care that no one carries you away with philosophy and empty deceit according to human tradition, according to the elements of the cosmos, and not according to Christ"? Well, perhaps not: the weight of scholarly opinion is against Paul's authorship of that letter, so immediately we encounter a problem with what counts as evidence.[1] And yet it is true that running through Paul's letters generally accepted as genuine is the stark contrast between human and divine wisdom, a reliance on revealed truths that cannot be achieved by human beings, and a claim to have had disclosed to him mysteries or secrets not previously available.[2] We will have to assess judiciously the implications of his apparent distaste

---

[1] Without entering debates about authorship, it suffices to draw our evidence for this chapter from the seven letters generally accepted as from Paul: 1 Thessalonians, 1 and 2 Corinthians, Galatians, Philippians, Philemon, and Romans. The translation used is the New Revised Standard Version, unless otherwise noted. Thanks to Nathan Ballantyne, Terry Donaldson, and Ann Jervis for helpful comments.

[2] Paul draws the distinction between human words and God's word (1 Thess. 2:13), contrasting human with divine authority (4:8). In Gal. 1:12, the source of his knowledge is not human; it is a revelation of the Gospel of Christ. The most sustained discussion on human wisdom, mystery, and revelation is 1 Cor. 2; see section IV.c of this chapter.

for philosophy, but however that turns out, it remains the case that Paul betrays very little interest in the philosophical activity of his day. Perhaps, given his background and likely education, he was acquainted with Stoics and Epicureans;[3] there is the famous account in Acts 17 of his debating in Athens with philosophers from those two schools, and in his speech before the Areopagus he quotes from Greek authors to buttress his argument. That would suggest not distaste but at least minimal acceptance of Greek wisdom; but then again, perhaps not. Questions of evidence reappear: while the author of Acts sometimes writes as a companion of Paul and eyewitness to events, he does not claim to have been at Athens; perhaps he is making his hero into an acceptable Greek debater, able to hold his own with the best of them.[4] So although the only two New Testament references to philosophy or philosophers are associated with Paul's name, one negative and the other not, we must tread carefully over this terrain.

There is another large problem midpath for this investigation: the problematic nature of Paul's awareness of the life and teachings of Jesus. When the assignment is to assess the influence of one thinker on a later writer, we want evidence of the latter's understanding of the mind of the former. In the case of the Jesus of the Gospels, post-Pauline readers have sayings, parables, miracle stories, disputations with opponents, and of course the evangelists' own presentations of the meanings of their narratives. This material has informed the understanding of the philosophers dealt with, or writing, elsewhere in this book on Jesus and philosophy. With Paul, though, we should assume that the source of his knowledge of Jesus was none of the four Gospels, given their likely composition after his own writings. Rather, he would have gained whatever he knew through oral accounts and traditions. Perhaps, as some believe, there was written material in circulation before the earliest of our Gospels, and if so one cannot be certain that Paul did not see it. That is mere speculation, though: the significant fact remains that Paul's letters betray very little direct evidence of such material.

In what is probably Paul's earliest letter, the facts about Jesus are sparse: in a sentence, "since we believe that Jesus died and rose again, even so, through Jesus, God will bring with him those who have died" (1 Thess. 4:14). In

---

[3] The exact nature of his acquaintance is not easily determined. See Abraham J. Malherbe, *Paul and the Popular Philosophers* (Minneapolis: Fortress Press, 1989); Troels Engberg-Pedersen, *Paul and the Stoics* (Louisville, KY: Westminster John Knox Press, 2000).

[4] James D. G. Dunn suggests that Paul's activities echo Socrates' and the "open air" teaching of Cynics (*The Acts of the Apostles* [Valley Forge, PA: Trinity Press International, 1976], 272). "The apostle is portrayed as the first Christian philosopher, using Stoic and Jewish arguments" (*The New Oxford Annotated Bible*, ad loc.).

Galatians, the resurrection of Jesus and his giving himself for our freedom are foundational for Paul (1:1, 4); this must be at the heart of the Gospel of Christ (1:7). Likewise with 1 Corinthians: the essential facts about Jesus are what Paul has handed on about the death, burial, and resurrection of Christ (15:3). The burden of his message is "Christ crucified" (2:2). Romans works out the meaning of the death and resurrection of Christ, revealing a couple of additional things about the actual life of Jesus: that he was descended from David (1:3; cf. Matt. 1) and that he "did not please himself" but bore insults (15:3; cf. Mk. 15:29–32).

There are echoes of the teachings or sayings of Jesus in Paul's writing, but his focus remains on the events of Jesus's death, resurrection, and anticipated return.[5] Compare Paul's knowledge and use of the Old Testament, and the contrast is striking: Paul is steeped in those texts and may well have often quoted them from memory.[6] The absence of Paul's explicit reflection on Jesus's words is a challenge for anyone trying to assess the influence of Jesus's teachings as we have them on Paul's own mind.

Of course we should be cautious about the nature of our evidence. We have an incomplete record of Paul's thinking,[7] and the surviving correspondence is intended to correct misapprehensions or misapplications of the Gospel of Christ, rather than to set out the content of Paul's understanding of that Gospel in a systematic way.[8] That said, it remains the case that Paul's consuming interest is in the identity of Jesus and in Paul's own relationship to him as present Lord rather than a historical master whose teachings are kept alive by

---

[5] On echoes and allusions to Jesus in Paul, see Dunn, "Jesus Tradition in Paul," in *Studying the Historical Jesus: Evaluations of the State of Current Research*, eds. Bruce Chilton and Craig A. Evans (Leiden: E. J. Brill, 1994), 155–78. Dunn argues that, though not fixed, the tradition shaped Paul's thinking at a deep level. David Wenham has argued vigorously for Paul's knowledge of the tradition, based on evidence ranging from the highly to the less plausible. For him, the cumulative argument turns parallels between Jesus and Paul into echoes of Jesus traditions known by Paul. See *Paul: Follower of Jesus or Founder of Christianity* (Grand Rapids: Wm. B. Eerdmans, 1995).

[6] According to E. Earle Ellis, Paul quotes the OT ninety-three times and makes numerous indirect allusions (*Paul's Use of the Old Testament* [Edinburgh: Oliver and Boyd, 1957], 11). See also Craig A. Evans and James A. Sanders, eds., *Paul and the Scriptures of Israel* (JSNT Supplementary Series 83; Sheffield: JSOT Press, 1993).

[7] Paul wrote a previous letter to the Corinthians now lost (1 Cor. 5:9,10). Colossians refers to a letter from Laodicea (4:16) not available to us, though it may not be Pauline.

[8] Paul's thinking is accessible, not in philosophical treatises, but in letters or epistles written for specific audiences. Alain Badiou calls the letters "interventions" rather than treatises (*Saint Paul: The Foundation of Universalism*, trans. Ray Brassier [Stanford University Press, Stanford, 2003], 31). Romans has some treatise-like characteristics, but is Paul's attempt to prepare the way for a visit to a church he did not found.

his followers. In order to advance our understanding of the influence of Jesus on Paul's thinking, then, we must next provide an account of this relationship.

In what follows our interest in Paul and his interpreters is dictated by the two large questions with which we began. We shall attempt to steer through the welter of opinions about sources or influences on Paul's thinking, nodding only occasionally to some of the many competing interpretations of his letters. Our overriding concern is not historical; it's about what does or does not follow for philosophical practice from the construction of the mind of Jesus in Paul's letters.

II. PAUL'S RELATIONSHIP TO JESUS

There is a simple clue to Paul's understanding of Jesus: Paul's modes of reference to him. The terms used include "Jesus," "Christ," and "Lord," individually or in various combinations. The last two are used alone many times; of the other combinations, "Christ Jesus" is the most frequent at four dozen occurrences in the generally accepted letters, followed by "Lord Jesus Christ" at three dozen.[9] But the simple name "Jesus" appears only seventeen times. Paul's dominant thinking about Jesus is not by that name: the person Jesus who died and rose again has a new identity for Paul, as *Christ* and *Lord*. These are the significant names for that person. Six of the simple uses of "Jesus" are in the context of his being Lord; eight refer the death or resurrection of the historical person.[10] Perhaps the identity shift is most straightforwardly expressed in Philippians 2. At the name of *Jesus* every knee should bend, for God has given him the name that is above every name; every tongue should confess that he is *Lord* (vv. 9–11).

To confess Jesus as Lord is to name him so. Unlike our use of proper names, this naming constitutes a relationship; one cannot call Jesus "Lord" except by the Spirit (1 Cor. 12:13). "Lord", then, is a relational term rather than a proper name like "Jesus." *Christos* (the Greek "anointed") is descriptive, having to do with role and function as God's chosen one, messiah, marked out for leadership. But for Paul, who never in his correspondence feels the necessity

---

[9] "Christ" appears, as name, close to 170 times in the undisputed Pauline correspondence. Of approximately 200 uses of "Lord", most refer to Jesus, but others may more naturally be read as referring to God. A quick count of "Jesus Christ" comes out at 26, and "Lord Jesus" at 22, whereas "Lord Christ" is used only once.

[10] The confession or identification of Jesus as Lord is found in 1 Cor. 9:10, 12:13; Rom. 4:24, 10:9; Phil. 2:10. References to Jesus's death or resurrection appear in 1 Thess. 1:10, 4:14; 2 Cor. 4:10, 4:14; Gal. 6:18 (the marks of Jesus on Paul's body); Rom. 8:11. That leaves only three other uses of "Jesus" (Rom. 3:26, 2 Cor. 4:5, 11:4) that may continue the historical reference.

to make the identity statement that Jesus is the Christ,[11] "Christ" is a proper name with both singular reference (no one else is Christ, though both Jesus and God are Lord) and descriptive meaning.

I propose, then, that Paul's lack of interest in using the single name "Jesus" betrays his relatively low level of interest in dwelling on traditions about the life of Jesus. It is not the mind of Jesus, disclosed in sayings, parables, disputes, and the like, that consumes Paul's thinking, so much as Jesus's identity, his relationship to God, and his salvific and eschatological roles. Who Jesus is now, for Paul and for Paul's readers, as Lord and Christ: this is the key issue. In a word, he wants to know the mind of Christ rather than the mind of Jesus.

The difference can be discerned in Paul's own comment on his present knowledge of Christ in 2 Corinthians 5:16: "From now on, therefore, we regard no one from a human point of view; even though we once knew Christ from a human point of view, we know him no longer in that way." The repeated phrase translated as "from a human point of view" is *kata sarka*, "according to the flesh." If not in that way, then how does Paul know Christ? The next verse speaks of a new creation where everything old has passed away (v. 17) and is now new "in Christ." So Christ is known not in "old" categories (as, for instance, a dangerously misguided and mistaken teacher, deservedly dead) but in the new light of resurrection. Paul has become acquainted with a person present to him, here and now, who is Lord.[12]

The hymn of Philippians 2 further works out the meaning of Paul's knowing Jesus not simply within ordinary human categories. In discerning the identity shift to Jesus as Lord, one finds what may be termed the "mind" of Christ that is to be emulated by his followers (v. 5). Indeed, Paul wants to know Christ in this way. It is insufficient to know *about* Jesus without "gaining" him (3:8), being in union with him (3:9). Paul's desire is to know Christ and the power of his resurrection, suffering with him in the hope of attaining resurrection (3:10–11).

---

[11] That Jesus is the Christ is the essence of the early Gospel proclamation: it is Peter's confession (Mk. 8:29) and Martha's (Jn. 11:27), and the reason for John's Gospel (20:31; cf. 1 Jn. 5:1). Peter's earliest preaching adds that Jesus is both Lord and Christ (Acts 2:36; cf. 10:36 in the first preaching to a Gentile). In the Acts accounts, Paul himself used the identity statement that Jesus is the Messiah, in Damascus after his conversion (9:22) and in Thessalonica (17:3); in 26:23 *Christos* is to be translated as "Messiah" (as it is once in Paul's own letters, in Rom. 9:6).

[12] Against the view that the passage supports a distinction between the "Jesus of history" and the "Christ of faith," see Wenham, *Paul: Follower of Jesus or Founder of Christianity*, 400–2. Paul, still interested in historical facts, sees them in new light.

In sum, Paul's knowledge of Jesus is best seen as his "knowing Christ" in a present relationship that imitates and incorporates in Paul himself a version of Jesus's own identity as crucified and risen.

III. HOW DOES PAUL COME TO KNOW CHRIST?

We must now think more directly about how Paul comes to know the mind of Christ. Given our evidence, we may agree that this knowledge is not exclusively *historical* knowledge, which though important and necessary is clearly not sufficient for the relationship Paul claims with Christ. We need in addition to invoke the category of revelation.

That category, though, is complex in Paul's case. As a Jew and Pharisee, he would identify the content of revealed knowledge with the law: Jews rely on the law and are instructed in it so as to know God's will and what's best (Rom. 2:17–18). Indeed, it was his zeal for God, the law, and the traditions of his ancestors that caused him to persecute the church (Gal. 1:13–14, Phil. 3:5–6). But something happened to Paul, or in him, that caused a mind-shattering reevaluation of his whole way of life. And he speaks of *that* experience, rather than of the law or the prophets, in the vocabulary of revelation.

Paul's own letters do not relate the actual experience he had on the Damascus Road, but whatever its details,[13] he is utterly convinced that God has revealed to him God's Son, Jesus Christ – or rather, the experience was the revelation of God's Son *in* Paul (Gal. 1:16). At the same time, he also refers to the content of what's revealed to him as *the Gospel.* The Gospel concerns, at heart, the death, resurrection, and return in judgment of Jesus, but not simply these events. For their meaning to be effective good news, they must be embraced in the affirmation that Jesus is Lord. As we saw earlier, for Paul no one can make this affirmation apart from the work of the Spirit. But there is more to the Gospel for Paul: in the revelatory experience he received a specific commission to take this Gospel to the Gentiles as well as the Jews. God revealed his Son in Paul so that he might "proclaim him among the Gentiles" (Gal. 1:16). Although the Judaism of Paul's day accepted Gentiles who were willing to observe some Jewish rituals and even permitted conversion with circumcision, it did not actively proselytize; so Paul's conviction that the

---

[13] The Acts accounts in chaps. 9, 22, and 26 are fairly consistent, though not identical. See Alan F. Segal, *Paul the Convert: The Apostolate and Apostasy of Saul the Pharisee* (New Haven: Yale University Press, 1990), especially chap. 1, on Luke's account of Paul's conversion. Terence L. Donaldson uses the notion of paradigm shift in his *Paul and the Gentiles: The Mapping of the Apostle's Convictional World* (Minneapolis: Fortress Press, 1997), 299–305.

Gospel was not just an essentially Jewish message for non-Jews but instead a new message for both Jews and Gentiles was shatteringly new.[14]

For that reason Paul is at pains to insist that the Gospel he proclaims was not received from human sources; he had it by a revelation of Jesus Christ (Gal. 1:11–12). What's crucial is that he is singled out in this revelatory experience, and singled out by no one other than God.[15]

He offers as evidence the fact that he did not discuss anything with any other apostle for three years, spent in Arabia after his conversion; only then did he meet in Jerusalem with Peter for fifteen days (and, he adds, with James).[16] Fourteen years later – in response to another revelation – he went back to Jerusalem to consult with leaders in order to set out the Gospel that he had been preaching. They did not contradict his conviction that his Gospel entailed that Gentile Christians were not required to assume a Jewish identity through keeping the law, especially with respect to circumcision and diet.

Revelatory experience for Paul, then, is complex. What happened on the Damascus Road was an eruption within Paul's own psychology, the recognition of an unmistakable singling-out. But it was also a revelation about religious identity: the Gospel was a double-pronged message that Jesus is risen Lord and that the good news is for Gentiles and Jews alike. From those convictions radiated deep and far-reaching waves of consequence for Paul's thought and practice. His practice, of course, was evangelism throughout as much of the known world as he could manage; but his thinking about the significance of the Gospel also ranged widely across the territory of religious belief.

While attempts to sort out Paul's thinking are daunting, our concern here is how Paul's mind, influenced by Jesus, worked on questions of philosophical

---

[14] On proselytizing, see Scot McKnight, *A Light among the Gentiles: Jewish Missionary Activity in the Second Temple Period* (Minneapolis: Fortress Press, 1991), and Martin Goodman, *Mission and Conversion: Proselytizing in the Religious History of the Roman Empire* (Oxford: Clarendon Press, 1994). Paul's convictions about the relationship of Jew and Gentile to the Gospel are, of course, subject to competing interpretations. John Gager, for instance, has argued that Paul's Gospel of salvation through Christ is only directed to the Gentiles; Jews continue to be saved through the Law (*Reinventing Paul* [New York: Oxford University Press, 2000]). Whether or not this is Paul's view, much of what I go on to say about Paul and philosophy could be adapted to it.

[15] Badiou does not accept a theistic account or explanation, but does see something unique in the Damascus Road experience. "In a certain sense, this conversion isn't carried out by anyone: Paul has not been converted by representatives of 'the Church'; he has not been won over.... Just as the Resurrection remains totally incalculable and it is from there that one must begin, Paul's faith is that from which he begins as a subject, and nothing leads up to it" (*Saint Paul*, 17).

[16] Badiou comments that Paul "leaves this subjective upsurge outside every official seal" (18); it has no authoritative sanction.

importance. We can now begin to appreciate how his experience of the Gospel raises some fundamental epistemological questions about the knowledge of God. If Gentiles are included in the Gospel apart from the law, how is their knowledge of God derived? If human beings are not capable of attaining such knowledge, can they be held responsible? Paul seems to want to insist on human culpability, but he also makes disparaging remarks about human wisdom that have been widely regarded antiphilosophical. Our next task, then, is to sort through these epistemological issues, postponing an assessment of their implications for philosophy until the next section of this chapter.

IV. PAUL ON THE HUMAN KNOWLEDGE OF GOD

We begin with a simple observation. Although Paul's Gospel comes through revelation, that experience has more to do with recognizing the identity and role of Jesus than with propositions about the existence and nature of God. Revelation is life-altering, but it may not do all the work required for the human knowledge of God. Of course, God has revealed himself in the law and the prophets, and some Gentiles may learn of God through their association with a synagogue (as in Acts 13:48); but what about others? Do human beings possess the ability to know God apart from revelation – and if so, has that capacity been corroded beyond use, as some later thinkers have argued on Paul's authority?

Paul makes strong claims about epistemological capabilities in his letters to the Romans and to the Corinthians. We'll consider Romans first, with an excursus about the presentation of Paul's practice in Acts, and then move to 1 Corinthians 1–4.

a. Natural Knowledge of God in Romans 1–2

The letter to the Romans is built on two convictions: that the Gospel of God is about his Son, so declared by resurrection from the dead, Jesus Christ the Lord, and that Paul's own apostleship is to bring obedience of faith among all the Gentiles (1:4–5). In setting out his Gospel, Paul begins immediately with the question of human accountability, recognizing at least implicitly that ignorance is an excusing condition.

Arguing that the Gentiles are without excuse before God, Paul claims that human beings do have requisite knowledge:

> For what can be known about God is plain to them, because God has shown it to them. Ever since the creation of the world his eternal power and divine

nature, invisible though they are, have been understood and seen through the things he has made (1:19–20).

The adjective and verb ("plain," "has shown") are from the same root; this is manifest knowledge, not obscure. What's knowable are invisible things about God – God's being God, that is, his divinity and his eternal power – and these *invisibilia* are understood through the things God has made. Whatever the character of this knowledge, it is sufficient both for honoring God and for giving God thanks. Insofar as human beings have failed to do this, they are responsible for their failing.

There is another kind of knowledge available to all human beings: moral knowledge.

> When Gentiles, who do not possess the law, do instinctively what the law requires, these, though not having the law, are a law to themselves. They show that what the law requires is written on their hearts, to which their own conscience also bears witness; and their conflicting thoughts will accuse or perhaps excuse them (2:14–15).

Those who have not received the revealed law not only act unconsciously in accordance with it; they also have an awareness of its rightness. How this comes about Paul doesn't say;[17] he is content to point to the fact of an interior law without providing further explanation as to its source. That lack of interest may itself be explained by Paul's paramount concern in these passages: he needs to establish that God rightly judges human transgressions (with respect to morality) and sinfulness (with respect to honoring God). For that purpose, the particular source of knowledge is unimportant, as long as it is reliable.

All the same, Paul does seem to assume that God has something to do with human knowing. In 1:19, it is God who has shown these plain things ("God has made evident"), and the metaphor of writing on the heart in 2:15 implies a scribe analogous to the divine author of the Mosaic law. His reasons for this assumption are not available to us, but it may well have been self-evidently

---

[17] What's "written on their hearts" is sometimes identified with conscience as a source of moral knowledge. The passage, though, does not make that claim; "conscience" (*suneidêsis*) is rather an awareness of noncompliance with that internal writing. See Paul W. Gooch, "Conscience." *The New Interpreter's Dictionary of the Bible*, vol. 1 (Nashville: Abingdon Press, 2006), 719–26. This text "does not treat *suneidêsis* as legislating right and wrong; that law is already written on the heart, and is the same for all human beings. Nor does *suneidêsis* act as moral judge: rather, the 'conflicting thoughts' do the accusing or excusing. Instead, *suneidêsis* performs the function of witness about whether or not the legislation has been observed. It is an internal, subjective awareness about one's shortcomings – and its operation leads to those conflicting thoughts over what one knows ought to be done and the bad feeling of not having done it" (725).

contained within his view of the world, and human beings in particular, as unthinkable apart from the creative care of God. Indeed, it may well be that Paul was not much interested in the question of whether human cognitive abilities are good enough to come to knowledge about God on their own, apart from revelation. It is enough for him to maintain that (a) Israel knows God through the law and prophets, and (b) though the Gentiles have neither of these sources, God has arranged it that they nevertheless have sufficient knowledge, attainable from the created world and moral experience.

b. Excursus: Paul's Practice according to Acts

If we suspend judgment about the kind of historical writing found in Acts, we may find it instructive to bring our epistemological interests to its accounts of Paul's message to Gentiles. The most famous is the Acts 17 story of his preaching to the Athenian Areopagus. Paul begins with creation and God's sustaining power, his sovereignty over the nations (God orders historical times and territorial boundaries), "so that they would search for God and perhaps grope for him and find him" (v. 27). From God's point of view, then, the divine intention to be discovered extends to all peoples. From the human point of view, the Athenians should realize that God is not far from them: their own writers bear witness to this.[18] Paul does not offer an opinion about the source of Greek knowledge that we live, move, and exist in God or are God's offspring. The point is simply that this knowledge is available, and sufficient for the realization that God cannot be the product of human artifice or imagination. That, in turn, is knowledge sufficient for human responsibility: "while God has overlooked the times of human ignorance, now he commands all people everywhere to repent" (v. 30), having appointed a man raised from the dead to judge the inhabited world. Paul does not refer to the Hebrew scriptures or name Jesus, but instead points to the Resurrection, an event revelatory for him and therefore, he believes, for his hearers.

The Athenian message is consistent with the Romans account of Gentile knowledge of God, though it is muted in some respects. For instance, Paul seems patiently didactic rather than condemnatory: the unknown God is not really unknown, if they would only think about it. He declares this God to them, but their own wisdom supports that declaration. Though Paul speaks of repentance, he does not engage in the Romans 1 critique of willful blindness

---

[18] The expression "in him we live and move and have our being" may, or may not, be from Epimenides; the source for being God's offspring is Aratus, *Phaenomena* 5. In 1 Cor. 15:33 Paul quotes Menander; cf. the quotation from Epimenides in Titus 1:12.

and arrogance, the rejection of God's being God, nor does he drive home the guiltiness of those who do not follow the inwardly inscribed law.

One other incident in Acts is worth comment. In Lystra, when the crowds wanted to sacrifice to Paul and Barnabas as gods, Paul tried to explain that the living God is creator of all, not a human being or a worthless idol. God has never left himself without a witness to the good he does: he sends rains, fruitful seasons, food, and joy in the heart (14:17). The common experiences of being provided for, and having a grateful heart, function as testimony to God's creative providence, and therefore to the basic nature of God as other than human. Again, this resonates with the expectation of Romans 1 that reflecting on the created order should lead to honoring and thanking God.

c. Cognitive Limitations in 1 Corinthians 1–4

On the evidence of Romans, and consistent with the presentation of Paul's practice in Acts, we may provisionally accept that Paul holds a view something like this: human beings enjoy, through the witness of common experience, sufficient theistic knowledge to honor and thank God, even knowledge apart from the particular expressions of the divine will to Israel in the law and prophets. Nevertheless, this is not the full story. We need to take more seriously Paul's claim in Romans 1 that human beings have not made proper use of their cognitive equipment. They have suppressed the truth (v. 18); they have become futile in their thinking and dark in mind (v. 21); claiming to be wise, they are fools (v. 22); they have exchanged truth about God for a lie (v. 25). So God's wrath has been revealed against them; they have been given over to their own lusts, to degraded passions and debased minds.

Although Paul insists on guilt and accountability, some readers have taken him to hold that sin has so corrupted our cognitive powers that we can no longer reliably gain knowledge of God.[19] Perhaps this was indeed his view, and the patiently reasoned approach he is made to take in Acts does not reflect his real mind. It's time to turn to 1 Corinthians 1–4, the most sustained argument Paul gives about human and divine wisdom. We will stay with the theme of the possibility of natural knowledge of God, reserving discussion of its implications for philosophical practice to the next section of the chapter.

---

[19] A possible explanation for how the ignorant may still be guilty could make use of the observation that the drunkard acts in ignorance but is still responsible for getting into a drunken state (Aristotle gives this example in *Nicomachean Ethics* 3.5). Just so (it could be argued), the human race has willfully placed itself into the state of blindness about God.

At first blush, things look bad for our capacity to gain theistic knowledge, especially in 1 Corinthians chapter 1. The world's wisdom (*sophia*) is diametrically opposed to the wisdom of God, which the world – the Greeks in particular – must think foolishness. And what the world – the Jews in particular – stumbles over as weakness, a crucified Christ, God makes powerful for salvation. Paul sets out serious oppositions between divine and human epistemological categories, in statements such as these:

(1) worldly wisdom cannot know God and is impotent to save (1:21);
(2) human wisdom is not as wise as God's foolishness (1:25);
(3) worldly wisdom is shamed by God's foolishness (1:27);
(4) faith must not rest on human wisdom but on God's power (2:5);
(5) human wisdom cannot teach what the Spirit of God reveals (2:13);
(6) the wisdom of this age is foolishness (3:18–20).

Some of this is paradoxical wordplay on what's really wisdom and what's not, but it is clear that Paul is convinced that human wisdom cannot achieve salvific knowledge of God.

The first-blush assumption of many readers is that Paul means, by human wisdom, the unaided or natural knowledge of God, but in order to test this supposition we must have a clearer understanding of what Paul's overriding intentions are in chapters 1 through 4. Does he mean to attack the capacity of human reason itself? Or, his own aims aside, does the impotence of reason for theistic knowledge follow from his critique of worldly wisdom?

In answering, we should remind ourselves that Paul is not writing a treatise on faith and reason, but addressing specific problems and misunderstandings in the Corinthian community. And in these opening chapters, his target is the mistaken self-perception of its members.[20]

That this is what weighs on the apostle's mind is disclosed in the stinging ironies of chapter 4:6–21. The Corinthians see themselves as far superior to the apostles: they are glutted, rich, royal, wise, strong, and honored, whereas the apostles are poor, meek, and weak in the world's eyes. So when Paul had commented earlier that among the Corinthians there were not many wise, not many powerful, not many noble (1:26), he was preparing the ground for his critique of their inflated self-importance: they think of themselves in just the opposite categories.

[20] The following five paragraphs reflect some elements in my reading of this text in chap. 2 of *Partial Knowledge: Philosophical Studies in Paul* (Notre Dame, IN: University of Notre Dame Press, 1987).

The Corinthian condition that Paul has diagnosed, then, is conceited knowledge, inflated self-importance. This is the root cause for the poisonous divisions among them, explaining their jealousy and quarreling (3:3); they are puffed up against one another (4:6). The antidote will turn out to be love, but for now Paul excoriates them for their pretense and complacency.

If we understand Paul's target to be what we might call epistemological hubris,[21] we will have an explanation for the repeated emphasis on boasting that pervades these chapters. That also explains the paradoxical plays on wisdom and foolishness, strength and weakness: what the world thinks foolish is in fact weakness, just because of its inflated self-assessment. The boaster thinks he is smart and powerful; God and the apostle know otherwise. But does this reading bring us any closer to figuring out what Paul might think about human reasoning itself?

Though it would be tempting to restrict Paul's critique to the particularities of Corinthian hubris, that critique may be built on an underlying assumption about human cognitive capacities. It might well be that Paul believes any attempt whatsoever, on the part of anyone, to come to a knowledge of God through human effort is hubristic because misuse has destroyed our abilities (as might be argued from Rom. 1). And indeed, these chapters have suggested such a view to some readers. From "The world did not know God by wisdom" (1:21), it is an easy step to "Human beings do not know God by human intellectual effort." And many have taken chapter 2 as support for this claim. There Paul argues that God's wisdom is secret, hidden from even the most powerful; it is understood only by God's own Spirit. Just as I can gain access to your private thoughts only if you reveal them to me, so God's mind can be known only if revealed by the Spirit to human learners (vv. 6–13). We may, following Paul, call the content of what's revealed "spiritual" (*pneumatikos*) knowledge, distinguishing it from "natural" (*psuchikos*) knowledge. Then that easy step will assign the sphere of faith to the former and the sphere of human reason to the latter.

Nevertheless, we must be cautious about taking that step on the basis of this Pauline distinction. The evidence will not take us that far, I suggest, for two reasons. First, the claims in chapter 2 are not exactly about "natural" knowledge in the sense of knowledge gained by unaided reason. What's opposed to "spiritual" knowledge is variously labeled as worldly, human, and natural,[22]

---

[21] Indeed, though I did not use "hubris" in *Partial Knowledge*, it is a good term for the Corinthian condition, since it links knowledge and power. Hubristic persons have an inflated estimation of their epistemological abilities as well as being convinced that their knowledge is superior.

[22] Some of the language suggests our natural capacities (as in "the heart of human beings," v. 9), but the phrase *psuchikos anthrôpos* (the "natural" person of v. 14) occurs in the context

so once again it is hubristic reasoning that is Paul's target. Second, the content of "spiritual knowledge" is not necessarily coextensive with everything that may be known about God. To play with Paul's analogy, even if one person needs to learn through disclosure the private thoughts of another, still the one may know many publicly accessible things about the other without that disclosure. It doesn't follow from chapter 2 that there is no naturally accessible knowledge about God. Further, Paul believes that the Corinthians lack mature "spiritual" knowledge because of their hubris, but this cannot mean that they are without any knowledge of God whatsoever. Being ignorant of the full purposes of God does not entail a complete incapacity to know anything whatever about God with ordinary human cognitive equipment.

From 1 Corinthians 1–4, then, we draw a couple of negative conclusions. First, on a defensible reading of the text, Paul's castigation of worldly or human wisdom does not necessarily extend to human reasoning itself. Second, Paul's account of "spiritual" knowledge as the product of revelation to "spiritual" believers does not entail that there can be no natural knowledge about God; the point is rather that the "unspiritual" are too filled with hubris to understand the things of God that are in fact revealed.

Put these chapters together with Romans, and we can understand why Paul would speak there of futile thinking and foolish minds being darkened: this again is the consequence of the epistemological hubris of those who turn away from God. But we are not required to conclude that Paul believes that our cognitive equipment is so damaged that it can deliver no theistic knowledge. Indeed, his insistence on culpability strongly suggests otherwise.

Since, however, a negative claim only creates space for a positive role for human reason on behalf of faith, there is more work to be done. We need to draw out some implications for philosophical practice from our study of the mind of Paul and his understanding of the mind of Christ.

V. THE MIND OF PAUL, THE MIND OF CHRIST, AND
PHILOSOPHICAL PRACTICE

Many of Paul's critics hold that by "human wisdom" he means what we know as the enterprise of philosophy; in Paul's mind, then, the mind of Christ is opposed to philosophy.[23] However, this opposition becomes groundless when

---

of concepts such as foolishness and the worldly and the human, all describing epistemological hubris.

[23] Calvin's commentary on 1 Corinthians seems so to assume; see appendix B to chap. 2 of *Partial Knowledge*, 49–51. Badiou styles Paul the "antiphilosopher," who holds philosophical wisdom in contempt, which is what got him into trouble in Athens (*Saint Paul*, 27). For common views

epistemological hubris is recognized as Paul's real target. Although there will be debates about what constitutes that condition, it can be argued that hubris is itself antiphilosophical; certainly Socrates, for one, so thought.

Although we can dismiss the warning in Colossians against philosophy on the grounds of authorship,[24] we must comment finally on one more Pauline text that has been read as antiphilosophical. Defending his apostolic authority in 2 Corinthians 10:3–5, Paul writes that he opposes those who think he conducts himself "according to the flesh" (*kata sarka*), then adds that he does indeed live "in the flesh" (*en sarki*) but does not wage war according to it. Our weapons of war, he says, are not "fleshly" (*sarkika*),

> but they have divine power to destroy strongholds. We destroy arguments and every proud obstacle raised up against the knowledge of God, and we take every thought captive to obey Christ.

Here the concept of *sarx* keeps its association with human pride, as in 2 Corinthians 5, but it also carries meaning beyond the moral; it has a flesh-and-blood, human vulnerability dimension. The complaint against Paul is that he acts as though inflated with authoritarian power, but in reality he is weak and ineffectual. Paul accordingly constructs this charge as his acting *kata sarka*, being bloated with power; he will in reply agree that he is *en sarki*, only humanly vulnerable. But he does not combat this charge with *hopla sarkika*, "fleshly" weapons. Both meanings of *sarx* inhabit this phrase: the weapons are not prideful, but they are not merely human either. In Paul's military imagery, fortresses and proud elevations and captives need to be taken. The

---

of Paul on human reason, one may turn to articles on fideism in reference works. Here are three: (i) Richard Popkin classifies Paul as an extreme fideist in the *Encyclopedia of Philosophy*, ed. Donald Borchert, vol. 3, 2nd ed. (Detroit: Macmillan Reference USA, 2006), 630–33. (ii) In "Fideism," in *The Stanford Encyclopedia of Philosophy* (summer 2005 edition), ed. Edward N. Zalta, Richard Amesbury writes: "Developing a theme articulated by the Apostle Paul in his First Letter to the Corinthians, Tertullian insisted that the truth of Christianity could be disclosed only by revelation, and that it must necessarily remain opaque to unregenerate philosophical reason" (http://plato.stanford.edu/archives/sum2005/entries/fideism/). (iii) And finally, for a truly "popular" or "open source" opinion: "This sort of fideism has a long history in Christianity. It can plausibly be argued as an interpretation of 1 Corinthians, wherein Paul says: For since, in the wisdom of God, the world did not know God through wisdom, it pleased God through the folly of what we preach to save those who believe.... For the foolishness of God is wiser than (the wisdom of) men. (1 Cor. 1:21, 25)" (http://en.wikipedia.org/wiki/Fideism).

[24] And also on the grounds that here *philosophia* means not right reasoning but any intellectual system opposed to Christ. For a fuller discussion of this verse, see chap. 1 of *Partial Knowledge*, where the argument is constructed to take account of the possibility of Pauline authorship.

strategy is to attack *logismoi*, arguments, and success is achieved by bringing every thought (*noêma*) into the obedience of Christ.[25]

Philosophers resonate with some of this imagery: defending and attacking arguments is our sort of business. However, other language may grate upon the philosophical ear: the claim, for instance, that there can be divinely powerful weapons or techniques, and especially the strategy of making the thoughts of opponents obedient to a religious authority.

But that concern may well mistake the object of attack. It can be argued, I think, that what's in view is not someone else's philosophical position, but epistemological hubris. And that makes Paul's language about destroying arguments and capturing thoughts more comprehensible and, indeed, instructive for philosophy.

For there is a way of doing philosophy that is *kata sarka*, self-important, focused on trouncing the opposing party by powerful and crushing argument that is merely destructive (to say nothing of the temptation to use facile counterexample or cheap shot). Even without having to spell out more fully what constitutes "sarkic" philosophical practice, we are able to recognize this behavior in others if not ourselves. Its practitioners are more interested in the triumph of their own ideas than in the pursuit of wisdom or a constructive and collaborative attempt to advance understanding.

a. Paul on the Mind of Christ: Christlike Philosophizing

So here is a proposed reading of 2 Corinthians 10:3–5 for normative philosophical practice, arising from Paul's language even if not intended by it. "Sarkic" opponents are not to be fought with "sarkic" weapons; the philosophically proud are not to be hoist with their own petard, satisfying though that may be. Instead, Christian philosophers may regard their opponents as "in Christ," the object of divine self-giving love. To bring thoughts into the obedience of Christ is to attempt to carry out thinking in a spirit of appropriate humility and self-emptying so that space is made for truth. In the language of Philippians, the mind of Christ at work in such thinking would

---

[25] This is a literal translation, "into the obedience of Christ." The phrase is rendered as taking every thought captive "to obey Christ" by the NRSV, and compelling every human thought to surrender "in obedience to Christ" by the REB. These translations take the genitive "of Christ" as objective, meaning the obedience concerned with or owed to Christ. Genitives can also be subjective – here, the obedience exhibited by Christ, Christ's own. The military imagery encourages the former reading because captives are required to submit to authority, but it is possible to reflect on the nature of Christ's own obedience in this context, as I shall do shortly.

be "kenotic" philosophical practice. The power of such practice is not fleshly, worldly, or hubristic; it is divine in that it is manifest in what the proud think of as weakness.

Perhaps this reading isn't right. Since it is Paul's opponents who are to be brought into "the obedience of Christ," and not just Paul's mode of arguing, surely he must mean that the content of their every *noêma*, thought, must line up with Christ's thoughts.[26] Indeed, Paul may have intended something like that. Nevertheless, nowhere does Paul provide us with a developed description of the beliefs that his opponents should obediently hold. He is more concerned with their hubris (manifested in the proud obstacles they raise up against the knowledge of God), in their modes of thinking. And Paul's use of *noêma* elsewhere is much better understood as a thought process rather than a particular thought.[27] So I suggest that it is legitimate to read our text as promoting the use of "non-sarkic," "kenotic" methods to bring about a like mind in one's opponents.

That would mean, however, that just as the Corinthian believers were afflicted with epistemological hubris, Christian philosophers could find themselves practicing "sarkic" philosophy. In that they were not participating in, and demonstrating, the mind of Christ in their work, they would be doing philosophy in an un-Christlike manner, regardless of the content of their philosophizing.

As one result of this investigation into the mind of Paul and the mind of Christ, then, I propose that Paul's understanding of the obedience of Christ serves as a model for "Christian" philosophy – as Christlike philosophical practice. This is Christian philosophizing in Pauline mode.

For an analogy, this mode is more like "Socratic" than "Platonic" philosophy. "Platonism" has come to mean a set of beliefs, mainly metaphysical and epistemological, associated with Plato's dialogues (even though Plato did not construct a systematic philosophy), whereas philosophizing that is "Socratic" refers to a way of doing philosophy in a dialogic conversation that questions beliefs, reveals inconsistencies, and generates serious epistemological paralysis, all with the intention of getting interlocutors to discover the truth

---

[26] That is, to use the distinction in footnote 25, Paul's mode of arguing should exhibit Christlike obedience and humility (the subjective genitive), but the subjection of his opponents' thinking is obedience to Christ (the objective genitive).

[27] In 2 Cor. alone, Paul uses *noêmata* in speaking of the "designs" of Satan, i.e., his plotting or scheming (2:11); "minds" or thought processes being hardened (3:14); "minds" of unbelievers being hardened, i.e., their mental capacities (4:04); and "thoughts" being led astray from devotion to Christ as was Eve's by the serpent's cunning (11:03). These are all epistemological attitudes and dispositions rather than items of belief.

for themselves.[28] The difference, undoubtedly, is that Socratic philosophizing employs a method, whereas Christian philosophizing displays an attitude, an approach of mind and heart, regardless of specific method or systematic content.

That, of course, makes this description of Christian philosophizing at once too broad and too narrow a characterization of the wider relation between Christian faith and philosophy. It's too broad, because all sorts of activities, not just philosophizing, should be marked for Christians by the possession of a Christlike mind. There are surely "sarkic" ways of parenting or doing high-level mathematics, and "kenotic" approaches to myriad creative and intellectual endeavors. But the emphasis on attitude is also too narrow, for even if there is no agreed-upon philosophical *method* that is demonstrably Christian, there are recognizably Christian *beliefs* that should form the subject matter of Christian philosophizing. Surely there is "Christian philosophy" as well as philosophizing by Christian thinkers. And is not Paul's attempt to seek the mind of Christ relevant to the content of this philosophy?

b. The Mind of Paul: Philosophy as Reflection on the Mind of Christ

The answer is not directly ascertainable from Paul's letters, given their character and Paul's lack of expressed interest in philosophy as he knew it. But we've done enough work to realize that Paul's understanding of revelation leaves room for the philosophical enterprise of natural theology. *Only* that, however; the room created does not yet host any activity. Whether Christian philosophers should argue on behalf of natural theistic knowledge is not a matter of faith or doctrine, but to be decided on philosophical grounds themselves. That's as far as Paul can take us.

Christian philosophers have of course spent a great deal of effort on this question, both *pro* and *contra*, and they have also defended the faith against attack from enemies, keeping them at the gate if not winning them over. However, even when carried out in a Christlike fashion, this work is not distinctively Christian in its content. Rather, much of contemporary analytic philosophy of religion is *broadly theistic* in its concerns. Without detracting from its great importance, we may wish to interrogate further Paul's concern for the mind of Christ for its philosophical implications.

---

[28] For an insightful discussion of Socratic philosophy as concerned with perplexity rather than results, see Gareth B. Matthews, *Socratic Perplexity and the Nature of Philosophy* (Oxford and New York: Oxford University Press, 1999), especially chap. 12 on philosophical practice.

As we have argued, Paul's experience of Jesus as the risen Lord for Gentile as well as Jew is a revelation about identity and relationship, not the disclosure of a comprehensive system of beliefs. Paul's intellectual and pastoral task is to work out the meaning of this revelation in new circumstances. Though he does not do this in a systematic way, he does raise a series of questions, and argue for answers, which are philosophically (and not just theologically) fruitful. This is not the place to go into detail, let alone attempt to create a comprehensive account. But let the following serve as reminders. In Romans, for example, Paul struggles with the problem of understanding divine purposes in history (what is the role and destiny of Israel?), theodicy (will the forces of evil win out in the end?), moral psychology (why do we do what we know we should not? and not do what we know we should?), and practical philosophy (must one obey the state? what are the limits on freedom, where others will misunderstand and be adversely affected?). Galatians works on the relation of freedom and law; 1 Corinthians deals with not only the epistemological issues we have discussed but also ethical questions and an important metaphysical question about the nature of resurrected persons.

These examples suffice to establish that Paul is not merely reflecting on questions set for him by his contemporary traditions, either Jewish or Greek, but is instead struggling with what it is to know the mind of Christ where familiar identities are being challenged by his experience of the risen Lord. And it's the mind of *Christ* he seek to express, not (let us remind ourselves) the mind of Jesus.

What is it to know "the mind of Christ" in a Pauline sense, not simply as kenotic attitude but for the convictions of faith and practice? The one occasion on which Paul uses this phrase, in 1 Corinthians 2:16, is instructive. In response to the divine inscrutability implied in the Septuagint version of Isaiah 40:13 ("Who has known the mind of the Lord?"), Paul adds, "[B]ut we have the mind of Christ." How so? Through the work of the Spirit in revealing the things of God. It is an openness to the Spirit that will form in Paul the mind of Christ. That Paul believes he can gain an understanding that goes beyond the actual teachings of Jesus is nicely illustrated in 1 Corinthians 7:40, at the end of a discussion of separation, divorce, and marriage. There he offers advice not specifically related to the Lord's sayings, adding that he thinks he "has the Spirit of God" in this advice.

More is said about the mind of the Spirit in Romans 8, where Paul states that believers in Christ must live not *kata sarka* (our familiar "according to the flesh") but *kata pneuma*, according to the Spirit (8:4). One's mind must be the mind of the Spirit, the Spirit of Christ, which is also the Spirit of God who raised Jesus from the dead and will give life to believers by dwelling in them (8:9–11).

However, to have the Spirit, and thereby the mind of the Spirit, is not to achieve full knowledge. It is to be adopted into a family relationship, as children of God who is *Abba*, and to know divine parental concern in the midst of one's troubles. Our knowledge continues to be limited: we don't even know how to pray. But God as Spirit wills all things for our good and assists our groaning spirits in articulating our needs to God as Father.

It seems, then, that to have "the mind of Christ" in a Pauline sense is to embrace and inhabit a way of life, within a set of divine and human relationships characterized by faith, hope, and love. To do philosophy with Christ's mind is, minimally, to have Christlike attitudes, but it is also to work out the meaning of faithful, hopeful, and loving relationships in one's present circumstances. A Pauline approach is not so much the construction of a comprehensive philosophical system, a full-blown "Christian philosophy," as it is a set of reflections on the meaning in one's present circumstances of distinctively Christian beliefs and practices. This involves philosophical activities that not only articulate and defend beliefs against skeptics and cultured despisers but also offer to Christian communities the clarification, interpretation, and critical appraisal of their beliefs.[29]

There will be debate about what should be on the philosophical agenda for contemporary Christian faith. Recent decades have seen a great deal of first-rate activity in the philosophy of religion, and there has in the last couple of decades been increasing attention to Christian philosophical theology as the articulation of philosophical themes, concepts, and arguments arising out of Christian beliefs. Anglo-American philosophers have written on central concepts such as trinity, incarnation, and atonement.[30] However, these endeavors have largely been directed to the question of the intelligibility of orthodox Christian doctrine, rather than to the interpretation of the mind

---

[29] A suggestion for further reflection: philosophizing in Pauline mode may be deeply related to prayer. Augustine and Anselm famously addressed God in their thinking, but one may reflect prayerfully on philosophical themes without using that explicit rhetorical form. For a discussion of how prayer may change philosophical questions, see Paul W. Gooch, *Reflections on Jesus and Socrates: Word and Silence* (New Haven: Yale University Press, 1996), 111–13, 157–60.

[30] These three themes are singled out, with relevant bibliography, by Michael Murray in "Philosophy and Christian Theology," *The Stanford Encyclopedia of Philosophy* (summer 2002 edition), ed. Edward N. Zalta (http://plato.stanford.edu/archives/sum2002/entries/christiantheology-philosophy/). Interestingly, the philosophical attention paid directly to Paul and Paul's texts has largely come from continental rather than analytic philosophers.

of Christ in new situations. There are many good reasons for this, including the fairly mild influence of philosophers on institutional Christianity
and the relative isolation of the academic guilds of theology and philosophy.
But these sociological and political factors should not blind us to the insights
that philosophers may be called upon to contribute to the understanding that
contemporary faith seeks.

Although setting an agenda for faithful philosophy requires a process of
discussion and discernment, permit me an observation. Among the pressing
questions facing institutional Christianity is the ancient one, faced by Paul, of
religious identity and difference, now in significantly changed circumstances.
These questions are both internal and external. Internally, whereas throughout
the history of Christianity, differences among Christians revolved around
doctrinal beliefs, we are now faced with divisions and alliances around moral
issues, primarily sexual morality. Christian groups who long denied each
other full recognition as members of the family of faith are reaching out
to one another to make common cause against other Christian groups that
hold contrary views on, for instance, abortion or homosexuality. The rhetoric
has sometimes grown extreme, making sexual ethics the measure of faithful
Christian identity.[31] At the same time, questions of identity arise externally.
Global mobility and immigration have brought different faith communities
into much closer contact with each other in North America and Europe. In
world politics, misunderstanding, prejudice, and hatred have been cloaked
in religious dress. It is difficult to underestimate the importance, for our
collective well-being, of sorting out issues of religious pluralism.

Constructing Christian identity in these circumstances calls for more than
quoting texts and citing authorities; it requires clear thinking and sensitivity to the Spirit. One might say, indeed, that the time is ripe for Christian
philosophers, taking their cue from Paul, to expose epistemological hubris
and to make their special contribution toward seeking the mind of Christ for
the twenty-first century. Strangely, since we may make more use of the mind
of Jesus than did Paul, and since we also have the insights into the mind of
Christ from Paul himself, the apostles, the saints, and our other predecessors,
the resources for philosophical work are all the richer.

It does not follow that every Christian philosopher should spend all, or
indeed any, professional time pursuing contemporary Pauline philosophical

---

[31] When I first drafted this, the national press reported a statement by Pope Benedict that
Canada had excluded God from the public sphere because it permits abortions and same-sex
marriage. The deep disagreements over homosexuality are at present threatening division in
my own denomination, the Anglican Communion.

issues. Like other academics, philosophers are employed to do what they're good at, and their talents may lie in areas without overt connection to distinctively Christian beliefs. Of course, again like other Christian academics, they may practice their profession "kenotically" rather than "sarkicly," exhibiting in attitude a Pauline understanding of the mind of Christ. Further, their continuing formation "into Christ" will include their minds as well as hearts, and they have a particular vocation to bring their skills to the discerning of the mind of Christ for their Christian communities, regardless of their particular professional areas of expertise.

There remains, however, a particular calling for some philosophers to engage in a form of Christian theological philosophizing that seeks to discern and reflect upon the mind of Christ, following the example of Paul. It might surprise Paul, the critic of worldly wisdom, to be co-opted as patron of these philosophers, but having been mightily surprised before, he just might be able to appreciate one more paradox in the workings of the Spirit.

PART TWO

❧

JESUS IN MEDIEVAL PHILOSOPHY

Jesus and Augustine

Gareth B. Matthews

Ludwig Wittgenstein opens his *Philosophical Investigations* with this quotation
from Augustine's *Confessions*:

> When they (my elders) named some object, and accordingly moved towards
> something, I saw this and I grasped that the thing was called by the sound
> they uttered when they meant to point it out. Their intention was shown
> by their bodily movements, as it were the natural language of all peoples:
> the expression of the fact, the play of the eyes, the movement of other parts
> of the body, and the tone of voice which expresses our state of mind in
> seeking, having, rejecting, or avoiding something. Thus, as I heard words
> repeatedly used in their proper places in various sentences, I gradually learnt
> to understand what objects they signified; and after I had trained my mouth
> to form these signs, I used them to express my own desires.[1]

Wittgenstein takes this picture of learning a language by "ostension," that
is, by having the teacher point to the objects that the words in that language
refer to, as a target for philosophical criticism. He offers several criticisms of
this picture. At one point he makes this comment:

> Augustine describes the learning of human language as if the child came
> into a strange country and did not understand the language of the country;
> that is, as if it already had a language, only not this one. Or again: as if the
> child could already *think*, only not yet speak. And "think" would here mean
> something like "talk to itself".[2]

But the main difficulty Wittgenstein finds with what he takes to be this
Augustinian picture of language learning by ostension is the problem of

---

[1] Wittgenstein (1967), 2e, fn. 1.
[2] Ibid., ¶32.

ambiguity. Here he explains the problem:

> Now one can ostensively define a proper name, the name of a colour, the
> name of a material, a numeral, the name of a point of the compass and so on.
> The definition of the number two, "That is called 'two'" – pointing to two
> nuts – is perfectly exact. – But how can two be defined like that? The person
> one gives the definition to doesn't know what one wants to call "two"; he
> will suppose that "Two" is the name given to *this* group of nuts! – He *may*
> suppose this; but perhaps he does not. He might make the opposite mistake;
> when I want to assign a name to this group of nuts, he might understand
> it as a numeral. And he might equally well take the name of a person, of
> which I give an ostensive definition, as that of a colour, of a race, or even of a
> point of the compass. That is to say: an ostensive definition can be variously
> interpreted in *every* case.[3]

The problem of the ambiguity of ostension seems to threaten any account of
language learning that relies on "ostensive definitions" to connect our words
to objects in the world, and to their qualities and the relations among them.
Wittgenstein implies that Augustine's account of language learning is based
on the, as he supposes, mistaken, assumption that ostensive definitions can
make unambiguous connections between our words and the world.

There is, however, a difficulty with this critique of Augustine. As Myles
Burnyeat pointed out a long time ago,[4] the quotation from Augustine's *Confessions*, with which Wittgenstein opens his *Philosophical Investigations*, omits
this crucial prefatory comment:

> Yet I was no longer a baby incapable of speech but already a body with power
> to talk. This I remember. But how I learnt to talk I discovered only later. It
> was not that grown-up people instructed me by presenting me with words
> in a certain order by formal teaching, as later I was to learn the letters of the
> alphabet. I myself acquired this power of speech with the intelligence which
> you gave me, my God (1.8.13).[5]

When this preface is added to the quotation Wittgenstein uses, the resulting
picture of language learning becomes something very different. The view is
now that boy Augustine is, "with the power of intelligence" that God gave
him, able to connect words to the things his elders use those words to refer
to. There is no longer any assumption that ostensive definitions can be a
trouble-free way to connect words to things. There is instead a claim that the

---

[3] Ibid., ¶28.
[4] Burnyeat (1987).
[5] Augustine (1991), 10.

power of intelligence that God gave to Augustine, and presumably gives to the rest of us, is what enables us to make the desired connection.

Setting the record straight on Augustine and language learning is all the more appropriate when one realizes that Augustine was himself aware of the ambiguity of ostension. He expresses that awareness in his dialogue *The Teacher*. Early on in that dialogue Augustine discusses with his son, Adeodatus, how one person can teach another the meaning of a word. Together they first try to explain the meaning of one word using other words or, as Augustine puts it, the signification of one sign by using other signs. But obviously our language will not offer us a way of talking about the world unless we can break out of our web of words and connect at least some of our words to the world and what is in it. "I would like you to show me the very things," Augustine tells his son, "of which these words are the signs."

Adeodatus responds with a very cheeky, but also astute reply:

> I'm surprised that you don't know, or that you're pretending not to know, that what you want cannot be done in my answer while we're engaged in discussion, where we can only answer with words. Furthermore, you're asking about things that, whatever they may be, surely aren't words – and yet you're also asking me about them with words! First raise the question without words, so that I may then answer under that stipulation of yours [i.e., that I point out the very things of which these words are the signs without using signs] (3.5).[6]

Augustine acknowledges the cleverness of his son's return challenge. However, he presses on, undeterred:

> But if when one says "*wall*" I were to ask what this one-syllable word signifies, couldn't you show me with your finger? Then when you pointed it out I would straightaway see the very thing of which this one-syllable word is a sign, although you used no words.[7]

Adeodatus accepts that idea of showing what "wall" means by pointing to a wall. There follows a discussion of whether the meaning of a color term can be shown by pointing to object of that color and whether the signification of terms for sounds, smells, flavors, weight, heat, and other things can be shown by pointing a finger. Adeodatus thinks not.

In this discussion Augustine and Adeodatus come close to worrying about the ambiguity of ostension. Thus as Adeodatus remarks, "Aiming a finger is

---

[6] Augustine (1995), 99–100.
[7] Ibid., 100.

certainly not the wall" (3.6).[8] However, annoyingly, neither Augustine nor his son asks how the learner is supposed to learn that "wall" doesn't mean *pointing a finger*, or perhaps just *finger*, rather than *wall*.

Three speeches later, however, they do confront the problem of the ambiguity of ostension directly. They are now discussing whether the meaning of a term for an activity can be shown by performing the very activity that the term names. "What if I should ask you what walking is," Augustine asks, "and you were then to get up and do it? Wouldn't you be using the thing itself to teach me, rather than using words or any other signs?"[9]

Adeodatus agrees. But then Augustine adds a troubling complication:

Augustine: Now do this: tell me – if I were completely ignorant of the meaning of the word ["walking"] and were to ask you what walking is while you were walking, how would you teach me?

Adeodatus: I would do it a little bit more quickly, so that after your question you would be prompted by something novel [in my behavior], and yet nothing would take place other than what was to be shown.

Augustine: Don't you know that *walking* is one thing and *hurrying* is another? A person who is walking doesn't necessarily hurry, and a person who is hurrying doesn't necessarily walk. We speak of "hurrying" in writing and in reading and in countless other matters. Hence given that after my question you kept on doing what you were doing, [only] faster, I might have thought walking was precisely hurrying – for you added that as something new – and for that reason I would have been misled (3.6).[10]

Unfortunately, Augustine and his son do not go back to reexamine their easy assumption that the meaning of "wall" can be given by simply pointing to a wall. How do we know, for example, that "wall" is not a name for a stone in the wall that the pointer is pointing to, rather than the wall itself. Or again, it could name the color of the wall being pointed to. The trouble the "walking" case introduces does not simply afflict cases in which we try to offer "ostensive definitions" for activities while we are performing them. The difficulty is a perfectly general one.

Later in *The Teacher* Augustine talks about learning what bird catching is by watching what a bird catcher does. He does not frame his question as one about the word for bird catching. But clearly it could have been put that way.

---

[8] Ibid., 101.
[9] Ibid.
[10] Ibid., 101–2.

And, as we can see, Adeodatus quickly associates the problem with the one about teaching what the word "walking" signifies.

> Augustine:... Consider this example. Suppose that someone unfamiliar with how to trick birds (which is done with reeds and birdlime) should run into a birdcatcher outfitted with his tools, not birdcatching but on his way to do so. On seeing this birdcatcher, he follows closely in his footsteps, and, as it happens, he reflects and asks himself in his astonishment what exactly the man's equipment means. Now the birdcatcher, wanting to show off after seeing the attention focused on him, prepares his reeds and, with his birdcall and his hawk, intercepts, subdues, and captures some little bird he has noticed nearby. I ask you: wouldn't he then teach the man watching him what he wanted to know by the thing itself rather than by anything that signifies [that is, by any words]?
>
> Adeodatus: I'm afraid that everything here is like what I said about the man who asks what it is to walk. Here, too, I don't see that the whole of birdcatching has been exhibited.
>
> Augustine: It's easy to get rid of your worry. I add that he's so intelligent that he recognizes the kind of craft as a whole on the basis of what he has seen. It's surely enough for the matter at hand that some men can be taught about some things, even if not all, without a sign.
>
> Adeodatus: I also can add this to the other case! If he is sufficiently intelligent he'll know the whole of what it is to walk, once walking has been illustrated by a few steps.
>
> Augustine: You may do so as far as I'm concerned (10.32).[11]

This happy resolution to the problem of ostensive learning may come to us as a disappointment. It seems insufficient to say that people who are smart enough learn what "walking" or "bird catching" means, even though any demonstration or pointing aimed at teaching them will be open to multiple interpretations.

However, Augustine's solution to the problem of the ambiguity of ostension is part of a more general and, at the same time, more radical thesis about teaching, learning, and knowing that Augustine argues for in this little dialogue. The radical thesis is that we learn what we come to know not through the instruction of an "outer" teacher but rather through inner illumination. The most an outer teacher can do is to prompt us to find the relevant truth within ourselves.

---

[11] Ibid., 134–5.

Augustine sometimes expresses his idea of inner illumination as learning from Christ, the Inner Teacher, as in this passage:

> Regarding each of the things we understand, however, we don't consult a speaker who makes sounds outside us, but the Truth that presides within over the mind itself, though perhaps words prompt us to consult Him [that is, Christ]. What is more, He Who is consulted, He Who is said to *dwell in the inner man* [Eph. 3:16–17] does teach: Christ – that is, *the unchangeable power and everlasting wisdom of God* [1 Cor. 1:24], which every rational soul does consult, but is disclosed to anyone, to the extent that he can apprehend it, according to his good or evil will. If at times one is mistaken, this doesn't happen by means of a defect in the Truth consulted, just as it isn't a defect in light outside that the eyes of the body are often mistaken – and we admit that we consult this light regarding visible things, that it may show them to us to the extend that we have the ability to make them out (11.38).[12]

Thus one philosophically important connection between Jesus and Augustine is that Augustine, in his dialogue *The Teacher*, takes Jesus Christ to be a sort of "Inner Sage." When we come to understand something, it is through the mediation of this Inner Sage that we are illuminated.

In the prefatory comment to the passage with which Wittgenstein begins his *Philosophical Investigations* Augustine speaks of "the intelligence which you gave me, my God." The idea there seems to be the same that Augustine appeals to when he assures Adeodatus that if one is "sufficiently intelligent he'll know the whole of what it is to walk, once walking has been illustrated by a few steps." And that idea, in turn, seems to be what Augustine wants to capture later on in the same dialogue when he speaks of the mind, "perhaps prompted by words," consulting Christ the Inner Teacher.

Faced with the problem about ostensive learning, Wittgenstein responds in a way that seems to be the very opposite of Augustine's response. Instead of trying to identify, or even just name, the power with which we learners are able to identify in a demonstration of walking what exactly the word "walking" refers to, Wittgenstein directs our attention to what he calls "language games." His idea seems to be that when we have developed an ability to play the language games in which, for example, the word "walking" is used, we will understand its meaning well enough. There need be no further question about how we manage to link its meaning to exactly the right activity in the world, namely, the activity of walking (as opposed to hurrying, taking a few steps,

---

[12] Ibid., 139.

strolling, or whatever). It will be part of the language game to discriminate walking from related, but differently specified, activities.

Wittgenstein tries to free us from a preoccupation with a problem about how the mind latches onto the right thing – the very thing that a given term like "walking" or "two" denotes. Instead of focusing on how we can ever "cut through" the ambiguity of ostension, we should focus on the contexts in which we use language and on the competence we acquire in using "walking" and "two" correctly. For a *large* class of cases – though not for all – in which we employ the word "meaning," Wittgenstein writes, "it can be defined thus: the meaning of a word is its use in the language."[13]

Augustine, by contrast, keeps our focus on how it is that we ever figure out what a general term, such as "walking," signifies, or picks out. Since no single occasion of ostensive learning, or indeed any series of such occasions, will remove all possibility of ambiguity, he supposes there must be an inner illumination, which he understands as instruction from Christ the Inner Teacher.

What exactly is at stake in this debate between Augustine and Wittgenstein? In particular, what does it matter whether we think of the ambiguity of ostension as being overcome in language learning by an inner illumination, identified by Augustine as coming from Christ the Inner Teacher, or whether, instead, we move our attention away from the alleged problem of how we ever learn the meaning of general terms and focus instead on how we come to play "language games" in which learning the accepted use of general terms is an essential part. Neither response to the problem of ostensive learning actually explains how we make precise connections between our language and the world.

One difference between the two responses is that the Augustinian response encourages us to take up a reverential attitude to the mystery of language acquisition. The needed connections are made, according to Augustine, with divine help. Wittgenstein, by contrast, tries to dissolve the problem by turning our attention from single word acquisition to linguistic practices more generally. Language learning is a social phenomenon and not necessarily anything of religious significance.

I hasten to add that although Wittgenstein's account of language learning is not itself religious, we should not conclude from this fact that Wittgenstein was a purely secular person. To the contrary, he was often preoccupied with religious questions throughout much of his life. He seems not, however, to have thought that religious faith might have anything much to do with the

---

[13] Wittgenstein (1967), ¶43.

phenomenon of language acquisition in general or, in particular, with the ambiguity of ostension.

There is, however, quite a different approach to the problem of ostensive learning that should be considered in company with Augustine and Wittgenstein. Finding the exact meaning of, say, "walking" can well seem to be a problem of how we could ever arrive at the appropriate necessary and sufficient conditions for a movement to count as an instance of walking, rather than strolling, hurrying, or whatever. Is it right to say that the physician who is standing only a short distance from the patient's bedside and takes only two steps to arrive at his or her bedside *walks* to the patient's bedside or only *steps over* to the patient's bedside? If taking two steps is enough for walking, what about taking only one step? And if two steps are insufficient, what about taking three?

Work during the last thirty years on the psychology of language acquisition suggests that children do not learn the meanings of words by coming to internalize necessary and sufficient conditions for their application. Instead, they learn what Eleanor Rosch and her associates call "prototypes," that is, paradigm instances of application.[14] Thus a child may associate a robin with "bird" and so have difficulty in recognizing that a penguin is also a bird.

Prototype theory suggests that the ambiguity problem is best solved by coming to realize that a certain indeterminateness belongs to our use of most all general terms. Taking three steps will certainly not be our paradigm for walking. We may have difficulty in saying how many steps are required for a genuine case of walking. Strolling across the room will more likely fit the paradigm. But there will always be borderline cases.

There may still be an element of mystery about how we grasp paradigms and how we apply them to other cases. Wittgenstein's advice to look for the actual use of words and to the competence a child develops in using words may be helpful. But it may well be that each of these three of these approaches – Augustine's Doctrine of Illumination ("Christ, the Inner Teacher"), Wittgenstein's admonition to look for the use of general terms in actual "language games," and Eleanor Rosch's prototype theory – complement the other two. Perhaps the most distinctive contribution of Augustine's solution is, as I have already suggested, the religious attitude it promotes toward what most philosophers and psychologists of language acquisition would consider a purely secular matter.

So far I have talked about the role of Jesus in Augustine's thinking as Christ the Inner Teacher. But obviously Jesus as "Outer Teacher," that is, Jesus as

[14] Rosch and Lloyd (1978).

the figure we encounter in the New Testament Gospel narratives, also plays an important role in Augustine's thought. Many of Augustine's sermons and commentaries attempt to deal with the sayings of the biblical Jesus. I want to focus now on how Augustine interprets a famous saying of Jesus from his Sermon on the Mount (chapters 5 through 7 of the Gospel according to St. Matthew).

In Augustine's *Commentary on the Lord's Sermon on the Mount*[15] we find a very important elaboration on this famous verse:

> You have heard that it was said, "You shall not commit adultery." But I say to you that everyone who looks at a woman lustfully has already committed adultery with her in his heart (Matt. 5:27–28).

Augustine's commentary on this verse puts forward what William Mann has called, quite appropriately, Augustine's "inner-life ethics."[16] Central to Augustine's thinking here is his account of what he takes to be a complete sin. According to this account, the components of a complete sin are these: (1) suggestion, (2) pleasure, and (3) consent. Here is the way he explains these components:

> The suggestion is made either through the memory or through the bodily senses – when we are seeing or hearing or smelling or tasting or touching something. If we take pleasure in the enjoyment of this [suggestion], it must be repressed if the pleasure is sinful. For example, if the craving of the palate is aroused at the sight of viands while we are observing the law of fasting, it arises only through pleasure; we do not consent to it, we repress by the law of reason, to which it is subject. But, if consent is given, then a sin is fully committed in the heart, and it is known to God, even though it be not made known to men, through the medium of any act. Therefore, these three successive stages are such as if the suggestion were made by a serpent, that is to say, it is made by a slimy and sinuous motion, namely, a transient action of the body. For, if any such images hover within the soul, they have been drawn from without, that is, from the body. And if, in addition to those five senses, any occult operation of a body comes into contact with the soul, it, too, is transient and moving quickly; therefore, the more occultly it glides into contact with thought, so much the more rightly is it compared with a serpent. Therefore, as I as beginning to say, these three successive stages may be likened to the action that is described in Genesis [3]. For the suggestion, as well as a kind of persuasion, is made as though by a serpent; the pleasure is in the carnal desire, as though in Eve; and the consent is in the reason, as

---

[15] Augustine (1951).
[16] Mann (1999).

though in the man [Adam]. And if a man passes through these three stages, he is, as it were, cast out from Paradise; that is to say, he is expelled from the most blessed light of justice and is cast unto death. And this is most strictly in accordance with justice, for persuasion is not compulsion (1.12.24).[17]

Augustine is not explicit about whether the first component by itself, that is, the mere suggestion of doing something illicit, counts as a sin or whether the first component and the second, that is, pleasure in the thought of performing an illicit act, count as a sin. All we learn is that nothing is a *complete* sin without all three components.

Augustine goes on:

Therefore, just as sin is reached through the three successive stages of suggestion, pleasure, and consent, so also there are three distinct degrees of the same sin, accordingly as it is in the heart, in a deed, or in a habit. These three degrees of sin are, as it were, three types of death. The first – when consent in the heart is given to lust – is as though typifying the home; the second – when assent becomes deed – typifies the dead man being carried outside the door; the third – by the weight of bad habit, the mind is pressed down as by a mound of earth – typifies the dead body rotting in the grave. Now, every reader of the Gospel is aware of the fact that the Lord restored life to these three types of dead men (1.12.35).[18]

The idea here seems to be that the three components make up a complete sin and that the action, if any, that follows from consenting to perform it is not an additional sin, but only the revelation of a sin already committed in the heart. To go back to Jesus's example of adulterous lust, the wrongness of an act of adultery does not consist in the consequences it may have for the person lusted after, or for that person's spouse or family, even though these consequences may indeed be great evils. The sin consists of the suggestion of having sex contrary to what is lawful, the pleasure in considering that suggestion, and the consent to perform the act of adultery. Even if the action consented to is never actually performed, even if the person lusted after is completely unaware of any lustful gaze, the sin can be complete. The actual deed consented to in the adulterer's heart, if it is actually performed, does not make the agent any more sinful than the inner action of giving consent had already made him or her. That point is suggested by a parallel passage in Augustine's *Commentary on Genesis against the Manicheans*:

[17] Augustine (1995), 53–4.
[18] Ibid., 55.

If, when the suggestion has taken shape, our desire or greed is not roused to sin, the serpent's cunning will be blocked; if it is roused, though, it's as if the woman has already been persuaded. But sometimes the reason valiantly puts the brake on greed when it has been roused, and brings it to a halt. When this happens, we don't slide into sin, but wins the prize with a certain amount of trouble. If, however, the reason does consent and decide that what lust or greed is urging on it should be done, then the man is expelled from the entire life of bliss, as from paradise. Sin is already put down to his account, you see, even if the actual deed doesn't follow, since the conscience incurs guilt just by consent (2.14.21).[19]

If we think of ethical theories as either consequentialist or deontological, and we think of Augustine's commentary on the Sermon on the Mount as giving us a Christian ethics, then the ethics we find here is purely deontological. The actions enjoined and forbidden are given in God's Law, including no doubt the Ten Commandments, and this summary that Jesus gives us of the Law:

You shall love the Lord your God with all your heart, and with all your soul, and with all your mind. This is the great and first commandment. And a second is like it, You shall love your neighbor as yourself (Matt. 22:37–39).

But, according to this theory, it is not the "outer" actions that are the primary object of moral assessment. Rather it is the "inner" activities of suggestion and pleasure in the forbidden, as well as the inner action of forming the intention to perform some forbidden action, that are the primary locus of moral assessment.

We can find Augustine trying to apply his inner-life ethics to various aspects of his own life. Particularly difficult for him is its application to his dream life. Of course, Jesus did not admonish us to have no unchaste dreams. But it is difficult for Augustine to convince himself that he is not sinful when he consents, in his dreams, to unlawful sex. He wrestles with this problem in at least two different passages, but more earnestly in this passage from *Confessions* 10:

You commanded me without question [O Lord] to abstain "from the lust of the flesh and the lust of the eyes and the ambition of the secular world" [1 John 2:16]. You commanded me to abstain from sleeping with a girl-friend and, in regard to marriage itself, you advised me to adopt a better way of life than you have allowed [1 Corinthians 7:38]. And because you granted me strength, this was done even before I became a dispenser of your sacrament.

---

[19] Augustine (2002), 85.

But in my memory, of which I have spoken at length, there still live images of acts which were fixed there by my sexual habit. These images attack me. While I am awake they have no force, but in sleep they not only arouse pleasure but even elicit consent, and are very like the actual act. The illusory image within the soul has such force upon my flesh that false dreams have an effect on me when asleep, which the reality could not have when I am awake.

Do I not exist that that time, Lord, my God? Yet how great a difference between myself at the time when I am asleep and myself when I return to the waking state. Where then is reason, which, when [I am] wide-awake, resists such suggestive thoughts, and would remain unmoved if the actual reality were to be presented to it?

Does reason shut down with the eyes? Does it sleep with the bodily senses?

If that were so, how could it come about that often in sleep we resist and, mindful of our avowed commitment and adhering to it with strict chastity, we give no assent to such seductions?

Yet there is a difference so great that when it happens otherwise than we could wish, when we wake up, we return to peace in our conscience.

From the wide gulf between the occurrences and our will, we discover that we did not actively do what, to our regret, has somehow been done in us (10.39.41).[20]

As I have suggested elsewhere,[21] there seem to be three ways Augustine could attempt to get out of responsibility for the consents of his dream self:

(1) He could deny that he is his dreaming self.
(2) He could insist that what happens in his dreams does not really happen.
(3) He could insist that he is not morally responsible for doing what his dream self does in his dreams, including consent to this or that course of action, on the grounds that he could not, in his dreams, do anything different from what he actually does in his dreams.

None of these three options can be very attractive to Augustine. The first option, denying that he is his dreaming self, would make problems for his famous response to Academic skepticism. To the global skeptic's challenge for him to point out at least one thing that he knows, Augustine replies that he knows he exists. The skeptic then follows up with the question "But how do you know that you are not asleep?" to which Augustine replies, "If I am mistaken, I exist" [*si fallor, sum*]. Augustine's idea that the skeptic's taunt, "You might be mistaken, as you often are when you are asleep," does not

---

[20] Augustine (1991), 203, Chadwick's translation, but somewhat modified.
[21] Matthews (2005), 71–2.

undercut the claim to know that he exists, since he would have to exist to be mistaken.

Augustine does ask, in the earlier quotation, "Do I not exist at that time, O Lord my God?" But this is for him a rhetorical question. Thus he goes on in the very next sentence to point to the difference between his dreaming self and his waking self. Though he wants to think that difference may relieve him of responsibility for what he consents to in his dreams, it does mean that he is not his dreaming self.

In the end Augustine does suggest that what we seem to do in a dream, such as engage in sex, is perhaps only something "in some way done in us" [in nobis quoquo modo factum esse], rather than something we do. But who is it that, in his dream, consents to illicit sex, if it is not he? He cannot say.

The second option – denying that anything really happens in dreams – is hardly more attractive to Augustine. He doesn't know how to distinguish (1) its merely seeming to him that he consents to having sex and (2) his actually consenting, inwardly, to having sex. When, in the very next section, he asks for God's help in ridding himself of immoral dreams, he says this:

> You will more and more increase your gifts in me, Lord, so that my soul, rid of the glue of lust, may follow me to you, so that it is not in rebellion against itself, and so that even in dreams it not only does not commit those disgraceful and corrupt acts in which sensual images provoke bodily emissions, but also does not even consent to them (10.30.42).[22]

So what he wants his soul not to consent to is illicit sex, even in the context of a dream. And he wants that because he has to allow that even dreamt consent is still consent. We must remember that we have completed a sin, according to Augustine, if we consent to an action that we never actually perform. And so, in his view, consent to something in a dream is a form of consent, even if it never finds expression in any action in waking life.

Augustine cannot accept the third option either. He supposes that each of us has free will. But he also supposes that we can do nothing good except by the grace of God.[23] So we cannot resist temptation, even in a dream, except by the grace of God. But with God's help we can certainly resist temptation, even in a dream. And, as we have already seen, God's help in resisting temptation, even in his dreams, is exactly what Augustine prays for.

Whatever you and I think about our responsibility for the actions and passions of our dreaming self, we should appreciate the stress the moral dream

---

[22] Augustine (1991), 203–4.
[23] See, e.g., Confessions 10.4.5.

problem places – not just on Augustine himself – but also on Augustine's inner-life ethics. If we think of what Augustine calls "consent" as a robust resolution to act on a suggestion to perform some unlawful act that one has taken pleasure in contemplating, the idea that one has sinned in one's heart may indeed be plausible. But when we consider the possibility that the consent may have been only dreamt consent, the idea of culpability be less plausible to us. However, the situation becomes much more complicated when we consider the whole range of possibilities from, on one extreme, the firm resolution to commit adultery to, on the other, the mere dream of consenting to illicit sex. For in between these two extremes are many other kinds of case. For one thing, there is the phenomenon of daydreaming. More generally, there is the question of how to evaluate, morally, one's fantasy life.

Can we easily say which of these is worse: (1) fantasizing that one is having illicit sex with someone every time one sees her, without ever taking any steps to make this fantasy real, or (2) consenting inwardly on a single occasion to have illicit sex, but never getting the opportunity, and later regretting having once formed the unrealized intention?

We can also wonder whether Augustine's theory of suggestion, pleasure, and consent really captures what Jesus had in mind when he spoke of committing adultery in one's heart. Jesus talks about looking lustfully at a woman who is not one's wife. Some men do that every day during their lunch break. We can suppose that some of them, perhaps most of them, never actually form an intention to lie with the women they ogle during lunch break. On a straightforward reading of the words of Jesus, these men have already committed adultery in their hearts. If this is right, then Augustine's inner-life ethics has not really captured the message Jesus meant to convey.

Of course, Augustine does not say that ogling without consent is no sin. What he says seems to imply that it is, at least, no complete sin. But to fill out the inner-life ethics that Augustine sketches in his commentary on the Sermon on the Mount, one would need to say something about the whole range of cases in which we consider, and take pleasure in considering, something that, if we actually did it, would be morally wrong.

Jesus himself seems not to have offered anything that a philosopher today would consider a moral theory. Augustine does at least offer the core of an ethical theory that is inspired by a famous saying of Jesus. Even though the theory Augustine offers is incomplete and even though it may not capture exactly what Jesus seems to have had in mind, it should force us to think more seriously about that famous saying of Jesus. It also challenges us to see if we could do a better job of developing a theory of inner-life ethics.

Augustine's work on ethics has another virtue. It extends ethical consideration to the assessment of our inner lives in a way that is not clearly provided for by the Kantian categorical imperative or by the principle of utility. Besides Kantian ethics and utilitarianism, the other main theory professional philosophers discuss toady is virtue ethics. The virtue ethicist may have an easier time accommodating our intuitions about the moral significance of our inner lives than the Kantian, let alone the utilitarian. But so far as I know, no virtue ethicist has made much of an effort to do so.

In many ways, then, Augustine's inner-life ethics does make a contribution to ethical theory, to biblical exegesis, and to anyone who finds it plausible to think that the quality of our inner lives is ethically significant, even when the drama of that inner life does not lead directly to action.

BIBLIOGRAPHY

Augustine. *Commentary on the Lord's Sermon on the Mount, with Seventeen Related Sermons.* Washington, DC: Catholic University of America Press, 1951.

Augustine. *Confessions.* Henry Chadwick, trans. Oxford: Oxford University Press, 1991.

Augustine. *Against the Academicians, and The Teacher.* Peter King, trans. Indianapolis: Hackett, 1995.

Augustine. *On Genesis.*, Edmund Hill, trans., Hyde Park, NY: New City Press, 2002.

Burnyeat, M. F. "Augustine and Wittgenstein *De magistro.*" *Proceedings of the Aristotelian Society,* suppl. vol. 61 (1987): 1–24; reprinted in *The Augustinian Tradition,* edited by Gareth B. Matthews, 286–303. Berkeley: University of California Press, 1999.

Haji, Ishtiyaque. "On Being Morally Responsible in a Dream." In Matthews (1999), 166–82.

Mann, William E. "Inner-Life Ethics." In Matthews (1999), 140–65.

Matthews, Gareth B. "On Being Immoral in a Dream." *Philosophy* 58 (1983): 47–54.

Matthews, Gareth B. *Augustine.* Oxford: Blackwell, 2005.

Monk, Ray. *Ludwig Wittgenstein: The Duty of Genius.* New York: The Free Press, 1990.

Rosch, Eleanor, and Barbara Lloyd, eds. *Cognition and Categorizatin.* Hillsdale, NJ: Erlbaum, 1978.

Wittgenstein, Ludwig. *Philosophical Investigations.* G. E. M. Anscombe, trans. Oxford: Blackwell, 1967.

6

∿

Jesus and Aquinas

. *Brian Leftow*

Jesus was to Aquinas what water is to a fish. Thomas's parents deposited him in a monastery at age five. His teenaged rebellion was to leave the monastery for the Dominicans. He thought, taught, and preached about Jesus for his entire adulthood. He saw other ways to live, but he knew no other life than one with Jesus at its core. When we ask about Christ's relation to Thomas's philosophy, however, some raise a difficulty: Thomas did not think of himself as a philosopher and wrote few purely philosophical works.[1] But the difficulty can be overstated. There are certainly in Thomas deliberately given answers to questions philosophers ask, understood as such, and arguments supporting these that do not take as premises authorities of the Christian faith – scripture, creeds, and so on. It is no misnomer to call Thomas a philosopher, even if he might have been uncomfortable with the label.[2]

I now discuss Christ's relation to that in Aquinas which is philosophical under three heads. I first note his metaphysical framing of what philosophy seeks and an argument he gives for accepting that Christ has the role in philosophy Thomas gives him. I next suggest how Christ actually affects Thomas's practice of philosophy. I finally consider some concrete ways Thomas reacted as a Christian to his most prominent philosophical source, Aristotle, suggesting that Thomas makes some effort to show that Christian theology completes thinking about God that Aristotle did not take far enough. Thomas differs sharply from Aristotle over how much God knows about what goes on in the world. Given some things on which Thomas agrees with Aristotle, it can seem unclear that he should disagree. I thus try to make sense of Thomas's account

---

[1] On this see Mark Jordan, "Theology and Philosophy," in *The Cambridge Companion to Aquinas*, eds. Norman Kretzmann and Eleonore Stump (Cambridge: Cambridge University Press, 1993), 232–51.

[2] Jordan, *Companion to Aquinas*, makes a case that he would.

of God's knowledge of creatures, differing en route with Eleonore Stump's recent discussion of this.

PHILOSOPHY SEEKS, CHRIST PROVIDES

Aquinas gave Christ a central place in philosophy in the first chapter of what some see as his "philosophical *Summa*," the *Summa Contra Gentiles* (henceforth *SCG*). Aristotle saw wisdom, the goal of philosophy, as the knowledge of first principles and causes.[3] *SCG* begins by echoing this, saying that it is the role of the wise to seek the truth about things' highest causes and last end, and then at once adds that divine wisdom took on flesh and came into the world to make the truth known.[4] Aristotle (Thomas continues) tells us that "first philosophy" – metaphysics – is the study of the truth about the ultimate source of all things: divine truth. Then Thomas writes that "divine truth . . . is truth *antonomastice*,"[5] that is, in the phrase "divine truth," "truth" names a person. He has in mind Christ, who said "I am the truth." Thus Thomas asserts that philosophy actually seeks *inter alia* knowledge of Christ, though philosophers do not know it. This is the right conclusion if orthodox Christianity is true and philosophy really does have as one of its goals knowing the highest causes as fully as possible.

I deal first with philosophy's access to the "highest causes." The non-Christian thinkers Thomas knew – Plato, Aristotle, Maimonides, Avicenna, Al-Ghazali, Averroes – believed in a divine highest cause. Aquinas, Aristotle, Maimonides, Avicenna, and Averroes were at one on its being atemporal, immutable, and simple. The fact of the Incarnation coupled with the fact that the incarnate Christ had someone to pray to make known another truth about its metaphysical attributes, which Thomas thinks those unguided by Christian theology could never attain, namely, that it contains more than one Person.[6] Thomas is surely right about this: even if the doctrine of the Trinity is true, it is not a conclusion a non-Christian philosopher would ever draw about God.

Christ taught about the moral and affective nature of God. Thomas of course follows him, but his differences with the writers just mentioned vary. Plato described the Demiurge as good, benevolent, and generous, but not as loving, just, or merciful.[7] Now Thomas sees God's love as largely consisting in

---

[3] *Metaphysics* A2.
[4] *SCG* I, 1.
[5] S. Thomae Aquinatis *Summa Contra Gentiles* (Turin: Marietti, 1909), I, 1, p. 2.
[6] *In Boeth. de Trin.*, q. 1, a. 4.
[7] *Timaeus* 29e-30a.

willing good to others – benevolence.[8] So he would have to concede that Plato got God's love at least partly right. But Thomas also holds that love includes willing union with the beloved, in an appropriate mode.[9] Christ taught that he was God incarnate – I say it, though some New Testament scholars dispute it – and the Incarnation is a mode of union with a beloved human race with no parallel in non-Christian religious philosophy. (Aristotle, as we see later, held that God did not even know that the human race exists.) Even leaving this aside, Christ taught that God wills a final eschatological union with those who believe – the great wedding feast. Christ also taught that God was going to greater lengths to provide good than any Greek or Roman philosopher imagined, insofar as he taught that God Incarnate's death was part of this. Thus even if a piece of Thomas's conception of God's love coincides with a claim Plato made, fidelity to Christ's teaching led him to claims about God's love with no parallel in Plato, which make God out to be more loving than Plato thought.

Aristotle calls the Unmoved Mover good, but it is not clear that this can have a moral sense, as the Unmoved Mover has no will and does nothing but think; Aristotle may mean no more than that it is something (likeness with which?) others find desirable. Maimonides accepted the Old Testament, from which Christ taught; he thus had open to him a doctrine of God's moral nature that could coincide with a Christian thinker's. But Maimonides also argued a strict negative theology: we cannot speak the truth if we speak positively of God's nature, on Maimonides' terms, unless we reinterpret what we say as a set of claims about his actions.[10] So in the end, Maimonides would not assert that God is by nature loving, just, or even good. The Muslim thinkers were influenced to varying degrees by the Koran, much of which to a Christian reads like a pastiche from and (heretical) commentary on the Bible. Given the biblical influence, it is not surprising if a Muslim thinker like Al-Ghazali says things about God's moral nature that echo Christianity. But Christians have reason to say that it is precisely an echo, dependent on Christ's teaching, and in some cases the Muslims' metaphysics undercuts it. Avicenna tries to argue that God is generous, since he gives good things to creatures without any ulterior motive.[11] But what he can mean by this is limited: as Avicenna sees it, God acts by necessity of his nature, without possibility of refraining, and further directly produces only a single effect, the rest of Creation unfolding

---

[8] *SCG* I, 91.

[9] Ibid.

[10] *Guide for the Perplexed*, I, 58.

[11] Avicenna, *Metaphysica*, trans. Parviz Morewedge (London: Routledge, 1973), 71.

from it without his direct effort. It is hard to see where divine love could fit into this picture. Averroes's doctrine of God stays close to Aristotle and (in some respects) Avicenna.

Philosophers can try to reason out God's nature a priori, by perfect being theology, or a posteriori, from his effects. Perfect being theology began with Plato, Aristotle, and the Stoics.[12] It ascribes to God the attributes that would characterize a perfect being, that is, a most great-making consistent set of attributes each of which individually is prima facie better to have than to lack. Thus perfect being theology takes as input a writer's intuitions about perfection. Given as input only the moral intuitions behind Platonic, Aristotelian, and Stoic moral philosophy, perfect being theology would yield a God whose moral nature is not much like the one Thomas describes. It is ultimately Jesus's input that accounts for the difference. Moving to a posteriori arguments, divine justice and mercy are not obvious among God's effects – or if there is evidence for them, it coexists with apparent evidence of their opposites. There would be no problem of evil were the world's character good evidence that God is perfectly benevolent, but in fact a case can be made that no possible created world could be evidence of a deity's perfect benevolence, for there is no best possible Creation. Thus any creation God could make could be surpassed, and so for any possible Creation, one could argue that a perfectly benevolent being would have made a better world than that.[13] Design arguments can conclude to a designing intelligence, but (as Hume noted) the mixed moral nature of the effect does not give strong reason to believe in a morally perfect cause. Cosmological arguments, just as such, have no implications at all about the first cause's moral nature. Christ taught that God is morally perfect.[14] Without Christ's teaching, it is unlikely that philosophers would have come up with the picture of God's moral nature that is now standard fare – unless Judaism had eventually diffused far more widely than its prospects by the first century A.D. would make likely.

If the wise seek knowledge of the last end and the way to happiness, as Aristotle also thinks,[15] then if the world and we ourselves were made, and made with a point, the wise cannot know the last end without knowing the point for

---

[12] See my "Concepts of God," in *Routledge Encyclopedia of Philosophy*, ed. Edward Craig (London: Routledge, 1998).

[13] William Rowe bases an argument against God's existence on this, in *Can God Be Free?* (Oxford: Oxford University Press, 2004). I block the argument in "No Best World: Moral Luck," *Religious Studies* 41 (2005), 165–81, and "No Best World: Creaturely Freedom," *Religious Studies* 41 (2005), 269–85.

[14] Matt. 5:48.

[15] *Nicomachean Ethics*, I, 1.

which we were made: the maker determines the end of the artifact. Christianity gives the fullest account of happiness and the last end, if Christianity is true, and the account goes so far beyond and is so counterintuitive relative to the contents of purely secular moral philosophy that it is safe to say that secular philosophy is radically incomplete if Christianity is true. Since he does believe Christianity is true, without any sense of incongruity, Thomas can say that he is taking up the office of the wise – the philosopher's task – and then say that this is "to make manifest . . . the truth professed by the Catholic faith."[16]

In making knowledge of Christ and the teachings he provided an unacknowledged goal of philosophy, or at least an unacknowledged indispensable route to acknowledged goals, Thomas just picks up a motif from Paul, who wrote of "Christ in whom are hidden all the treasures of wisdom and knowledge" (Col. 2:3). Wisdom is partly a practical matter, having to do with the right organization of life. So this is partly an allusion to Christ's role as an ethical teacher. But it is also ipso facto an allusion to the authority we must ascribe to him if we are to take his teachings seriously. For so much of what Christ taught about the good, best, and required is so unintuitive relative to purely secular moral philosophy that if we do not see him as at least a prophet, revealing God's authoritative will, we will have little reason to take it seriously – and so reap the advantage of acting as it dictates.

Wisdom and knowledge also seek to grasp the true natures of things, a body of necessary truths. For Thomas as for any medieval Christian, realities in God finally determine creatures' natures. Many medievals would have said that God's nature and ideas, the Christian transform of Plato's Forms, determine the truths philosophers can hope to know. What it is to be a substance, many would say, is determined by the nature of the primal instance of substance, God. (On some versions of Aristotelianism and all versions of nominalism, what content an attribute has is determined by what its instances are like.) Many medievals followed Augustine's Christian transform of Platonism into the claim that what it is to be a dog is set first by the content of God's idea of a dog. For Thomas, what it is to be a dog is set by the power of God, which contains the nature of dogs as it contains the nature of all its possible effects – and since the content of God's power is an aspect of his nature, for Thomas all necessary truths have truth makers ultimately in the divine nature.[17] Thus for Thomas, all that philosophers seek to know is bound up

[16] S. Thomae Aquinatis *Summa Contra Gentiles*, I, 1, p. 2.
[17] On this see my "Aquinas on God and Modal Truth," *The Modern Schoolman* 82 (2005), 171–200.

with the nature of God – which is more fully revealed in the Christian tradition than anywhere else, if orthodox Christianity is true.

AN ARGUMENT FOR AUTHORITY

But why think Christianity true? Aquinas points to miracles, which certify prophets as prophets and so their doctrines as true: "a visible action which can only be divine points out an invisibly inspired teacher of the truth."[18] Thomas claims as a miracle the writing of eloquent scripture by simple, untutored men.[19] But this can be mirrored in other faiths and presumes that scripture's human authors were untutored, which we do not in fact know. The chief contemporary miracle Thomas points to is the acceptance of Christianity despite its teaching things beyond full human understanding and demanding the renunciation of the world's pleasures.[20] These are not without candidate natural explanations; whether the disjunction of these is more plausible than the explanation of miraculous divine agency is a good question. Further, the phenomenon does not conform to Thomas's own definition of miracle. Thomas writes that "those things are properly called miracles which are done by divine agency beyond the order commonly observed in nature,"[21] and even if Christian faith is always implanted by divine agency, (a) it crops up far too frequently to count as an uncommon occurrence, and (b) belief in doctrines not transparent to reason and that demand renunciation of worldly pleasure is more common still, being a feature of Hinduism, Sufism, and Buddhism. Thus Thomas's best candidate miracles are those in scripture. But we know about these only if we accept that scripture tells the truth. Aquinas also points to fulfilled prophecies, but here we depend in a double way on the truthfulness of scripture.[22]

Ultimately, then, Thomas's argument for Christ's role boils down to what he has to say in favor of the truthfulness of certain books. Thomas does (I think) have an argument for this: SCG is in part an extended argument that Christian authorities are reliable on subjects connected with God. To establish the reliability of a witness, we check his or her testimony where we are able to. SCG's first three volumes do just this for Christian authorities. In these volumes Thomas argues on purely philosophical grounds for an elaborate theory of God's nature and relations to the world. Many of SCG's chapters end

---

[18] Ibid., I, 6, p. 6.
[19] Ibid.
[20] SCG I, 6.
[21] SCG III, 101.
[22] SCG I, 6.

with citations of Christian authorities, chiefly scripture, showing that these teach what Thomas has (he thinks) established by philosophical argument. If the arguments work and Thomas reads his authorities correctly, what emerges is that the Bible and the Christian tradition it inspired get it right about God every time. In *SCG* IV, Thomas proceeds to doctrines about God's nature and Christ's person that can't be supported by purely philosophical argument – things accepted ultimately on the basis of Christian authorities, that is, because one believes in the truthfulness of books that proclaim them. Why think the books truthful? Because they have been truthful about God's nature (Thomas has tried to show) in every instance where we have an independent basis for assessing what the truth is. This is a good way to establish the reliability of a witness, and once a witness is known to be reliable, whatever else it tells us is rationally taken to be probably true. Thus *SCG*'s validation of biblical testimony extends also (though to a lesser degree) to biblical testimony to historical events, which are after all an easier subject to get right – including purported miracles.

CHRISTIANITY IN PHILOSOPHICAL PRACTICE

So far I have explained how Christ figures in Thomas's metaphysical framing of what philosophy is about, and the character of an extended argument Thomas presents for granting Christ this role. But despite the place Thomas gives Christ in philosophy, in most areas, Christ's impact on Aquinas's philosophy was indirect and mediated. Jesus had much to say in ethics. His ethical teachings led Thomas to major transformations of the Aristotelian material he wrestled with. But that is a story for someone else to tell. Jesus did not teach metaphysics, epistemology, or philosophical theology. Jesus's significance for these parts of Aquinas's philosophy was as the ultimate guarantor of an entire tradition from which Thomas drew. The New Testament drew its authority for Thomas from the presumption that its authors spoke from their memory of Jesus's teaching and the prompting of the Spirit he sent. The Old Testament too had its authority due ultimately to Jesus: had he not sent a mission to the Gentiles, Thomas would have had no reason to take this collection of Hebrew writings as relevant to his thinking, and its prophecies were part of the argument for Christianity's truth. The Fathers and earlier medieval theologians drew what authority they had for Thomas from the presumption that in and through them church, led by the Spirit, was sifting out the right interpretation of the apostles' words. These authorities occasionally dictated a metaphysical position: Thomas rejects Platonism as "contrary to the faith,"[23] though he

---

[23] *ST* Ia 84, 5.

also endorses what Aristotle had to say against it. They more often directed Thomas to a view in philosophical theology.

Thomas's account of what omnipotence is, for instance, is often excerpted in textbooks in philosophy of religion as a stand-alone bit of philosophical analysis. But he adopts the definition he does ultimately because he sees it as the best way to be adequate to scripture. There we read that "the Lord ... can do all things" (Job 42:2), that "nothing is impossible with God" (Lk. 1:37): Aquinas's thesis that God has power to produce at any time all states of affairs it is absolutely possible to produce at that time[24] was just a philosophically precise reading of these claims. I say that Christian authorities "directed" because the statements of scripture did not dictate a particular philosophical explication of them – thus the plethora of definitions of omnipotence in the centuries prior to Thomas.[25] But given that Thomas accepted scriptural claims as true, the true account of omnipotence had in his eyes to consist in the best philosophical explication of these claims, not in something that could not be suggested and ultimately justified by these claims. The claims Thomas found in Christian authorities – which is to say the claims he took as true due ultimately to their relation to the words or person of Christ – provided the data he tried to explicate, and in many cases the propositions he sought to show true by philosophical means. Many philosophers Thomas read did not think God omnipotent, and the view was current in his own day because of the influence of Averroes. Thomas gave independent arguments that God is omnipotent, but he looked for them because he accepted first as a Christian that God is. It is in this sense that despite his explicit way of distinguishing philosophy from theology, Thomas gives us a Christian philosophical theology. His arguments are philosophical. His authorities are not, and the authorities suggest what to argue for.

It might seem odd to speak of philosophy as done subject to or within constraints dictated by or at the behest or inspiration of authorities. But this has analogues few philosophers today would question: few philosophers are physicists or evolutionary biologists, and all accept the dictates of physicists and evolutionary biologists as authoritative. These authorities, moreover, play much the role Aquinas did and have the same sort of source for their authority. Naturalist philosophers take the dicta of scientists as data, sometimes requiring interpretation, but never to be overturned from their own epistemically inferior position. They take remaining faithful to and within the bounds of these data as a condition of doing properly responsible philosophy, and take

---

[24] *ST* Ia 25, 3.
[25] On which see my "Omnipotence," in *The Oxford Handbook of Philosophical Theology*, eds. Thomas Flint and Michael Rea (Oxford: Oxford University Press, forthcoming).

it to be part of philosophy's job to give the most adequate philosophical explication of these data – taking it for granted that to do so will be a way to get
at the truth. And the dicta of scientists are not accepted because the scientists
are presumed to be intrinsically capable of delivering truth: it is rather that
they directly possess the evidence for the things they say and are properly
equipped to appreciate its significance, for physicists and biologists substitute
the prophets and apostles, and the result is Thomas's approach.

DRAWING THE PHILOSOPHERS ALONG

The Christian tradition led Thomas to argue against positions he might not
have thought to resist or challenge had not Christian revelation told him
that they were false. When he does, he sometimes seeks quietly to show
that Christianity completes what philosophy has to say about God. Thomas
agreed with much of Aristotle's concept of God – that he is eternal, immutable,
purely actual, simple, and an intellect that is wholly one with that which it
understands, which is its own act of understanding. But Aristotle seems also
to have held that God knows only himself, since God thinks only of what is
best – justifying this in part by a claim that there are things it is better not to
know, and God in particular knows none of these.[26] If this is true, of course,
then if Aristotle's God loves, he loves only himself – something no Christian
can accept. The *Magna Moralia* has it that

> Friendship . . . exists only where there be a return of affection, but friendship
> toward God does not admit of love being returned, nor at all of loving. For
> it would be strange if one were to say that he loved Zeus.[27]

This book's authorship by Aristotle has been questioned, but if it is not his
own work, it is an abstract of his views by a sympathetic later author (who
overlooked Aristotle's claim that God produces the motion of the heavens by
being loved[28]). But it is not clear that Aristotle's God can love even himself.
Aristotle nowhere speaks of the Prime Mover as having will, affections, or
emotions.

Thomas offers a variety of arguments that God has a will, and that he loves,
and some proceed from the premises Aristotle accepted. Aristotle granted that
God is good and understands himself.[29] But (says Thomas) the understood
good is necessarily loved[30] – a claim rather close to Aristotle's "the good is

---

[26] *Metaphysics* Λ9, 1074b25–34.
[27] II, 11, 1208b28–31.
[28] *Metaphysics* Λ7, 1072b3.
[29] *Metaphysics* Λ7 1072b18–21, 28–9; Λ9.1074b34–5.
[30] *Compendium Theologiae* I, 32.

what all desire."[31] Thus God must be able to love. For Thomas, love is the first act of the will.[32] Thus it is for him much the same argument when he reasons that the understood good is necessarily willed.[33] Given the thin, abstract nature of what Thomas is willing to count as love and volition, the argument's not-quite-Aristotelian premise amounts to little more than that one who understands that something is good necessarily has an attitude of approval toward it. Aristotle could just stand pat – this is necessarily so, he could say, only if the one understanding is the sort of thing that can have attitudes, and that, Aristotle might say, is precisely the point at issue; the "all" in the Aristotelian quote was intended to cover only humans. Again, Aristotle grants that God's life is pleasant.[34] But (says Thomas) intellectual pleasure is through the intellectual appetite, the will, even as sensible pleasure is through the sense-appetites.[35] Thomas's extra premise here seems more debatable: perhaps there is some phenomenology to intellectual pleasure, something like a sensation that one can have whether or not one wants anything. But it is clear what Thomas is up to, in any event. He wants to present what Christians believe as a reasonable extension of what Aristotle held on purely philosophical grounds, that is, to present what scripture teaches as the completion of what philosophy had arrived at independent of revelation. He is also (of course) presenting purely philosophical premises, which might commend themselves to any save one dogmatically insisting on not going beyond Aristotle's *ipsissima verba*.

On the question of whether God is aware of anything beyond himself Thomas is less successful in (as it were) drawing Aristotle along with him. God knows only himself, says Thomas, in the sense that the direct objects of his knowledge, which account for his knowing what he does, include nothing distinct from him. But it does not (Thomas thinks) follow from this that God has knowledge only of himself: God knows himself perfectly, and so understands his effects perfectly, and since all things in nature depend on God, God understands all things in nature.[36] It's clear how Aristotle could resist this. Thomas's argument rests on the claim that effects can be understood by understanding the powers of their sources.[37] It's not clear that Aristotle's God has any power other than the power to think – Aristotle's God produces all his effects by final, not efficient causation. And it would be enormously

---

[31] *Nicomachean Ethics* I, 1, 1094a1.
[32] *ST* Ia 20, 1.
[33] *SCG* I, 72.
[34] *Metaphysics* Λ7, 1072b15–6.
[35] *SCG* I, 72.
[36] *In XII Meta.*, l. 11, ##2614–5.
[37] Ibid.

implausible to hold that final causes somehow have written within themselves
what they finally cause: there is surely nothing within me that would permit me
to read out whether someone acts out of love from me, even in principle. But if
one granted this implausible premise, it might well follow only that Aristotle's
God would necessarily understand only his immediate effect, the motion of the
outer heavenly sphere: for Aristotle, God has no direct responsibility at all for
what happens further down in the world. Thomas also suggests that because
God understands all things in understanding himself, God can know base
things without being infected by their baseness: understanding the base is to be
avoided only if it would detract from one's attention to higher things,[38] or lead
to an inordinate affection for the base.[39] This tacitly denies one of Aristotle's
premises: there really isn't anything it is intrinsically better not to know; as
Thomas suggests elsewhere, everything has some nobility and is called lowly
or base only in comparison with still higher things.[40] It is not hard to hear in
this the echo of Genesis 1, in which God calls all things he has made good.

Given Aristotle's other views, it was reasonable of him to hold that God
knows nothing outside himself. For Aristotle holds that God is purely actual
and so has no passive (i.e., receptive) potentialities. A being with no passive
potentialities cannot be caused to be in any state and so cannot perceive
anything outside itself. A being that cannot efficiently cause anything cannot
come to know anything about the external world by its knowledge of its own
agency there. So on Aristotle's terms, a divine belief about the external world
could only be true by luck – and it is a moral of Gettier cases that beliefs true
by luck are not items of knowledge. Aquinas agrees with Aristotle that God
has no passive/receptive potentialities.[41] He also takes it as a general metaphysical truth that nothing corporeal can make a causal impact on anything
incorporeal.[42] So he no more than Aristotle can hold that God is caused to
know by anything outside himself, and this rules out any claim that God
literally perceives external realities. He speaks frequently of God as having
"knowledge of vision" of external things, but also says things suggesting that
all vision talk entails is that the knowledge is of things outside him:

> Things which are, were or will be . . . He knows with "knowledge of vision":
> because that properly is seen which has being outside the one seeing.[43]

[38] Ibid., #2616.
[39] SCG I, 70.
[40] SCG I, 70.
[41] De Potentia, 1, 1.
[42] ST Ia 84, 6.
[43] Super Sent., lib. 3 d. 14 q. 1 a. 2 qc. 2 co.

"[S]imple knowledge" and "knowledge of vision" introduce no difference on the side of knowledge, but only on the side of the known. "Knowledge of vision" is said in God's case in likeness of bodily sight, which sees things outside itself.[44]

"[S]imple knowledge" is said not to exclude a relation of knowledge to the known . . . but to exclude its mixture with anything outside the genus of knowledge – e.g. the existence of things, which "knowledge of vision" adds.[45]

Eleonore Stump suggests that nonetheless

God's intellect would not be perfect if it weren't somehow timelessly in receipt of what its "seeing" discloses . . . even in the case of the human intellect, the intellect understands by itself acting on data, not by being acted upon. So it seems that it is possible to hold consistently with Aquinas's other views that God's intellect as it were sees things but without undergoing and without being acted upon.[46]

Stump suggests that this is possible because God (for Thomas) is timeless: "real potentiality is time-bound . . . the undergoing of cognition . . . takes time."[47] However, it is hard to see how a mind could be "in receipt" without being a receiver or how a mind could be a receiver without being passive to that from which it receives. Thomas holds that "a thing is passive to the extent to which it is in potentiality" and that passive potentiality is just "the principle of being acted on by another."[48] So there doesn't seem to be space within Thomas's views for the possibility Stump holds out, however attractive it might be as a position on its merits. Stump reads Aquinas as saying that God's intellect, like the human intellect, acts on data with which it is in "epistemic contact," but saying nothing about in just what this epistemic contact consists.[49] Stump tells us that epistemic contact is

a component in perception or in divine analogues to perception (which in us is) the result of the central nervous system's processing of sensory data (but) does not include the matching of the data to information stored in associative memory . . . in Aquinas' terms (it is) the apprehension of the accidents of

---

[44] *DV* 2, 9 ad 2.
[45] *DV* 3, 3 ad 8.
[46] Eleonore Stump, *Aquinas* (London: Routledge, 2003), 186.
[47] Ibid.
[48] *ST* Ia 25, 1 and ad 1, trans. of Stump, *Aquinas*, 121.
[49] Stump, *Aquinas*, 186–7.

some extra-mental thing without any apprehension of the thing's *quod quid est*.[50]

Concepts or mental representations have to be applied to what the cognizer is in epistemic contact with . . . although (in the human case) what is cognized acts causally on the cognizer's senses, for that causal connection to count as *epistemic* contact . . . the sensory data produced in that way must undergo some processing by the central nervous system. Causal contact between some object and, say, an eye in a vat would not constitute epistemic contact. But sensory input by itself underdetermines the result of the central nervous system's processing. How is the result of that processing related to the thing cognized, then? Or, to put it another way, how is it that the result of the processing constitute epistemic contact with the external things that generated the sensory input? . . . nobody knows. The incompleteness of Aquinas' account of God's knowledge looks less surprising when we recognize that contemporary accounts of human knowledge are incomplete in the same way.[51]

Being in "epistemic contact" seems to amount to possessing a representation of an individual, in virtue of possessing that one has some knowledge of it, which is (in us) the result of causal contact with that individual and low-level cognitive processing. It seems to be that in virtue of which being in a low-level mental state constitutes possessing some information about an extramental particular (and here the Thomist connotations of "information" are apt), and in virtue of which higher-level mental states can also constitute being informed about it. Now in God's case, it's obvious how (in Aquinas's eyes) he comes to have the representation: it's innate, as all "divine ideas" are. There is no question of acquiring it causally. The rest of the issue about epistemic contact amounts to this: in virtue of what relation between that divine idea and something outside God does God through that representation possess information *about* that thing? What gives that representation a knowledge-yielding relation to some extramental particular? Stump thinks Aquinas never says. I'm not so sure. I think he gives us at least some definite hints. A belief is about a particular thing, and so knowledge we have via believing it is knowledge about that thing, in virtue of a relation of reference between some representation that is a component of the belief and the thing. So a look at Aquinas on singular reference may turn up what Stump thinks goes missing in his account. I discuss first the human case, then the principle on which we can extrapolate from it to the divine.

---

[50] Ibid., 509n50.
[51] Ibid., 187.

AQUINAS ON SINGULAR REFERENCE

Thomas holds that to think that Smith is human, we "turn to" Smith's "phantasm."[52] Our thought somehow brings together Smith's phantasm (a physically realized representation of Smith, stored in the brain[53]) and the concept of humanity. Because the phantasm is the phantasm of Smith, the thought refers to Smith:

> inasmuch as our intellect . . . turns back upon the phantasm from which it abstracts the species, the phantasm being a particular likeness, our intellect gets some kind of knowledge of the singular.[54]

So we need to see how phantasms are *of* individuals to see how Thomas thinks human singular reference works.

Thomas writes of the "sensible species" from which phantasms originate that it "is a likeness only of one individual – whence the individual alone can be known through it."[55] "Likeness" is for Thomas a broad term; my photo is a pictorial likeness of me, but so too is anything that represents me nonpictorially. Let's ask how Thomas means it here. If the species represents the individual (quasi-) pictorially, by its content somehow resembling what it represents, Thomas has problems. One species might picture many different particulars equally well. So if a species is *of* what it pictures, a species I acquire from Socrates is of Socrates only if Socrates happens to resemble its content more than anything else does. But even at the time, there might have been more than one item maximally like its content – perhaps Socrates had a twin, who at that moment was against the same sort of backdrop – and since then Socrates might have changed, so that a Socrates imitator now looks more like what my species pictures. The species is now of Socrates, if it is, only by chance, the chance that what I've just said isn't so. But then (as emerges later) my beliefs, on Thomas's account, are of Socrates only by chance, and so I cannot *know* about Socrates by way of this species or a "phantasm" that arises from it at all.

Thus charity bids us seek another reading of Thomas's claim. For Aquinas, sense faculties, in sensing, take on in their own way the very form they sense in the object they sense: the seeing eye in some way takes on the form of the color

---

[52] *ST* Ia 86, 1 (see also *DV* 10, 5c and 5 ad 3). Thomas's example is puzzling: when Thomas referred to Socrates, never having perceived him, what served as phantasm of Socrates?

[53] *In IV Meta.*, l. 14, #693; *ST* Ia 78, 4.

[54] *DV* 2, 6.

[55] *ST* Ia 14, 12. See also Ia 84, 7 ad 2.

it sees.[56] This is always a "spiritual" taking-on (though there may sometimes be some literal physical taking-on as well, as when my finger, sensing the heat of a fire, is also heated by it).[57] This amounts merely to coming to represent the external form in an appropriate way.[58] Presumably what it represents is the particular's own case of the form in question; it is Socrates' paleness that the eye seeing Socrates "takes in." But what makes it Socrates' paleness rather than his twin's that the eye "takes in"? It's hard to see what answer there could be save that Socrates' paleness caused the representation. Thus Thomas writes that

> the likeness in sense is abstracted from the thing as from an object of knowledge, and consequently the thing itself is directly known by means of this likeness.[59]

It is because the causal chain ending in the species begins at Socrates that the species is of Socrates. Thomas seems, then, to hold that if one has sensory knowledge of x through a sensible species, one acquired it via the right sort of causal relation to x, because he thinks that being acquired via the right sort of causal relation to x is one necessary condition for a species' being *of* x. Now phantasms are not sensible species. But they result from these by further cognitive processing and are equally sense "likenesses"; one faces broadly the same problem in saying what they are phantasms *of*, and it needs broadly the same solution: the causal chain beginning at x goes one step further to yield the phantasm, and the phantasm is of x, I suggest, precisely because of this causal fact. If so, then if phantasms are his vehicles of singular reference, Thomas's account of singular reference includes a causal component: Thomas writes in *De Veritate* that

> phantasms are related to our intellect as sensible objects are related to sense . . . just as the species in the sense is abstracted from things them-selves and by its means the cognition of the sense is extended to the sensible things themselves, so also our intellect abstracts the species from the phan-tasms and by means of this species, its cognition is extended in a certain sense to the phantasms.[60]

The intellect hooks onto the phantasm because of the causal relation between its "species" and the phantasm, and this causal relation is just one more link in a causal chain stretching back to the extramental particular. Thomas

---

[56] *ST* Ia 78, 4.
[57] *ST* Ia 78, 3.
[58] *DV* 2, 3 ad 9.
[59] *DV* 2, 6.
[60] *DV* 2, 6.

continues, as we have seen, that the intellect "turns back to" the phantasm and thereby acquires knowledge of the singular.[61] Later in *De Veritate* Thomas calls this the intellect's mingling with sense,[62] then asserts that this mingling explains our ability to form propositions about individuals.[63] Thomas's picture of singular reference thus seems to include the claim that in a singular proposition "S is P," "S" refers to A only if "S" expresses a phantasm[64] whose content represents A's sensible forms because it ends the right sort of causal chain from A.

DIVINE SINGULAR REFERENCE

Let us now ask what for Thomas gives God's thought-contents *their* reference to singulars. For Thomas, the conceptual content of God's thoughts consists wholly of shareable attributes. Arguing that God thinks, Thomas writes that

> whatever is incomplete is derived from something complete, for complete things are naturally prior to incomplete . . . forms existing in particular things are incomplete, because they exist there partially, not in the commonness of their nature. So they must derive from complete, non-particularized forms. Such forms cannot exist save as understood, for no form is found in its universality save in an intellect. Consequently it is proper to them to be intelligent, if they subsist . . . So God . . . is intelligent.[65]

Forms God understands are his ideas' conceptual content. Thomas treats these forms as not particularized – only so do they provide an argument for God's being a thinker. So for Thomas, God's idea of Socrates is (as it were) composed not *inter alia* of Socrates' wisdom and Socrates' piety, but wisdom and piety *simpliciter*. Now a set of shareable attributes can pick out an individual if only one possible individual can co-exemplify all of its members. But Thomas denies this:

> something singular is not constituted from a collection of universal forms, however many they be, because the collection of these forms can be understood to be in many.[66]

---

[61] *DV* 2, 6.

[62] *DV* 10, 5.

[63] *DV* 10, 5 ad 3.

[64] For the claim that conventional words primarily signify "passions of the soul" – species, concepts, phantasms – and only through them signify external things, see, e.g., *In de Interpretatione*, lect. 2.

[65] *Summa Contra Gentiles* I, 44. Surprisingly, Thomas is here just a hairsbreadth from arguing God's very existence from the reality of universals. I translate "perfecta" as "complete things" following the suggestion of Thomas' odd "partialiter."

[66] *DV* 2, 5. See also *QD de Anima*, a. 20.

Thus it is not their conceptual content that gives God's thoughts their singular reference.

For Thomas, the conceptual content of God's idea of a creature c is purely general – yet it is an idea of c, not just of a c-like creature.[67] How can this be? Consider some of Aquinas's remarks about how God's knowledge differs from ours:

> Natural things from which our intellect gets its knowledge measure our intellect. Yet these things are themselves measured by the divine intellect, in which are all created things- just as all works of art find their origin in the intellect of an artist. The divine intellect, therefore, measures and is not measured ... But our intellect is measured, and measures only artifacts, not natural things.[68]
>
> The relation implied in divine knowledge does not involve dependence of the knowledge upon the things known, but rather the dependence of the thing known upon the knowledge. The opposite is true of us ... "knowledge" when used of us indicates a dependence of our knowledge upon its object.[69]

Thomas stresses that since God is Creator, the relation between God's knowledge and facts of nature is the reverse of the relation between our knowledge and facts of nature.

Singular knowledge involves reference. We know that Socrates was a philosopher only if we are disposed to assert a proposition one of whose terms refers to Socrates. For Thomas, a tokened term refers to Socrates only if the tokening's causal history links it to Socrates in the right way. God knows that S is P via his idea of the particular to which "S" refers.[70] That idea's referring to S is part of God's knowing this. Thomas holds that God's knowledge of nature differs from ours because its causal relations to nature reverse our knowledge's. Suppose, then, that God's singular knowledge involves reference (as ours does) and that Thomas's account of God's singular reference, as of ours, has a causal component. I suggest that Thomas's claim that the causal chains God's knowledge involves reverse the direction of ours is more

---

[67] This may be why Thomas describes God's ideas of creatures this way: "so ... far as God knows His nature as imitable in such a way by such a creature, He knows it as the ... idea of this creature" ("inquantum Deus cognoscit suam essentiam ut sic imitabilem a tali creatura, cognoscit eam ut ... ideam huius creaturae" [ST Ia 15, 2]). Thomas describes the idea's content as general – "His nature as imitable *in such a way* by *such* a creature." Yet he then calls it the idea of *this* creature, and one most naturally reads the demonstrative "*hic*" as picking out one *particular* creature.

[68] *DV* 1, 2. See also *SCG* I, 62.

[69] *DV* 2, 5 ad 16.

[70] *ST* Ia 15, 2. This does not imply that God knows by affirming propositions – rather, he knows what propositions affirm, in a different way (*ST* Ia 14, 14).

specifically a claim that the causal chains God's reference involves reverse the direction of ours. If for Thomas our token of "Socrates" refers to Socrates partly due to a causal chain from Socrates to our tokening, God's idea of Socrates will refer to Socrates due to a causal chain from God's thinking that idea to Socrates himself. For Thomas, I have suggested, "S" refers to a singular A in "S is P" iff "S" expresses a phantasm-content that ends the right sort of causal chain from A. So for Thomas, I submit, God's thinking of "S" in "S is P" refers to a singular A iff it expresses (or is God's having) a divine idea that *begins* the right sort of causal chain *ending* at A.[71] In short, God's idea of a sometimes-actual creature c is an idea of c partly because it is the idea by which God made and conserves c. This is not to say that if God knows that S is P, God causes it to be the case that S is P, let alone that he causes it by knowing it. For Thomas, God's causal relation to creatures is most fundamentally that he creates and sustains them. This is the relation that carries his reference. It does not, as such, account for anything more than their existing.

Conversely, for Thomas, to be c is to be the c-type creature God intended to make, that is, the creature that resulted from God's intentionally instancing his idea of a c-type creature. In God's case, there can be no referential misfires. God's ideas cannot fail to be about the creatures he means them to be about, because to be a particular creature is just to be the creature God made to instance a particular divine idea. Speaking of ideas of creatures God actually makes, Thomas writes that God's

> ideas are multiplied according to the different relations they have to things existing in their own natures.[72]

That is, ideas of sometimes-actual creatures are paired 1:1 with sometimes-actual creatures. For each such creature, there is a distinct idea by which God knows it. Thomas adds that

> although an exemplar implies a relation to something outside, it is related as a cause to that extrinsic thing.[73]

---

[71] For Thomas, God has but one thought, in which is all he ever thinks (*SCG* I, 21 and 45). Thus for Thomas, any thought in which God tokens "S is P" is identical with the thought whence stems the (one-link) creative causal chain from God to A. Those willing to allow God many thoughts will correspondingly want to loosen this requirement, and say that it is enough to forge the referential chain that A is what resulted when God said "let there be S." I note that for Thomas, any deliberate action begins with the intellect's presenting some end or act as good (*ST* Ia 82, 3 ad 2 and 4 *ad* 3). Thus the causal chain in any such action starts from a thinking.

[72] *DV* 3, 2 ad 7.

[73] *DV* 3, 3 ad 3.

For Thomas, divine ideas' relation to "things existing in their own natures" is causal. The idea paired 1:1 with a creature c is paired with c because it is the idea by which God made c. I suggest that for Thomas, this is also why it is an idea *of* c. Thomas's view of divine reference includes a reverse causal-chain component. For Thomas, God's thought of a creature refers to whatever creature terminates a causal chain starting from God's thinking the divine idea involved in that thought.

Thus Thomas writes,

> What an agent effects is in some way in the agent. Moreover whatever is in another is in it in the manner of its recipient.... If the agent is an immaterial active source, the effect will be in it immaterially... something is known by another according as it is received immaterially in it. And so... every immaterial active source knows its effect. Whence it is that in the *Book of Causes* it is said that an intelligence knows what is under it, insofar as it is its cause. Whence, because God is an immaterial active source of things, it follows that there is in Him knowledge of things.[74]

> we place something in the divine cognition... according as He Himself... is its cause.[75]

These texts do not imply that God's knowledge is itself causally efficacious.[76] But neither do they seem only to use God's causation as an argument that he does somehow have knowledge of creatures. The first tells us that God knows his effects because he is immaterial and they are his effects: God's causing what he does is part of what explains his knowing what he does, and the rest of the explanation is just his own intrinsic nature. It is plain that the sort of causation here is efficient: the principle appealed to concerns *agents*. We have here, I think, the missing account of what gives divine ideas their epistemic contact with creatures.

If we say that God knows what happens in Creation *inter alia* by making a causal contribution to it, it might seem that if God knows our sinful acts, he is causally responsible for them, or that if he knows our acts at all, he causes them and so we are not free. Thomas's account of epistemic contact, as I read it, does not have either consequence. God causally contributes to sin by conserving the agent and his or her powers and helping in using them; he conserves the sinful act insofar as it is a being.[77] However, for Thomas,

[74] S. Thomae Aquinatis *Quaestiones Disputatae* v. 3 (Turin: Marietti, 1931), *QD de Veritate* 2, 3, p. 37.

[75] *De Veritate* 2, 4, p. 41.

[76] Stump shows well that this cannot be Thomas's view. See *Aquinas*.

[77] *ST* I–IIa 79, 2.

the act's being evil consists in its lacking something, in the nonexistence of a due good about it. The effect of conservation is existence, not nonexistence. This is a conceptual truth. So if an act's being evil consists in the nonexistence of something, it is a conceptual truth that the relation by which God has epistemic contact with the act does not cause it to be evil. Thus Thomas argues that although God knows our sins, God causes not sin but the good to which sin is opposed[78] and by which it is known,[79] and in which it inheres, and so knows evil (as it were) indirectly and without causing it. Thomas's claim is that although God causes the sinful act to be, God does not cause it to be sinful: that is to be traced no further than the sinner's will.[80] Because God is in constant causal contact with the act as it happens, he knows about it. (He has an idea of it; the act is in a broad sense an accident of its agent, and Thomas believes that God has ideas of accidents.) But God does not causally determine everything about the act with which he is in causal contact, and he need not do so to know about it. For Thomas, God does not *cause* everything to which he *causally contributes*. The agent brings it about that the act that derives its being from God is a sinful act, determining the character of what God conserves. The agent causes it to be a lying act. God causes the lying act to be. In understanding the causal relata here, stress matters. A proposition becomes true – that this act is a lie. The agent brings it about that this is *a lie*. God brings it about that it *is* a lie. This is a case not of overdetermination but of joint causation: had the agent not contributed, the act would not have been a lie, but had God not contributed, the act would not have been at all, and God's contribution does not determine whether it is a lie or a truth-telling.

Thomas's thought seems to be that causal and so epistemic contact with a sinful act is enough to provide knowledge of its sinful character without determining it, by way of knowing where the good in it ends (so to speak). If this makes sense, the move is applicable to free agency generally; as I determine that what God knows and cooperates with is a lying, I determine too that what he knows and cooperates with is a telling of one lie rather than another. On this picture, it is not that God knows that I lie because I do something to him, but that he knows this because he is doing something with me; the causal connection runs from rather than to God. I do not make him know. He knows simply because he knowingly creates and conserves. I only bring it about, given that he is so acting as to know, that he knows this rather than that. We do not bring this about by acting on him. In no way can I act on an

---

[78] *De Veritate* 2, 15 ad 1.
[79] *ST* Ia 14, 10 ad 2.
[80] *ST* I–IIa 79, 2.

immaterial, atemporal being: I can't touch it, heat it, electrify it, and so on. The only causal connections we have any reason to believe possible here run in the other direction. We bring it about that God knows what he does simply by acting on ourselves and the world.

One may wonder how I can determine that God knows this rather than that but not act on him. But states of affairs can depend counterfactually without depending causally. Were it not the case that $1 + 1 = 2$, it would not be the case that $2 + 2 = 4$, but the first does not cause the second; were it not the case that the slaves were freed, it would not be the case that the North won the Civil War, but the first did not cause the second. So too, were it not the case that I choose to do A, not B, God would not know that I choose A, but this does not entail that I cause God to know the latter. Still, even if we accept that the inference fails, that does not tell us how what Thomas is saying about God can be so.

If God does not know what he is cooperating with by knowing what he first willed to be cooperating with, and yet we do not cause him to know what he knows, one wonders how he can know what he is cooperating with. It is hard to answer this question because in the nature of this case, common-sense analogies mislead. They come from a material realm in which every action has an equal and opposite reaction. So they inevitably suggest that any action toward us to bring it about that he knows what we do will carry with it our doing something to him in virtue of the fact that we determine the content of his knowledge. But if the relation that accounts for God's epistemic contact with creatures is creative and sustaining, there is no question of "pushing back" or an equal and opposite reaction. Either can take place only if that on which one acts is there prior to one's action to resist and react. But what God creates is not there prior to his creating it. And the effect of conservation is continued existence; because what creates is not there to resist prior to its creation, what is conserved is not there later to resist later prior to being caused to be there later.

Bearing in mind that the equal-and-opposite reaction feature of the analogy must be edited out, what Thomas suggests about God's knowledge can be pictured this way. God is like a water-hose jetting being, one that feels what happens to the water it emits as long as the water stream is continuous with its nozzle. When I act, I shape or direct the stream with my hand, without ever touching the hose. The hose feels what my hand is doing in virtue of feeling which way the stream goes. The hose does not cause the water to go one way rather than another. The hand does that. The hand does not act on the hose. But the hose's cognitive state depends counterfactually on what the hand does with what the hose contributes.

A stranger but closer analogy might run this way. Imagine that there are Platonic Forms and they are conscious: Plotinus, for one, believed this, and many might accept "conscious Platonic Form" as a rough partial description of Thomas's God. Let's say that a Platonic Form of F is a particular that is intrinsically, essentially, and underivedly F and such that anything else's Fness – a trope – is a sharing in the nature of the relevant Form. Let's not say with the middle-period Plato that the Form of the Good is simple, being nothing but good, but say the closest thing to this, that goodness is the essential property that makes it what it is, the rest – being particular, one, a substance, and so on – being the minimum necessary to (as it were) set it up in being as a particular bearing some essence or other. Each Form is fully aware of its own character: the Form of the Good is aware of goodness. It is not the case that its goodness causes the Good to be aware of it. Nor is it even the case that its being good is one state, its awareness of being good another, for were this true, we'd have to say (wouldn't we?) that the first caused the second. What we want, rather, is a picture of its being good as a mental state of such a sort that being in the state includes being aware of the state's content, like the state of being aware of phenomenal redness. Let's say that this is because it is the Good's nature to be aware of goodness, wherever it is, and because goodness just is a phenomenal quality the Form perceives. If all this is so, the Form will also be aware of the goodness tropes existing in things participating in goodness, and other things' being good will be a state of other things such that it is included in that state that the Good is aware of their goodness.

If I am to some degree good, then, but so act as to lessen my goodness, the Good will be aware of my goodness lessening. But I will not act on the Good. Nor for that matter will I act on my goodness. Tropes aren't the kind of things we can act on, even indirectly. By acting on the things we can act on, we bring it about noncausally that our tropes change, in virtue of noncausal, determinative connections between our properties and the concrete parts of us that directly instantiate them. I can't talk to my goodness, but I can talk to you, and by telling you a lie, I bring it about that I am more disposed to tell lies in the future and have a moral record marred by one more lie. In virtue of these things my goodness is less intense, but these things do not *cause* my goodness to be so. The relation involved is more in the broad order of the constitutive; I have altered the concrete world in such a way that the relevant portions of the world as resulting from these changes constitute my being in certain nonmoral states, and my being in certain moral states supervenes on this, changes in my goodness being noncausally determined by changes in the concrete world due to my agency.

I do not act on my trope. Nor does my trope act on the Good. The connection between any case of goodness and the Good is not efficient-causal. It is rather that any case of goodness is of such a nature that the Good is by nature aware of it – as it were by an awareness that is extended into other things when the nature of which it is naturally aware is extended into other things. I have noncausally accounted for a certain change in a trope, and on the strange metaphysics I've set out, this change includes a change in the Good's awareness: so I have noncausally accounted for the Good's being aware of something new. Those aware that for Thomas, God is *esse ipsum*, existence itself, and aware of how closely Thomas models God and his relations to the world on that between a Form of existence and existent things participating in it, may well think what I've said a fairly good analogue to what Thomas actually thinks. Now this is a wild, crazy story. But I do not think it counts as in any sense incoherent. If it is not, neither, perhaps, is Thomas's account of God's knowledge of creatures.

PART THREE

JESUS IN CONTEMPORARY PHILOSOPHY

7

ᘯ

The Epistemology of Jesus: An Initial Investigation

William J. Abraham

We do not naturally turn to Jesus of Nazareth when we go in search of epistemological resources. On the one hand, he is seen canonically in the church in such exalted theological categories that we naturally feel it is demeaning if not insulting to pull him down to the level of our mundane puzzles about the nature of rationality, truth, warrant, justification, and knowledge. On the other hand, our ruminations on epistemic issues have a proper life of their own, with their own carefully developed themes and insights, so that dragging in Jesus of Nazareth initially seems incongruous and artificial. To speak of the epistemology of Jesus is an oxymoron, a category mistake.

No doubt there are additional historical considerations from the Enlightenment onward that confirm and strengthen our discomfort. To appeal to Jesus is simply question-begging if we are looking for a serious account of our central epistemological concepts. Why should we look to Jesus for epistemological insight? Have we not already cooked the books in advance if we appeal to Jesus? Have we not already deployed various epistemic intuitions and assumptions that allow us to bring Jesus into the discussion in the first place? Did not Descartes and Locke teach us once and for all that theological disputes required some kind of independent adjudication if they were to be resolved without recourse to violence? So from the side of philosophy the whole enterprise seems hopelessly doomed before it even begins. Epistemology belongs first and foremost within philosophy rather than theology, so surely we can set Jesus aside.

We can come to a similar conclusion from the side of theology. Jesus came to save the world and baptize us in the Holy Spirit;[1] he did not come to resolve our epistemological worries. To turn Jesus into a philosopher is to misread his

---

[1] This is the agreed testimony of John the Baptist that is appropriated by all the synoptic Gospels.

ministry and mission; it is to reach for an inflated and pseudo-pious vision of his real work. He did not come to be a judge over our epistemological theories any more than he was a judge over our domestic disputes about inheritance.[2] God has already equipped us with the necessary intellectual resources for this work in our creation as agents made in his image. To look beyond these for special help is misguided and ungrateful.

Once we narrow the field to the epistemology of theology, however, the landscape changes dramatically. Here the exalted theological categories come into play immediately. If Jesus is the one and only incarnate Son of God, then appeal to Jesus is decisive for theological topics. Karl Barth drove home this claim with a vengeance for twentieth-century theology; one does not have to be a Barthian to agree, for it has been a commonplace observation in the history of theology.[3] It is surely no accident that the richest theological account of Jesus in the Gospels, that of John, is laced with epistemological material.[4] We might invent an aphorism: the higher the Christology the higher the role of Jesus in the epistemology of theology. That aphorism then opens the door to exploring the wider implications of Christology for epistemology generally.

Yet we must move cautiously. There is a logically prior question to be addressed: How do we come to believe and know that Jesus is the Son of God? Clearly the earliest disciples did not start from an exalted theological vision of Jesus. They started, as we all do, with their ordinary cognitive capacities of perception, memory, testimony, judgment, and the like. These were not accepted because they were derived from some kind of high Christology, for that was not in their initial repertoire of responses to the ministry of Jesus. Moreover, they were drawn into that vision over time and were only then able to explore the epistemological ramifications of their conversion and commitments. It is that initial move in their encounter with Jesus that I want to explore in this paper. In order to execute this goal I shall provide an epistemological reading of the Gospel of Mark that seeks to ferret out how we

---

[2] Thus speaking of a dispute between two brothers over their inheritance, Jesus asks, "Who made me a judge or a divider over you?" See Lk. 12:14.

[3] The opening verses of the epistle to the Hebrews capture the issue succinctly. "Long ago God spoke to the fathers by the prophets at different times and in different ways. In these last days, He has spoken to us by His Son, whom He has appointed heir of all things and through whom He made the universe." See Heb. 1:1–2.

[4] For an interesting review see Howard Clark Kee, "Knowing the Truth: Epistemology and Community in the Fourth Gospel," in *Neotestamentica et Philonica, Studies in Honor of Peder Borgen*, eds. David E. Aune, Torrey Seland, and Jarl Henning Ulrichsen (Leiden: Brill, 2003), 254–80.

might begin to mine the life and teaching of Jesus for epistemic insight.[5] With that behind us I shall briefly explore the wider ramifications of our findings both for theology and for epistemology more generally.

Mark's Gospel is not, of course, an essay in epistemology. It is first and foremost an exercise in narration and proclamation. Like scripture as a whole, its primary aim is soteriological and evangelistic.[6] Thus we must work indirectly by exploring the epistemological assumptions, insights, suggestions, and proposals that show up en route to ends that are not directly epistemological. What strikes the reader forcefully on a careful reading of the book as a whole is the extraordinary intellectual journey represented by the disciples. Indeed the journey into serious discipleship clearly involves significant growth in understanding, intellectual discovery, and personal commitment. Piety (or spirituality) and insight are clearly intimately related. Moreover, the journey into greater understanding is accompanied by second-order reflection on how to make progress in faith and knowledge. It is particularly in the latter arena that the search for epistemic ore should be mined.

It is helpful to begin our excavation with the confession of Peter in Mark 8:29. Peter there confesses that "Jesus is the Messiah." It is surely no accident that this intellectual turning point follows a story where we are presented with a miracle of healing that takes place in two stages.[7] A blind man goes through a phase of seeing human agents as trees walking before he sees correctly. Peter has come to see that Jesus is the Messiah, but his conception of the Messiah needs radical reworking if it is to fit with that owned and made manifest in the life of Jesus. When Peter objects to the idea of a suffering Messiah, he is roundly rebuked as being on the side of the Enemy, attending not to the things of God but to merely human affairs. The tacit epistemic rationale that comes to mind at this point is obvious: Peter is not functioning properly as an epistemic agent. His sight is not entirely reliable; it is altered for the worse by inappropriate background beliefs, interests, desires, anxieties, and expectations. The epistemic map that best makes sense of this phenomenon is clearly that of externalism. It is not that Peter has failed to move by means of explicit valid and sound reasoning from premise to conclusion; Peter is failing as a properly functioning cognitive agent. While he is on the way to

---

[5] I shall assume for the sake of the argument in this chapter that Mark gives us reliable access to the life and ministry of Jesus. The faint of heart on this score can simply treat what follows as a commentary on the epistemology of Mark.

[6] This vision of scripture is deployed in one of the early classical texts on the subject, 2 Tim. 3:16.

[7] It has often been noted that the section in which this unit is embedded and that deals with the blindness of the disciples ends with the healing of a blind man. See Mk. 10:46–52.

the truth about Christ, his spiritual sight is badly affected by his spiritual and moral vices. He cannot and will not see how the Messiah can suffer and be crucified.[8]

In this context it is profoundly important that he and the other disciples are confronted immediately with the inescapability of a suffering that mirrors that of Christ himself. Their cognitive malfunction is surely directly related to their false hopes and dreams that accompany their vision of Christ as the Messiah of Israel. The matter is not simply pedagogical; it is also epistemic. It is true, of course, that following Christ will mean self-denial and cross bearing as conditions of their salvation; equally, however, it is only as they enter into such moral and spiritual renovation that they will be able to discern the truth about Christ and what it means to be Messiah. To echo Calvin, knowledge of God is correlative with knowledge of ourselves.[9] Not surprisingly Matthew adds the gloss that Peter's confession is causally related to the work of divine revelation given to Peter by the Father.[10] It is not just a matter of human discovery; it is a matter of divine revelation. Mark signals something like this when he links the sight of the blind man to the miraculous activity of God. The cognitive malfunction in Peter and the disciples is so deep that it cannot be cured without significant divine assistance.

It is also important to see that the need for radical reorientation in thought and action is followed sequentially by the transfiguration of Jesus to a small selection of disciples confined to Peter, James, and John, three pivotal leaders in the early tradition. Read epistemically, this episode operates as providing robust confirmation that Jesus rather than Peter is in the right about what it is to be Messiah. The place (on a high mountain), the background conditions (presence of clouds), and the appearance of Jesus (in clothes of dazzling light) readily signify the guidance of God as signaled by God's earlier dealings with Israel. The conversation of Jesus with Moses and Elijah clearly indicates prophetic endorsement. Finally the testimony of the voice of God ("This is my Son, whom I love. Listen to him."[11]) provides riveting, climactic approval. To be sure, Peter is frightened and flabbergasted, but he has

---

[8] The theme of the suffering Messiah is so important that it is repeated no less than three times in the second half of Mark. See Mk. 8:31; 9:30; 10:33. The incomprehension of the disciples is also reiterated. It is powerfully expressed in their depiction during the passion narrative, where they are warned by Jesus to keep awake no less than three times. The matter is well brought out in Marcus, "Mark 4:10–12 and Marcan Epistemology," 569.

[9] Calvin announces this theme forcefully right at the beginning of Book One of the Institutes: "Without knowledge of the self there is no knowledge of God." John Calvin, in *Institutes of the Christian Religion*, ed. John T. McNeill (Philadelphia: Westminster Press, 1960), I, 35.

[10] Matt. 16:18.

[11] Mk. 9:7. Cf. Mk. 1:11.

enough inchoate, puzzling evidence to stay the course and hang on for further illumination and more accurate perception up ahead. He accepts for the moment but does not really believe that Jesus is the Messiah as presented by Jesus; he believes an important half-truth rather than the whole truth about Jesus.

The justification of Peter's beliefs is as much diachronic as it is synchronic. It is not just a matter of the evidence currently available but also a matter of coming to see things differently over time. Peter, James, and John have access to divine revelation represented here by divine speaking; yet even with data of this high order at their disposal they fail to see for themselves who Jesus is.[12] Given who God is, it would be epistemically inappropriate not to believe what God tells us. It is no accident that theories of divine dictation and inspiration as applied to scripture have led to great confidence and certitude about scripture on the part of those who espouse them. However, this kind of move focuses much too narrowly on the synchronic aspects of justification. Once we bring externalist considerations into play, then we can understand why even what is reported as high forms of divine revelation is not received immediately as warranted manifestations of divine approval. There is a necessary, diachronic dimension that fits naturally with an externalist reading of the journey to faith and within faith. Cognitive malfunction is not usually overcome in an instant; it requires a temporal process in which data and warrants undergo radical reinterpretation over time. We are aware of this when we attend to, say, the history of science, and note there the way in which our visions of what counts as evidence change across the generations.[13] It is surely also commonplace in our own intellectual development; we change our minds as to how to read relevant data, as to what counts as data, and as to how best to think of relevant warrants for our beliefs. Yet we have paid next to no attention to the temporal, diachronic dimension of justification in epistemology.[14]

What I have just asserted about the conditions for the appreciation of divine revelation applies to the other data that justify Peter's confession of Christ as the Jewish Messiah. Thus it applies to the testimony of John,[15] Jesus's teaching with special authority,[16] the testimony of demons,[17] Jesus's

---

[12] I assume here that what God tells us can be stated as significant rather than trivial propositions.

[13] The concept of probability, for example, only came into play in the seventeenth century. Inferential statistics and experimental design show up even later.

[14] For an exception that proves the rule, see Richard Swinburne, *Epistemic Justification* (Oxford: Clarendon, 2001), chap. 7. Even then, Swinburne takes the discussion in a direction that is radically different from the one I am prosing here.

[15] Mk. 1:7–8.

[16] Mk. 1:22.

[17] Mk. 1:24; 5:7.

offer of forgiveness,[18] his authority to interpret the law of the Sabbath,[19] his exorcisms,[20] and his miracles.[21] None of these constitute proof of the theological identity of Jesus. What happens initially is that in varied ways they raise questions about who Jesus is and what God might be doing in his life and ministry. Thus they surely constitute good reasons for pursuing a line of interpretation that leads to the confession of Jesus as Messiah and Son of God. For those who insist on hard evidence such as we find in deductive proof they are hopelessly unsatisfactory. Clearly the data can be described and explained in more than one way. His hometown neighbors see him in entirely parochial categories as one of their own and therefore liable to have put on airs about himself.[22] The teachers of the law who have come down from Jerusalem to check out Jesus see his exorcisms as evidence of possession by Beelzebul.[23] This particular way of taking the evidence is immediately countered by Jesus as implausible on the grounds of internal consistency, for it is foolish to think that the demons are at war with one another. On the contrary, the exorcisms point to the presence of a power that is greater than Satan. To take another example, Herod, touched by superstition, perhaps, and clearly influenced by a bad conscience in his ordering the beheading of John the Baptist, thought the miracles were evidence of the work of John. "John the Baptist has been raised from the dead, and that is why miraculous powers are at work in him."[24] No one but Herod was likely to take this option seriously; so this way of handling the relevant evidence was a dead end. Peter and the disciples take most of the same evidence in the end as good reasons for believing that Jesus was the Messiah of Israel. What began as puzzling phenomena accumulate over time to justify in a soft but genuine way a constructive theological vision of Jesus. The data come to be seen in a new light, justifying but not proving that Jesus is the Son of God as attested by divine revelation.

Jesus is quite explicit in Mark about the factors that make possible the shift in perception and relevant conclusions reached over time. On the one hand, he indicates why some people read the evidence inappropriately; on the other, he makes clear what positive factors come into play. In both cases the critical factors have to do with the state of the heart, that is, with the various moral and spiritual dispositions that come into play in assessing the data at hand.

---

[18] Mk. 2:5.
[19] Mk. 2:28.
[20] Mk. 1:34; 5:1–20.
[21] Mk. 1:34; 2:12; 3:5; 4:35–41; 5:21–43; 6:30–56; 7:29–30, 31–37; 8:6–10, 22–26.
[22] Mk. 6:2–3.
[23] Mk. 3:22.
[24] Mk. 6:14.

Thus Herod is presented as a pathetic figure who is interested in the truth about God[25] but who cannot withstand the pressures against his pious interests from his wife. He is also a public figure who dares not lose face in the presence of friends and party guests. The Pharisees are depicted as formally religious but inwardly not committed to the will of God.[26] Like Herod, they have hardened hearts that act as yeast that causes their cognitive capacities to malfunction.[27] The disciples for their part are also seen as hardhearted and inattentive.[28] They are depicted as ambitious, competitive, and exclusivist.[29] In line with these instances of unbelief, the underlying causes of unbelief are depicted as moral in nature in the famous parable of the soils. Some are so caught up in evil that they barely hear what is said to them.[30] Others cannot handle trouble or persecution. Still others are taken up with worries of this life, the deceitfulness of wealth, and the desire for other things.[31]

On the positive front, it is clear what is needed if folk are to hear and perceive aright. The desiderata begin with repentance, that is, with a readiness to change their lives in the wake of a change of mind as called for in the acceptance of the good news of the arrival of the Kingdom of God.[32] The call to repentance is really a call to be radically open to new possibilities breaking through into reality. This appeal is supplemented by a call to hear, that is, to pay attention and to use the capacities they already possess.[33] "Consider carefully what you hear.... With the measure you use, it will be measured to you – and even more. Those who have will be given more; as for those who do not have, even what they have will be taken away."[34] The very choice of parables as a means of teaching dovetails with these admonitions. Those who do not take the time to ponder and unpack them will miss what is being said; parables only work for those who are prepared to explore what they mean. They provoke intellectual inquiry but leave it to the hearer to unravel and seek out the meaning. Equally, those who hope to hear and see

---

[25] "Herod feared John and protected him, knowing him to be a righteous and holy man. When Herod heard John, he was greatly puzzled; yet he liked to listen to him." See Mk. 6:20.

[26] Jesus draws on the words of Isa. 29:13. "These people honor me with their lips, but their hearts are far from me." See Mk. 7:6.

[27] The image of yeast, normally seen as a symbol for sin, is deployed by Jesus to describe both Herod and the Pharisees and by extension applied to the disciples. See Mk. 8:15.

[28] Mk. 8:17–21.

[29] Mk. 9:33, 38; 10 37.

[30] "Satan comes and takes away the Word." See Mk. 4:15.

[31] Mk. 4:17–19. The issue of wealth is also taken up in Mk. 10:22.

[32] Mk. 1:15.

[33] Note the repeated insistence, "If anyone has ears to hear, let them hear," in Mk. 4:9, 23. Note that the text does not say, "If anyone has truly spiritual ears to hear, let them hear."

[34] Mk. 4:24–25.

aright must give heed to their inner lives and the host of vices that well up from within.[35] They also need to expect God to do the impossible[36] and to take up the disposition of a child who is not preoccupied with questions of self-aggrandizement.[37] They have to switch from merely human concerns and have in mind the concerns of God.[38] Above all they have to be prepared to lead a life of self-denial, cross-bearing, and the following of Jesus. They must value the salvation of their souls over everything else. This in turn will require them not to be ashamed of Jesus and his words in the public arena in the midst of a sinful and adulterous generation.[39] More positively, they will need to be committed to living a life governed by love for God and neighbor.[40]

From these negative and positive observations it is clear that for Jesus proper intellectual formation and functioning is tied to the practice of virtue and the elimination of vice. The virtues and vices at issue here at not merely moral; they are also spiritual, that is, they involve appropriate dispositions to attend to one's relationship with God. Put more generally, there is a connection between cognitive capacities and character. This connection in turn explains why there is a connection between proper cognitive functioning and divine action. The underlying assumption is that human agents need robust forms of divine assistance if they are to make intellectual progress. We do not readily discard our longstanding theories about God, the world, and ourselves; this is most especially so when these theories serve our manifold desires, interests, power positions, and economic status. What we see, hear, and believe is radically affected by our character and by our prior identities. It is not too strong to say that human agents are often caught in a web of convictions, dispositions, and habits that require radical intellectual therapy and surgery if they are ever to get beyond them. They are often enslaved to self-serving ideologies and worldviews that they cannot abandon without significant assistance and reformation from within.

We are faced at this point by *the law of inverse rationality*. Merold Westphal captures this nicely in this way: "the ability of human thought to be undistorted by sinful desire is inversely proportional to the existential import of the subject matter."[41] In the light of this we need to expand our range of doxastic

---

[35] Mk. 7:20.
[36] Mk. 9:23.
[37] Mk. 9:35; 10:15.
[38] Mk. 9:33.
[39] Mk. 9:34–38.
[40] Mk. 12:29–31. It is surely no accident that the interlocutor of Jesus who approves of this is described as not being far from the kingdom of God.
[41] Merold Westphal, "Taking St. Paul Seriously: Sin as an Epistemological Category," in *Christian Philosophy*, ed. Thomas P. Flint (South Bend: University of Notre Dame Press, 1990), 205. Westphal borrows the language of *the law of inverse rationality* from an unnamed teacher.

mental states. It is not just that we believe or do not believe; it is also the case that we vehemently reject various beliefs, up to and including the elimination of those whose beliefs we deem offensive.[42] If this is correct, then we need to see belief and unbelief as two possibilities on a continuum that runs all the way from brutal rejection to martyrdom. The standard convention in epistemology of settling simply for belief and unbelief is much too narrow if we are to do justice to the full range of doxastic possibilities.

The relevant observation to pursue at this point is that Jesus speaks forcefully of the need for the availability of divine action in coming to believe. It is not just that the disciples come to believe on their own; rather "the secret of the kingdom of God has been *given* to you."[43] The deployment of agricultural imagery fits neatly in this context. The coming of the kingdom is like a seed that grows secretly in the ground. "All by itself the soil produces grain – first the stalk, then the head, then the full kernel in the head."[44] From very small beginnings, the kingdom is like a mustard seed that starts small and surprisingly becomes a gigantic garden plant "with such big branches that the birds can perch in its shade."[45] In these parables the emphasis falls initially on factors other than that of the agent's capacities and actions,[46] so much so that there is even a strong hint of predetermination. "But to those outside everything is said in parables so that "they may be ever seeing but never perceiving, and ever hearing but never understanding; otherwise they might turn and be forgiven."[47] This text is often taken as implying a monocausal origin of belief, that is, that human agents have no causal role in the process that leads to their believing; God in the end does everything.[48] This interpretation

---

[42] This last option surfaces as early as Mk. 3, where a group of Pharisees and Herodians begin plotting the death of Jesus. The pace quickens from chap. 11 onward. The reasons for the opposition to Jesus are, of course, manifold, but they clearly involve vehement opposition to his believing that he is the Messiah, the Son of the Blessed. See Mk. 14:61–64.

[43] Mk. 4:11. Emphasis mine.

[44] Mk. 4:28.

[45] Mk. 4:32.

[46] John's Gospel is very explicit on the critical significance of divine action. Thus none can come to believe in Christ unless the Father enables them. There is a drawing, teaching, enabling, and giving that is predicated of the Father in relation to belief in the Son. See Jn. 6:39, 44, 45, 65. As in the case of Mark, John 6 also makes clear that there is an ineradicable human element represented by the action of eating the flesh and drinking the blood of Christ.

[47] Mk. 4:11–12.

[48] See the interpretation developed by Joel Marcus in "Mk. 4: 10–12 and Marcan Epistemology," *Journal of Biblical Literature* (1984), 557–74. Marcus wobbles somewhat on whether to allow for any genuine human or Satanic agency. On the one hand, he says that "the autonomy that can be ascribed to human agents in matters of perception is severely limited" (562); on the other hand, he insists that God unleashed "the powers of darkness to blind human beings so that they oppose the [that] kingdom" (567). In his account of the parable of the soils, he insists that in the case of the state of soils "God's will, it must be assumed, determines that" (566). There are in fact only two actors, God and Satan, at work; Satan works in turn through

is clearly incompatible, however, with the stress on human agency that I have already identified as central in the epistemology of Jesus.

A better reading is to see Mark 4:11–12 as ironic. At one level it emphasizes the critical role of divine action in creating the conditions that bring about healthy cognitive functioning. It is not the case, however, that this or that individual is predestined to believe or not to believe; rather it is the method of teaching through parables that is predetermined by God. There is a divine design plan governing the pedagogy of parables. Those who, for whatever reason, are not interested in accepting forgiveness can decide whether they will or will not take the parables seriously. If they do not do so, then they will see but never perceive and hear but not understand. They will become even more blind and hard than they currently are. If they do take them seriously, then the parables work according to a divine design plan to bring about understanding; if they do not take them seriously, then in keeping with the divine design-plan they will be judged and become even more blind that what they are. Thus this enigmatic text speaks of a complex synergism of divine and human action in the use of our cognitive capacities.[49] This reading clearly fits with the whole tenor of the section in which it is embedded; the text does not at all take us toward a vision of double, unconditional predestination. God takes the initiative in reaching out to us in revelation and salvation, of course, and God also provides ample resources to hear, understand, and respond.[50] However, there is an inescapable element of human action in coming to believe; God does not do our repenting, hearing, and believing for us.

We can see by now that it is possible to read the teaching of Jesus in Mark as driving us in an externalist direction. The focus is not on deducing conclusions from premises but on the proper renovation and use of our cognitive faculties. Those faculties involve interaction with appropriate data as represented by divine testimony, the parables of Jesus, various miracles, exorcisms, his offer of forgiveness, his reinterpretation of Sabbath law, and the like. So it is not as if

the agency of tribulation, persecution, and the cares of the age. But God is the crucial causal agent. God "causes some to bear fruit for him while he hardens others by the mediation of Satan and Satan's agents" (566). It is God's action that creates perception and blinding (561). God stands behind the eye-opening and blinding (561). Behind both there lies divine destiny and divine appointment (561). Thus God's will stands behind the illumination and blinding of groups of people. "[P]art of the 'mystery of the kingdom' is precisely the division of humanity into the blind and *illuminati*, a division which God, for unfathomable reasons of his own, both wills and calls into being" (564).

49 The human dimension comes out very strongly in Matthew's use of the quotation from Isa. 6:9–10, which is in play here. See Matt. 13:15.

50 And the resources as represented by the parables are given in an appropriate manner. "With many similar parables Jesus spoke the word to them, *as much as they could understand.*" See Mk. 4:33; emphasis mine.

relevant evidence is not germane. However, the evidence is not coercive. The correct reading of the evidence requires the proper function of the recipient's cognitive capacities as represented by spiritual perception, sensitive hearing, apt judgment, and the ability to arrive at accurate explanations.[51] It also requires the reception and use of appropriate divine assistance that reorients the desires and interests of the believing subject. There is clearly an internalist element at work in the coming to believe and justify belief. The beliefs of the disciples were justified by internal factors that were available to consciousness. When asked to reflect on what and why they believe, they could cite this or that reason or experience as justifying, say, their belief that Jesus is the Messiah. However, there is also an externalist element, for there are also factors beyond those available to consciousness that affect their ability to see the justificatory status of the relevant evidence. I have cashed out this externalist element here in terms of the proper functioning of their cognitive capacities.

The mention of externalism also helps us to appreciate another aspect of externalism that shows up in the epistemology of Jesus in Mark, namely, the crucial importance of context both for understanding and of justifying our beliefs. Context in this instance is both culture-relative and person-relative. In leading the disciples into the truth about himself, Jesus does not start from scratch. He assumes that the God of Israel exists; and he accepts the reliability of Jewish prophecy and scriptural teaching. Thus the scriptures are relied on as giving access to truth about God and his promises in human history. There is no question of starting from the bottom up; new revelation is placed automatically in an agreed but contested arena. The default position is one of epistemic generosity rather than doubt. On the personal level, the disciples are selected to be the recipients of information that is not shared with the multitudes until it has been firmly established in their case and that requires attending to their very particular subjective situation. Jesus proceeds in a way that works with the grain of previous progress in the culture and in the journey of the individual. Equally important, there is an element of secrecy and concealment that prohibits the reporting of actions of Jesus that might well be misunderstood and precipitate more aggressive opposition and thus

---

[51] C. S. Lewis captures the issue of how to avoid God in an age before modern television with felicity. "Avoid silence, avoid solitude, avoid any train of thought that leads of the beaten track. Concentrate on money, sex, status, health and (above all) on your own grievances. If you must read books, select them carefully. But you'd be safer to stick to the papers. You will find the advertisements helpful; especially those with a sexy or snobbish appeal." See "The Seeing Eye," in *Essay Collection and Other Short Pieces*, ed. Lesley Walmsley (London: HarperCollins, 2000), 59.

prevent the initiation of the disciples into the proper interpretation of his life and ministry.[52]

Nowhere is there here a hint of radical skepticism or of nonrealist relativism. By skepticism I mean here a general strategy of doubt, and by nonrealist relativism I mean a version of relativism that insists that to see our beliefs as relative to their immediate context renders them suspect, or false, or as failing to be reality-depicting. Jesus assumes in his teaching of the disciples that there is no need to go back over previously secured knowledge. Nor does he call into question earlier progress in the cognitive attainments of the disciples. There is a staging process where the disciples move from initial impression to the perception of half-truth to the believing of fuller truth. Even then, there is a tendency to go back to unbelief.[53]

This not to say that skepticism or nonrealist relativism are inappropriate in their own time and place. As a general strategy skepticism and nonrealist relativism are, in fact, self-defeating and incoherent. Neither are absolute or self-starting in that they depend on prior certainties and securities. Thus skepticism depends on holding firm on the reliability of our cognitive capacities and powers of reasoning when we doubt this or that proposition. The acceptance of nonrealist relativism presupposes the accuracy of our initial contextual descriptions and the legitimacy of our concluding that the relevant context undermines our access to truth. In fact, skepticism and nonrealist relativism are entirely appropriate in contexts where previous traditions have been legitimately called into question, or where our cognitive dissonance is acute as, say, when we think that our beliefs are entirely dependent on their context and thus determined by their context.[54] Applied in context, we can rightly feel the force of skepticism and nonrealist relativism and seek out

---

[52] The theme of secrecy shows up repeatedly in Mark. See Mk. 1:34, 44; 3:12; 5:43; 7:36; 8:30; 9:9. The issue was dramatically pursued in modern scholarship in W. Wrede, *The Messianic Secret* (1901; trans. Cambridge: James Clark, 1971). Once diachronic and externalist dimensions of epistemology are taken into account, the theme of secrecy fits very naturally into the plot of the narrative as a whole. Just as some things can only be said after other things have been said, so some things must be kept secret until other things can be revealed. There is an apt order or progression in the delivery and reception of radically self-involving information.

[53] This applies especially if we hold that Mark ends enigmatically at 16:9, where the women witnesses to the empty tomb flee in a state of trembling and confusion. However, it also holds if we consider the longer canonical ending to the Gospel where the disciples refuse to believe the varied testimony to the resurrection of Jesus and are roundly upbraided for their unbelief. See Mk. 16:11, 13, 14.

[54] For this reason I dissent aggressively from the negative reading of Descartes that is common in theological circles. On the contrary, Descartes exposed the crisis in the epistemology of his day, a crisis that was in part engendered by a crisis in the epistemology of theology after the Reformation. He was right to worry that context seemed to determine belief and to sense that the whole tradition was in trouble. We need not agree with his solutions to grant that a

better options. They are poisonous when they are made foundational practices but useful when applied in appropriate contexts.

My aim thus far has been to provide an epistemological reading of the teaching and actions of Jesus as these show up in Mark. In doing so it is important to understand what is and is not being claimed. I am not claiming that the epistemological proposals I have unearthed are warranted by an appeal to Jesus or by an appeal to scripture. If these epistemological insights are correct, they are not correct because they are taught by Jesus or in scripture; rather they are taught by Jesus and in scripture because they are correct. In other words, I am not initially looking to Jesus or to scripture as warrants for this or that move in epistemology. If there are epistemological treasures here, then they should be accepted because they are intrinsically persuasive or because they help us resolve our epistemological worries and queries. It is not as if these proposals are dropped from heaven and we are asked to take them or leave them. This way of describing the enterprise in hand in no way undercuts or disparages, however, the status of Jesus or of scripture. In their own way Jesus and scripture have much more important functions to play in our life; we are not downgrading their exalted place in the universe if we do not make them a judge over our epistemological disputes.

Some will pause at this point and wonder whether this way of construing what is at issue really does justice to the place of Jesus in our intellectual endeavors. After all, once we have confessed that Jesus is the Son of God, does that not have important epistemological implications? If we put epistemology outside the reach of his teaching are we not restricting his Lordship over all creation? Should not our epistemology be thoroughly theological? And, once we allow that option, should not our epistemology be governed by our Christology?

Bruce D. Marshall has pressed the issue with pleasing clarity, rigor, and abandon. "Ordering all our beliefs around the gospel of Christ requires a massive reversal of our settled epistemic habits and inclinations, of our usual ways of deciding what is true."[55] As Marshall notes, the issue can also be expressed in terms of a vision of scripture. He cites Anselm to good effect on this score: "[H]oly scripture contains within it authority over every truth which reason gathers, since scripture either openly affirms it or at least does

---

genius had emerged and that he is rightly seen as central in the canon of epistemologists over time.

[55] Bruce D. Marshall, *Trinity and Truth* (Cambridge: Cambridge University Press, 2000), 124. A similar position, in part inspired by Marshall, is developed in Robert Barron, *The Priority of Christ: Towards a Postliberal Catholicism* (Grand Rapids: Brazos Press, 2007).

not negate it."[56] If this is the case, then we need to find an epistemology that will capture and preserve the epistemic primacy of those theological beliefs that are central to Christian identity and practice. By epistemic primacy Marshall means "a normative relation, such that for any beliefs A and B, A is epistemically primary with respect to B if and only if, should inconsistency arise between A and B, A is held true, and B rejected or modified."[57] Not surprisingly, this drives Marshall to embrace a coherentist account of justification as initially developed in the work of Donald Davidson. In turn this allows him to insist that "no true belief can contradict the narratives which identify Jesus and the Trinity."[58] If we find that this or that claim contradicts the doctrine of the Trinity, then that claim must of necessity be false. It is not as if the opposing, alien claim in question posses epistemic independence and can stand in judgment over the doctrine of the Trinity; the relation must be reversed if the doctrine of the Trinity is to stand as possessing epistemic primacy.

How might we relate this kind of claim to what I have suggested heretofore? In line with earlier intimations of where I want to go in answering this question, some distinctions and interpretative comments must be made immediately. It is one thing to explore the teaching of Jesus for epistemic insight; it is another to look to Jesus for foundational work in epistemology; and it is quite another to develop a theological epistemology on the other side of confessing that Jesus is the Son of God, the second Person of the Trinity. Furthermore, in the nature of the case, all of these projects depend on prior epistemological and philosophical theories that cannot themselves be secured by theological premises. Neither Jesus nor the church is in the business of epistemology; they have more important work on their hands. Moreover, epistemological meals must be paid for in epistemological coinage, and that coinage is not initially theological in nature.

The crucial arguments that secure these observations are as follows. First, if we are to appeal to the life and teaching of Jesus epistemologically, or if we are to draw epistemological inferences from his status as Son of God, then we have to assume a host of epistemic practices and principles. In both cases we shall have to rely on those basic practices that give us access to the world: memory, perception, testimony, judgment, and the like. We will have to take for granted from the outset those cognitive capacities without which we would not be able to understand who Jesus was, what he did, and how we should work out the

---

[56] Cited in Marshall, *Trinity and Truth*, 126.
[57] Ibid., 119.
[58] Ibid., 120.

full ramifications of his significance. It is not the case that we can rely, say, on memory and perception because Jesus tells us that memory and perception are reliable. We already rely on our memories and our perception to find out what Jesus tells us in the first place in that we have to trust the memories and perception of the first witnesses to give us accurate information, and we have to rely on our own memories and perception to hear and understand what Jesus is reported to have told us. Equally, to argue that holding to a high Christology requires us to accept the epistemic primacy of the Trinitarian faith of the church presupposes that we can rely on our bedrock intuitions about relevant inferences and implications. There is nothing in the claim that Jesus is the Son of God that tells us we can rely on the practice of inferring one proposition from another or on our intellectual perception that proposition A implies proposition B.

Second, any appeal to Jesus or to the church's teaching as giving us insight into epistemology will have to either assume that these constitute privileged means of access to truth in epistemology or provide arguments for that privileged position. If we take the former route and simply assume they give us insight, then our proposal will be arbitrary and question-begging. We will have cooked the epistemological books from the outset by our appeal to Jesus and the church's teaching; we will have posited in advance that they are normative for epistemological inquiry. We will have assumed the authoritative status of Jesus and the church for epistemological issues. Others will surely be free to substitute their own favored historical figures and communities and to develop the appropriate the epistemological theory that is governed by the teachings that are given epistemic primacy in their vision of the universe. If we take the latter course and argue for their special status, we will have to give arguments that do not presuppose such privileged status and these arguments and whatever governs them will constitute crucial logically prior steps in epistemology. We will have to give an account as to why Jesus and the church figure as privileged norms in epistemology, but this in itself will mean that we already have access to ways of adjudicating crucial issues in epistemology, most significantly how we can secure our norms in epistemology.

This line of argument fits aptly with the way in which theologians have often framed their appeals to Jesus, scripture, and the church in the epistemology of theology. These have been designated as having privileged access to the truth about God because they are held to be crucial sites of special divine revelation. Appropriate epistemological and historical arguments have then been deployed to secure their normative status. Over the last century it has become fashionable to eschew any and all arguments in favor of these as norms in theology. In part this is because many fear that any attempt to offer arguments in favor of, say, Jesus, as the final revelation of God will ultimately undermine that appeal to Jesus by making any arguments deployed the final norm of truth in theology. To use conventional rhetoric, reason will have triumphed over revelation, when revelation should stand in judgment over human reason. The worry here is not that conventional arguments fail as a matter of fact to secure Jesus as the final revelation of God; it is to say that any argument to this end will fail of necessity to secure its goal and ultimately ruin the whole theological enterprise.

This whole line of reasoning rests on an obvious mistake, however. To give reasons for proposing that Jesus is the final revelation of God is not at all to make reason triumphant over revelation; it is to argue for revelation as an appropriate epistemic norm in theology. Consider analogies. To argue that testimony should be taken as an appropriate norm of truth in the law courts is not to argue that we can now ignore testimony in the law courts and rely, say, on reasons or evidence that ignore testimony. It is to insist that it is right to rely on testimony. To argue that results of experiments should be taken as normative in deciding between theories in physics is not to conclude that arguments in physics should eschew the results of experiments; it is to make a case for relying on experiments. Equally, to argue that special revelation in Jesus is final revelation from God is not to imply that he can then be ignored in revolving disputes in theology; it is to uphold precisely the opposite of this. Similar considerations apply *mutatis mutandis* to appeals to scripture and to the church.

Let's assume with the tradition that special revelation rightly identified has a privileged position in the epistemology of theology. Clearly the full exploration of that topic is a weighty exercise that deserves extended exploration in its own right.[59] Can we go further and claim that special revelation has anything of importance to contribute to epistemology in general? Can the concept and the content of special revelation contribute in any serious way to the field of epistemology as a whole? In pursuing this question I shall circle back around to our earlier reflections on Jesus as a resource for epistemology.

Everything hinges at this point on the content of divine revelation. It is surely a truism that it is God who determines the content of divine revelation; we cannot tell God in advance how or what he should reveal. What God has made manifest in Jesus is first and foremost his kingdom and how we may enter into it for ourselves. The governing goals of divine revelation are first and foremost redemptive and soteriological; God has manifested his own life in

---

[59] I have explored the place of divine revelation in the epistemology of theology at some length in *Crossing the Threshold of Divine Revelation* (Grand Rapids: Eerdmans, 2006).

his Son through the agency of the Holy Spirit in order to save the world from sin and death. Thus in and through the life of Christ we are introduced to the very life of God. God did not send his Son to adjudicate epistemological disputes between rationalists and empiricists, foundationalists and coherentists, internalists and externalists, or fideists and natural theologians. When we read the narrative of Christ's life we shall inevitably import into our readings our varied epistemological assumptions insofar as these are evoked by the texts. However, this is not the end of the matter. Our reading of the texts themselves will then foster further reflection on our native epistemological platitudes and theories. The content of divine revelation and its media may well enrich our epistemological visions in various ways. Christian believers who happen to be philosophers will naturally want to pursue such enrichment with flair and self-criticism. We can be sure that there will be lively disagreement and debate, but we can also hope that there will be fresh and original lines of investigation and discovery.

In commenting on Mark I made ready use of insights from externalism in order to illuminate the assumptions about belief and evidence that are clearly evoked by the teaching and practice of Jesus in his interaction with the disciples and others. The intuition that informs this move is that any serious vision of epistemology must take with radical seriousness the place of bedrock cognitive capacities in sorting out our natural queries about the nature justification, and knowledge. There is no noncircular justification for reliance on such basic capacities as memory, hearing, sight, reflection, and judgment. We either trust these or we do not. The default position is that for there to be any justification and any knowledge we cannot get below or beneath reliance on these basic capacities. This is not a matter of dogmatism or of appeal to common sense. For one thing, any argument against the use of our cognitive faculties, say, that of memory, will never be stronger than the proposition that we should rely on our memories unless we have good reason to believe otherwise. For another, any argument we muster will have to rely on some or other track of our cognitive capacities and will therefore assert what it seeks to deny.

The deliverances of our cognitive capacities should be taken as innocent until proven guilty. We are entitled to our beliefs as they stand unless we have good reason to believe otherwise. These capacities are clearly fallible; they are reliable rather than perfect. Their use is person relative and community relative. Their deliverances are subject to background formation in human culture and community. They involve complex input and output mechanisms. Their usage is governed by sophisticated tacit rules that involve overriders where our initial beliefs and judgments are undermined by exposure to new experiences, data, and reflection. Their outputs are governed by varying degrees of subjective certainty and doubt. Our basic repertoire of cognitive abilities is subject to malfunction in a host of ways. They can also be brought back into good working order. Our cognitive practices are radically altered by anxieties, passions, desires, expectations, grievances, habits, intellectual policies, and past deliberations. Cognitive success and failure are intimately related to vice and virtue, and to character, behavior, and habits. Success and failure is also subject to the role of friendships, social relations, intellectual background music, peer pressure, mentors, perceived heroes and heroines, tradition, and training. Some capacities are given by nature; others are learned by complex processes of teaching and initiation. Some are not subject to our control; others are developed over time and involve hidden mechanisms that are partially under our control.

When we relate the epistemic material that we have noted in the life of Jesus it suffices for my purposes here to make only a few salient observations so as to take note of the larger issue that they exhibit. First, Jesus expands our vision of human capacities to include the capacity to hear the Word of God and see the activity of God in creation, in our own lives, and in his life and ministry. This is clearly taken up in the tradition of spiritual senses that plays such an important role in the epistemology of theology from the time of the New Testament writers to the present. Second, Jesus expands our account of the sources of malfunction to include not just ordinary vice like the lust for power but also spiritual rebellion against God. Thus there is warrant to take with radical seriousness the potential depths of human fallibility. No doubt this applies more to the epistemology of morality than to, say, chemistry, but it calls for radical intellectual humility across the board. Third, Jesus expands our account of the background conditions affecting the use of our cognitive capacities to include demonic agency and action.[60] Again the relevance of this point will be limited, but it provokes us to be far more alert to the possibilities of self-deception and delusion than we might otherwise be. Fourth, Jesus teaches that the use of our cognitive capacities involves a divine-human synergism that highlights both divine assistance and human responsibility. On the one hand, this undercuts any general skepticism in that we gratefully take our cognitive capacities to be created by a generous and competent Creator. On the other hand, it counters all forms of intellectual sloth and laziness, most especially on the part of those who might be tempted to take divine assistance as an intellectual labor-saving device.

---

[60] The theologically skeptical may want to demythologize the demonic, but even in that form my point still stands.

What is at issue in these brief observations is this. Once we make human capacities a central epistemological category then our description of the origins and nature of those capacities will be drawn up into a wider vision of creation that will affect how we articulate the range, function, formation, and exercise of those capacities. We can begin our articulation with an account that is entirely natural in the sense that it will not invoke or depend on theological concepts. However, a full description of those capacities will involve for the Christian believer a richer account whose ramifications cannot be anticipated in advance. We move from a naturalized epistemology to a supernaturalized epistemology, where our description of what is involved in justifying our beliefs or in gaining knowledge will reflect the wider theological commitments that arise out of being a disciple of Jesus.

This whole way of thinking will come as a shock to many contemporary epistemologists. They are liable to see this whole enterprise as silly or even poisonous. The reasons for this hostility are personal, historical, and metaphysical. At a personal level, they find the whole theological enterprise distasteful and offensive to their sense of their own autonomous independence. In some cases their own encounter with the Christian religion and with contemporary followers of Jesus leaves them angry or even outraged. At a historical level, they have been tutored in a tradition that highlights the violent effects of theological disputes after the Reformation and that readily draws attention to the dangers of renewed religious violence across the world over the last generation. For them the Enlightenment represents a thoroughly secular liberation from the Dark Ages of theology, so that to drag in theology is to return to the darkness and dreariness of the past. At a metaphysical level they are convinced that naturalism, suitably tutored by natural science, is the best hope of intellectual progress in the future. Adding in theological concepts and reflection to epistemology is naturally seen, then, not as enrichment of our descriptions and practices, but as a poisoning of our best insights and intellectual endeavors. Not surprisingly most contemporary epistemologists will think that supernaturalizing epistemology destroys rather than enriches or perfects nature.

Those who look to Jesus and to theology for epistemological insight should keep their nerve and take this kind of opposition in their stride. In fact, it is precisely at this point where we should take careful note of the work of current theologians like Bruce Marshall. One does not have to agree with his central proposals to appreciate the reverse revolution that he is pioneering. Marshall's work is thoroughly modern and contemporary; it is the by-product of a deep and rigorous immersion in one trajectory of recent analytical philosophy. It will and should evoke a response as contested as the subtle and complex epistemological resources he deploys. However, Marshall is also engaged in something thoroughly refreshing and that should come as no surprise to the informed theologian and to philosophers who take seriously the full canon of Western philosophy. He is expanding our background beliefs about creation to take into account the full revelation of God and God's work in the world that has been opened up to us by the church's deepest reflection on the confession that is at the heart of the Gospel itself, namely, that Jesus of Nazareth is Messiah of Israel and Son of God. He is developing an epistemology that has crossed over the threshold of redemption.[61]

It is no accident that Marshall is a brilliant student of Aquinas and of medieval theology and philosophy. He has learned there that in the end theology is not just the study of God but also the study of everything insofar as it relates to God. This "everything" must be taken with the utmost seriousness to include the study of ourselves as cognitive agents and of the complex categories and practices that we develop in order to gain belief-justification and knowledge. Like the great medieval thinkers he rightly admires, Marshall is not afraid to deploy the full contours of a Trinitarian ontology in order to think through to the end what may be at stake in epistemology. It is precisely this whole world, of course, that has been rejected by modern epistemology. However, just as the ruminations of Greek epistemology were absorbed and enriched by medieval followers of Jesus, so can contemporary epistemology be absorbed and enriched by his contemporary disciples.

---

[61] Marshall is not the only contemporary philosopher to develop a theistic epistemology. The same can be said of Alvin Plantinga in his work in epistemology. See his *Warrant and Proper Function* (New York: Oxford University Press, 1993).

ᴗ

Paul Ricoeur: A Biblical Philosopher on Jesus

David F. Ford

In 1979 Paul Ricoeur published a short article, "The Logic of Jesus, the Logic of God."[1] Paul, in his Letter to the Romans, repeats four times the phrase "how much more" (5:9, 10, 15, 17), and Ricoeur takes Paul's rhetoric to indicate the "divine logic" of Jesus. This is a logic not of equality and equivalence but of the excess and superabundance "that one hears in the voices of the prophets, in Jeremiah, in Ezekiel, and in the Psalms" and also in the teaching of Jesus – as in Matthew 5:39b–42 on turning the other cheek, going the extra mile, and never refusing to lend, or in the extravagance of a parable about the Kingdom of God or the hyperbole of a camel passing through the eye of a needle. Ricoeur goes on to argue that "Paul says the same thing as Jesus but at another level of language" but adds something new:

> that Jesus Christ is himself the "how much more of God." For the Gospel, Jesus was at first the one who spoke and spread the good news. Now he is announced as the one who, by the folly of the cross, breaks the moral equivalence of sin and death . . . . [T]he church, through the mouth of Paul, gives a *name*, the name of Jesus Christ, to the law of superabundance. But even then, this proclamation of the church would remain an exclusive saying if we could not attach this supreme "how much more" to the enlightening paradoxes of the rabbi Jesus.[2]

The article concludes by reflecting on the possibility of giving signs of the logic of abundance and generosity in the areas of penal law and economics.

Only a small proportion of Ricoeur's writings are directly about Jesus or other explicitly Christian topics. Yet, that short article can be paralleled by

---

[1] *Criterion* 18 (1979), reprinted in Paul Ricoeur, *Figuring the Sacred: Religion, Narrative, and Imagination*, trans. David Pellauer (Minneapolis: Fortress Press, 1995), 279–83.
[2] Ibid., 279, 282f.

other works in which he shows himself to be a Christian thinker.[3] Since it is
hard to demonstrate major inconsistencies in his philosophy, it is appropriate
to try to discover how his philosophy coheres with his Christian faith. His
affirmations of God, Jesus, and the law of superabundance make him rather
unusual among leading twentieth-century Western philosophers, and one
legitimate way to approach the work as a whole is to read it as the philosophy
of a Christian – it would be surprising if such affirmations as those about God
and Jesus did not have ramifications in all areas of his thought. I will do this
primarily by showing how his thought fits with John 1:1–18.

I am also concerned to set him in a wider context of Christian thought.
Ricoeur was alert to many schools of Christian theology and scholarship of his
own and previous periods. I will set him alongside Karl Barth in particular,
seeing them as largely complementary. I will then comment on three highlights of his thought about Jesus, concerning parables, the transformation of
the self in relation to Jesus, and John 1:18. Next, I will attempt to characterize
the distinctiveness of his biblical philosophy as it is shown through his treatment of Jesus. Finally, as an interpreter, Ricoeur himself always asked what is
"ahead of" or "in front of" the text, rather than being limited to what is
"behind" or "within" it. In developing philosophical ways of dealing with
Jesus, what might he have to teach philosophers who come after him?

First, I will introduce his thought about Jesus through its relationship to
one New Testament text.

RICOEUR AND JOHN 1:1–18

If anything stands out in Ricoeur's approach to Jesus, it is his engagement
with the Bible. Perhaps the single most influential text in Christian thought
is the Prologue of the Gospel of John (1:1–18). Ricoeur in fact commented on
it in several writings, but more important now is how it is possible to read his
work as being in line with it.

In contrast to Barth (see the subsequent section "Ricoeur and Barth"),
whose interpretation is explicitly Christological throughout, Ricoeur might
be seen as resisting too immediate an identification of the Word, the *Logos*
(Jn. 1:1, 14) with Jesus Christ (first named in 1:17). He takes seriously John's
delay in making the name explicit and revels in thinking about the Word in

---

[3] Cf. Paul Ricoeur, *Essays on Biblical Interpretation*, ed. Lewis S. Mudge, trans. various (Philadelphia: Fortress Press, 1980); idem, *Figuring the Sacred*; idem, *The Symbolism of Evil*, trans.
Emerson Buchanan (Boston: Beacon Press, 1969); Andre LaCocque and idem, *Thinking Biblically: Exegetical and Hermeneutical Studies*, trans. David Pellauer (Chicago: University of
Chicago Press, 1998).

its many forms, whether overtly linked to Jesus Christ or not. Most of his philosophy could be related to the first sixteen and a half verses before Jesus is named:

- "In the beginning . . . " (1:1) is a quotation from Genesis 1:1 in the Septuagint (the Greek translation of the Hebrew Bible). Ricoeur is fascinated by texts and intertextuality and defines himself as a philosopher who is first of all a hearer, a listener, and a reader. "To confess that one is a listener is from the very beginning to break with the project dear to many, and even perhaps all, philosophers: to begin discourse without any presuppositions. (We could speak simply of the 'project of beginning,' for to think without presuppositions and to begin to think are one.) Yet it is in terms of one certain presupposition that I stand in the position of a listener to Christian preaching: I assume that this speaking is meaningful, that it is worthy of consideration, and that examining it may accompany and guide the transfer from the text to life where it will verify itself fully."[4] He admits to presuppositions and is willing to name them, and, in the article from which that is quoted, the meaningfulness of the Bible is clearly his main one and its "beginning" is reinterpreted in John 1:1.

- " . . . was the Word . . . " (1:1). Language has been a core concern of Ricoeur, especially metaphor, symbol, narrative, the interplay of genres, and the superabundance of meaning that can flow through them. *Logos* might also be seen as the headline for a project that runs through all his works – the interrelation of the Hebraic and the Hellenic strands in Western thought and civilization.[5] John's use of *Logos*, with its extensive resonances in Hellenistic culture as well as in the Jewish Septuagint, was itself an inspiration of the Christian church in its early centuries, as it tried to relate affirmatively as well as critically and transformatively to the civilization within which it was born. Ricoeur carries on this tradition into modernity and beyond.

- " . . . and the Word was with God, and the Word was God" (1:1). For Ricoeur it is vital that the New Testament *continues* to name God. I will not hesitate to say that I resist with all my strength the displacement of the accent from God to Jesus Christ, which would be the equivalent of substituting one naming for another. I hold that what Jesus preaches is the kingdom of *God*, which is inscribed in the naming of God by the prophets, the eschatologists,

---

[4] Ricoeur, "Naming God," in *Figuring the Sacred*, 217.

[5] Compare his rejection of the "simplistic opposition of Jerusalem and Athens," in Paul Ricoeur, "Myth as Bearer of Possible Worlds," in *States of Mind: Dialogues with Contemporary Continental Thinkers*, ed. Richard Kearney (Manchester: Manchester University Press, 1984), 35.

and the apocalypticists. What is the cross without the cry, *"My God, my God, why have you forsaken me?"* inscribed into the naming of God by the psalmist? And what is the resurrection if it is not an act of God homologous to that of the exodus? Hence a Christology without God seems to me as unthinkable as Israel without Yahweh.... Jesus's humanity is not thinkable as different from his union with God. Jesus of Nazareth cannot be understood apart from God, apart from his God, who is also the God of Moses and the prophets.[6] Ricoeur's concern with God might therefore be seen as underlining the Prologue's naming of God in its opening verse, long before any explicit mention of Jesus, and with specific reference to an Old Testament text, Genesis 1:1. "Naming God comes about only within the milieu of a presupposition, incapable of being rendered transparent to itself, suspected of being a vicious circle, and tormented by contingency. This is the presupposition: naming God is what has already taken place in the texts preferred by my listening's presupposition."[7] The first text is the Old Testament, and Ricoeur comments on the "biblical polyphony" through which God is named there: in third person narrative; in the "double first person" of the "I" of the prophet and of God; in the second person instruction of Torah; in wisdom wrestling with the silence or absence of God, especially in face of unjust suffering, and seeking God as the meaning of meaning; in the "double second person" of psalms of celebration, supplication, and thanksgiving. "The word 'God' says more than the word 'being' because it presupposes the entire context of narratives, prophecies, laws, wisdom writings, psalms, and so on. The referent 'God' is thus intended by the convergence of all these partial discourses. It expresses the circulation of meaning among all the forms of discourse wherein God is named.... It is also the index of their incompleteness. It is their common goal, which escapes each of them."[8]

• "All things came into being through him . . . " (1:3). "All things" is the horizon for Ricoeur's wide-ranging philosophy. If there is this conviction that everything came into being through the *Logos*, then there is *carte blanche* for a Christian thinker to be interested in all things and their interrelations, and for an academic philosopher to explore as many disciplines as Ricoeur did – linguistics, literature, hermeneutics, theology, biblical and religious studies, and several of the human and natural sciences. "Self-understanding in the face of the text will have the same amplitude as the world of the text.

[6] Ricoeur, "Naming God," 230f.
[7] Ibid., 218.
[8] Ibid., 227f.

Far, therefore, from being closed in upon a person or a dialogue, this understanding will have the multidimensional character of biblical poetics. It will be cosmic, ethical and political."[9] Ricoeur's freedom in exploration is not constrained by any sense of wanting to prove a connection with the *Logos*. This is not apologetic Christian thought; rather there is a confidence that truth-seeking investigations, however diverse, are worthwhile for their own sake and need not worry that they might end up somewhere other than the *Logos*. He specializes in the "detour of thought" that takes the long way to a destination, thoroughly covering even distantly related areas so as to enrich the position eventually reached.

- " . . . and the life was the light of all people" (1:4). "All people" make up the horizon of his thought together with "all things." He has especially been concerned with people of the past, in particular with those who figure in the Bible, with ancient Greek and more recent European thinkers, and also with those in the contemporary West. In addition, he has engaged at length with characters in fiction.

- "The light shines in the darkness, and the darkness did not overcome it" (1:5). "The symbol gives rise to thought," and Ricoeur has thought thoroughly about symbols and their superabundant meanings, not least the symbolism of evil.[10]

- "[John] came as a witness to testify to the light, so that all might believe through him" (1:7). "Emmanuel Levinas: Thinker of Testimony" is the title of an essay by Ricoeur, and it is true of himself too.[11] He explores the ordinary, the judicial, and the religious meanings of testimony, drawing on biblical prophets and the New Testament, including John 1:7.[12] This testimony to "the light" has an absolute character, yet is inextricably connected with contingent events. Ricoeur takes the concept of testimony as the pivot for his response to the "scandal of particularity," the great ditch that Lessing saw between the universal truths of reason and the particular truths of history. In testifying to the divine in historical signs (above all, in Jesus), the self divests itself before what is witnessed and renounces absolute knowledge (such as in Hegel). Testimony can be tested, put on trial, but not proven; rather, it generates continuous interpretation. In a dense summary statement that requires the rest of the essay for its interpretation he says: "[O]ne can indeed say paradoxically that the hermeneutics

---

[9] Ibid., 235.
[10] Ricoeur, *The Symbolism of Evil.*
[11] Ricoeur, "Emmanuel Levinas: Thinker of Testimony," in *Figuring the Sacred*, 108–26.
[12] Ricoeur, "The Hermeneutics of Testimony," in *Essays on Biblical Interpretation*, 137.

of testimony is *absolute-relative*. It is twice absolute and twice relative. It is absolute as original affirmation in search of a sign, absolute as the manifestation in the sign. It is relative as the criteriology of the divine for philosophic consciousness, relative as the trial of idols for historical consciousness."[13] Part of what leads to that statement is a discussion of the unity-in-tension of event and meaning that is found in testimony to Jesus as the Christ:

> The first witnesses of the Gospel confess the significance of Christ directly on the Jesus event: "*You are the Christ.*" There is no separation between the Jesus of History and the Christ of Faith. This unity is written: Jesus-Christ. This is the shortcut of meaning and event which gives something to interpretation and which demands to be interpreted. How? In that this fusion signifies also a tension, the event is both apparent and hidden . . . . [T]he manifestation of the absolute in persons and acts is indefinitely mediated by means of available meanings borrowed from previous scripture. It is in this way that the primitive church continuously interpreted the "testimony of Christ," to pick up on a Johannine expression, with the aid of names and titles, figures, and functions, received for the most part from the Hebraic tradition, but also from the mystery religions and from Gnosticism. In calling Jesus Son of Man, Messiah or Christ, Judge, King, High Priest, *Logos,* the primitive church began to interpret the relation of meaning and event.[14]

Through his conception of testimony one can best understand why Ricoeur is a listening, hermeneutical philosopher (rather than, for example, an empiricist or idealist), how he sees the relation between faith and reason,[15] and what he makes of the incarnation.[16]

- " . . . his own people did not accept him" (1:11). John is the Gospel that is hardest on what it identifies as "the Jews." Ricoeur is extremely sensitive to the dangers of Christian anti-Judaism and supersessionism, and his understanding of Jesus is informed by the emphasis on "Jesus the Jew" that was part of the post–Second World War reconsideration of Christian-Jewish relations. The Jewish thinkers Franz Rosenzweig and Emmanuel Levinas were especially influential on him, and within the Christian Bible, he has more to say about the Old than the New Testament (cf. previous comments on God and subsequent comments on 1:17a).

---

[13] Ibid., 151.
[14] Ibid., 145.
[15] Cf. ibid., 153.
[16] Cf. ibid., 139, on John's testimony to Jesus, including Jn. 1:14.

- "And the Word became flesh and lived among us, and we have seen his glory, the glory as of a father's only son, full of grace and truth"(1:14). Ricoeur's programmatic essay on religion, "Manifestation and Proclamation," sets out from a contrast between a phenomenology of manifestation, focussed on signs that "show" the sacred, and a hermeneutic of proclamation, in which "the word outweighs the numinous," theology is organized around basic discourses, and the religious axis passes through speech-acts that have a tendency to desacralization.[17] He then asks a characteristically Ricoeurian question about whether these are as opposed as they appear and, if not, how they might be mediated in relation to each other. He takes seriously yet critiques the analysis that because of science and secularization, Western culture has outgrown the sacred, arguing that "humanity is simply not possible without the sacred. . . . Are we not on the verge of a renaissance of the sacred, at least if humankind itself is not to die?"[18] He finds the key to an answer in John 1:14, quoting it in support of his statement: "That word and manifestation can be reconciled is the central affirmation of the Prologue to John's Gospel."[19] The incarnation for him grounds the dialectic of preaching and sacrament that runs through Christian history: "The sacrament, we could say, is the mutation of sacred ritual into the kerygmatic realm. . . . Only the incarnation of the ancient symbolism ceaselessly reinterpreted gives this word something to say, not only to our understanding and will but also to our imagination and our heart; in short, to the whole human being."[20]
- "From his fullness we have all received, grace upon grace" (1:16). Here is an affirmation of the overflowing superabundance that is so central to Ricoeur's philosophy and faith, as exemplified in "The Logic of Jesus, the Logic of God" quoted in the opening paragraph. It is also about the radical transformation that the generosity of God embodied in Jesus makes possible as the grace is given and received. In theological terms, the "who" of Jesus articulated in Christology is for Ricoeur always inseparable from the transformation involved in soteriology, and I will comment further on the significance of his way of maintaining this.
- "The law indeed was given through Moses . . . " (1:17). As noted already on 1:1 and 1:11, and as is evident in my opening paragraph and on 1:7, the Old Testament plays a large part in Ricoeur's understanding of Jesus and of

---

[17] Ricoeur, "Manifestation and Proclamation," in *Figuring the Sacred*, 49–61.
[18] Ibid., 64.
[19] Ibid., 65.
[20] Ibid., 67.

Christianity as a whole. This is, of course, in line with the New Testament, and the intertextuality between the two testaments, which is at the heart of what he calls "the first Christian hermeneutic,"[21] is a frequent concern for him. Perhaps his most important hermeneutical statement on it concerns the second half of this verse:

- "... grace and truth came through Jesus Christ" (1:17). Here, finally, the Prologue names Jesus. Ricoeur's essay "Naming God" only arrives at the naming of Jesus Christ in relation to God by way of a thorough consideration of the naming of God in the Old Testament, and he vehemently rejects any substitution of the name Jesus for God (see on God in 1:1). How then does he understand the naming of Jesus? "The Logic of Jesus, the Logic of God" gives one approach – Jesus incarnating the "how much more" of God, which coheres well with John 1:16–17 on fullness and grace. The essay "Naming God" moves through the Old Testament naming into the New Testament, emphasizing in particular how God is named indirectly through "limit-expressions" in Jesus's parables, proverbs, paradoxes, hyperboles, and eschatological sayings, thus offering a "matrix for theological language inasmuch as this language conjoins analogy and negation in the way of eminence: God is like..., God is not...." [22] Ricoeur then poses the question "Poem of God or Poem of Christ?" and, after insisting on the unsubstitutability of names, gives an answer that formally has much in common with the classic Trinitarian concept of coinherence (Greek *perichoresis*, Latin *circuminsessio*) but that is articulated in terms of the history of naming God and the relation of power and weakness. He writes:

> Some may say that the relation between the Christological ground and this mediation through the history of the names of God is circular. Certainly it is circular. But this circle itself must be courageously assumed. Everything, in one sense, begins with the cross and resurrection. But the cross does not allow itself to be spoken of as the relinquishment of God except in relation to all the signs of God's weakness that belong to the whole naming of God. And the Resurrection may be understood only through the memory of God's liberating acts and in anticipation of the resurrection of every human being. Hence, it is perhaps the task of Christology to maintain, in the interior of the *same* meaning space, as the two antagonistic tendencies of the *same* naming, the celebration of total power, which seems to dominate the Old Testament, and the confession of total weakness, which seems to be declared by the New. It would then

---

[21] Ricoeur, "The Bible and the Imagination," in *Figuring the Sacred*, 148.
[22] Ricoeur, "Naming God," 230.

be necessary to discover that, on the one side, the total power of the biblical God, once stripped of Greek ideas of immutability and impassivity, already leans towards the total weakness signified by the contestation and failure of God. But it would also be necessary to understand symmetrically that the kenosis, signified by the cross, ceases to be the simple idea that some today would like to draw toward the idea of the death of God, as soon as it is put in relation with the power expressed through Jesus's preaching of the kingdom and the Christian community's preaching of the Resurrection. In this way, the New Testament announces a power of weakness that needs to be dialectically articulated along with the weakness of power that the other namings of God suggest.[23]

Then comes Ricoeur's challenge to Christian thinking today (which will be discussed later), as he acknowledges the difficulty of this "dialectical labour" in trying to "avoid the constraint of the logic of identity as much as the license of the logic of difference, as well as any false appeasement of the dialectic. The doctrine of the Trinity did this labour for one epoch of thought. A similar labour ought to be undertaken today, one that would take up the whole space of the naming of God and its discordant concordance" (ibid., p. 232). By the end of the essay, this has been developed to include the "precious dialectic of poetics and politics" and an accompanying "ethics of conviction," thus characteristically embracing the transformation of personal and social life.

One striking result of this positioning of Ricoeur's thought in relation to John's Prologue has shown the extent to which Ricoeur, sometimes almost in passing, affirms essentials of mainstream Christian teaching about Jesus.

RICOEUR AND BARTH

Were Ricoeur and Barth the two leading Protestant Christian thinkers of the twentieth century?[24] Many would agree on Barth being one, but the argument for Ricoeur would be harder to sustain. Yet I think the case could be plausibly made, especially if he is seen as complementary to Barth. Of course, if only theologians are counted as Christian thinkers then there is no case for Ricoeur. As a philosopher, he dealt with a remarkable range of disciplines,

---

[23] Ibid., 231f.

[24] There could of course be a further discussion as to whether these two members of the Protestant Reformed tradition made more important contributions than any Lutherans, Roman Catholics, Orthodox, and so on, but the wider the scope of the comparisons the more the problems of commensurability increase. Nothing much hangs on such "league tables," but I would minimally propose Ricoeur alongside Barth as a classic Christian thinker of the twentieth century, well worth repeated rereading.

including at times theology, but he always resisted the label of theologian. Barth likewise dealt with many disciplines, including philosophy, yet would never have wished to be called a philosopher.

Barth, like Ricoeur, commented on the Prologue of John and returned, explicitly or implicitly, to it at many points in his *Church Dogmatics*. Barth's theological understanding of John 1:1–18 centers on Jesus Christ,[25] and this sets the agenda for an extraordinary tour de force as one doctrine after another (God, election, creation and reconciliation) is thought through in explicitly Christological terms. So the most striking contrast that emerges is Barth's concentration on Jesus Christ and on thinking through the whole of theology with explicit reference to him. Yet both could argue that they are in line with John 1:1–18 and not in ways that are contradictory or even necessarily in tension. I suggest that they are complementary within what Ricoeur might call the superabundant meaning of John's Prologue.

Both are agreed in beginning from the position of listening to the text, and indeed Ricoeur says that he is indebted to Barth for teaching him this basic posture.[26] As his title, *Church Dogmatics*, suggests, Barth the theologian is concerned primarily with the teaching and preaching of the church. Ricoeur is a listener to that preaching who is a philosopher concerned with the *Logos* and "all things," "all people." Barth's Christian witness is strongly centered on teaching explicitly in the name of Jesus Christ. Ricoeur is equally keen on witness and frequently names Jesus Christ, but his testimony is often implicit or incognito, corresponding to those verses in the Prologue before the *Logos* is named. Neither is especially apologetic about his faith in Jesus Christ, and each displays strikingly daring free speech (New Testament *parrhesia*), but Barth is more concerned to propose and defend doctrinal positions. Ricoeur is not negative toward doctrine but neither is he interested in doing it. This is one of the most instructive contrasts between these two figures who might yet be seen as complementary, and it deserves further analysis.

Ricoeur's approach to doctrine has at least three elements. First, he revels in the polyphony of the Bible, with its many genres, moods, and voices. As he tries to do justice to the richness of scripture the impression is not that he considers much theology to be wrong but rather that it is inadequate to scripture, less lively and polyphonous, seeking univocal or overdefined meanings where these are not appropriate. His habit is to show, when necessary, that he is

---

[25] Cf. Karl Barth, *Church Dogmatics*, eds. G. W. Bromiley and T. F. Torrance (Edinburgh: T&T Clark, 1956–1975), vol. 1, pt. 2, 122–71, and vol. 2, pt. 2, 95–9.

[26] "It was in fact Karl Barth who first taught me that the subject is not a centralizing master but rather a disciple or auditor of a language larger than itself." Ricoeur, "Myth as Bearer of Possible Worlds," 27.

sure-footed on important doctrinal matters but then to spend most energy on interpreting scripture and accompanying hermeneutical reflection. He returns to reread the scripture to which doctrine appeals, and the result is that doctrine is tested and opened up in ways that challenge theologians and others to rethink them – as in his remarks on the Trinity quoted earlier on 1:17.

Second, he sees theologians using philosophy, and especially hermeneutics, to articulate their teachings and so being partly accountable to philosophical critique.

Third, as a Christian thinking about the *Logos* and "all things," his philosophical enterprise is like the creation of an intellectual and imaginative environment in which theologians can breathe freely and have some confidence. This is achieved neither by expounding and defending doctrines nor by demolishing atheist or other philosophies and ideologies that are hostile to Christian faith. Rather, he generously affirms yet stretches beyond the elements of truth in other positions, opening up possibilities of conceiving as true an understanding of reality that goes against much conventional secular wisdom. Here his pièce de résistance is at the end of *Oneself as Another*, where he sets the scene for a Christian continuation (which in fact he delivered in two further lectures that were not included in that book) but strictly limits himself as philosopher to raising possibilities. The central theme of the book has been the way in which otherness is part of selfhood. Now in conclusion he sees

> the need to maintain a certain equivocalness of the status of the Other on the strictly philosophical plane . . . . Perhaps the philosopher as philosopher has to admit that one does not know and cannot say whether this Other, the source of the injunction, is another person whom I can look in the face or who can stare at me, or my ancestors for whom there is no representation, to so great an extent does my debt to them constitute my very self, or God – living God, absent God – or an empty place. With this aporia of the Other, philosophical discourse comes to an end.[27]

Beyond being philosopher as philosopher, Ricoeur is not philosopher as theologian but philosopher as Christian thinker. As Christian thinker, he has so far appeared to be complementary with Barth the Christian theologian. But there is one massive question about their compatibility that is also of

---

[27] Paul Ricoeur, *Oneself as Another*, trans. Kathleen Blamey (Chicago and London: University of Chicago Press, 1992), 355. For a theological appropriation of *Oneself as Another* that responds to this passage, see David F. Ford, *Self and Salvation: Being Transformed* (Cambridge: Cambridge University Press, 1999), chap. 4.

great importance for the accounts they each give of Jesus. I will tackle it in
dialogue with its treatment by Kevin Vanhoozer.

Vanhoozer is a perceptive theological commentator who appreciates well
Ricoeur's philosophical achievement in nonapologetically making space for
theological ideas and exploring philosophical ideas that approximate to
them.[28] He sees the primacy of the *Logos* for Ricoeur and concludes his
book:

> The Word is Ricoeur's kingdom, and his hermeneutic philosophy is at the
> service of this sovereign. Ricoeur marshals all the resources of his philo-
> sophical anthropology and hermeneutics to come to the aid of this Word
> in a critical time. The kingdom of the Word appears weak in a deaf and
> unbelieving world. It is not the least of Ricoeur's service, then, that he makes
> space for a new hearing and appreciation of this Word. Such a hearing is
> vital, for humanity receives its meaning, the scope of possibilities for indi-
> vidual and social being, from this Word. Ricoeur does not serve his own
> word, but a regenerating Word, a freeing Word. However, Ricoeur is not
> principally a Proclaimer. His is the more humble task of "making space" for
> this proclamation and of rendering this proclamation intelligible by pro-
> viding philosophical approximations. But I repeat, Ricoeur is not himself a
> Proclaimer – neither preacher nor prophet. A hermeneutic philosophy that
> stays within the limits of reason cannot announce the Christian possibility.
> Ricoeur does not proclaim the Gospel. Rather, like John the Baptist, Ricoeur
> serves the Gospel by baptizing our imaginations, philosophically preparing
> the way for the Word.[29]

That conclusion is, in my judgement, correct in its affirmations but not
nuanced enough in its negations and indeed internally shows a degree of
vacillation in the shift from "not principally a Proclaimer" to "not himself a
Proclaimer." I would agree with the first statement, but the either/or structure
of Vanhoozer's assessment, which recurs elsewhere in his book, fails, in my
opinion, to do justice to the "both-and" character of much of Ricoeur's
thinking.

---

[28] Ricoeur does not see this approximation as a kind of backdoor apologetics, however: "If God
speaks by the prophets, the philosopher does not have to justify His word, but rather to set
off the horizon of significance where it may be heard. Such work has nothing to do with
apologetics" (Ricoeur, *Essays on Biblical Interpretation*, 97). "Ricoeur probably overstates his
disclaimer here, for though philosophy does not have to argue for the factuality of the central
claims of Christianity, it does argue for their meaningfulness. To defend the meaningfulness
of Christianity rather than its truth may certainly be seen as a kind of defense of the faith."
Kevin Vanhoozer, *Biblical Narrative in the Philosophy of Paul Ricoeur. A Study in Hermeneutics
and Theology* (Cambridge: Cambridge University Press, 1990), 128.

[29] Ibid., 288.

This is most serious in Vanhoozer's theological interrogation of Ricoeur. He questions Ricoeur sharply from what in many respects is a Barthian position, often with reference to Hans Frei (who was close to Barth in many respects). For Ricoeur, are the Gospels testimonies to historical events or tales about human historicity? Is his concept of salvation about a comprehensive change or just a change in self-understanding? Is he envisaging response to specific divine action or only a universal possibility of faith and freedom? Is he offering a Romanticist humanism rather than mainstream Christian thought? Does he privilege manifestation over proclamation? Is this from the start a Christian, Biblical understanding that frames everything else, or does the Bible provide illustrations within a more general philosophical framework? More sharply, and of particular concern here, is the person of Jesus indispensable or is he illustrative of general human experience and possibilities? One aspect of that point is Frei's judgement that Ricoeur, together with David Tracy, is "far closer to traditional allegorical than literal reading."[30] To respond by doing justice to Ricoeur's distinctive ways of engaging with such binaries without either choosing one or falling into ambiguity would be the work of a monograph, but Vanhoozer's critique of Ricoeur comes to a head in the way he contrasts him with Barth, and it is to this contrast that I will limit my comments.

Vanhoozer finds Ricoeur and Barth in opposition to each other on three fundamental points, on each of which I read their relationship differently. Each can also be related to the previous discussion of their interpretations of the Prologue of John and therefore to their understandings of Jesus. I will discuss Vanhoozer's points in turn before suggesting a constructive mediating interpretation of their relationship.

Vanhoozer's first point is:

> For Ricoeur the NT narratives disclose the religious dimension in human experience. For Barth, on the other hand, no form of human language has the innate capacity to accomplish such a feat.[31]

Another interpretation might see Ricoeur setting the Gospel narratives in the context of a world and humanity created through the *Logos* of John 1:1, and not needing to make any claim against Barth, concerning innate capacity.

Vanhoozer's second point is:

> For Ricoeur, poetic narratives manifest a world of human possibilities. The world disclosed by the Gospel narratives "is the world of a human, temporal existence permeated by a divine presence" [Thompson, *The Jesus*

---

[30] Quoted in Vanhoozer, *Biblical Narrative*, 160.
[31] Ibid., 180.

Debate, 127]. For Frei and Barth, the NT announces a new possibility that is ineluctably tied to an unsubstitutable and an indispensable person.[32]

Another interpretation might see Ricoeur's Jesus (who, as has already emerged earlier in the chapter, is the Jewish rabbi of Nazareth; is the preacher of the Kingdom of God; cried out to God on the cross as he died; was resurrected by God; is the Christ or Messiah; is at the same time and inseparably the Jesus of history and the Christ of faith; is, as John 1:14 says, the incarnation of God; is for humanity the "how much more" of God; embraces the power of weakness and the weakness of power; enables the transformation of personal and social life; is in union with God; and is appropriately, though not exhaustively, affirmed in his relationship to God through the doctrine of the Trinity) as both unsubstitutable and indispensable. Ricoeur does read the Gospel narratives as poetic and opening up a world of possibilities, but he also sees them as testimony to historical events.

Vanhoozer's third point is:

> For Ricoeur, the NT narratives manifest the way that the world is always-already graced by God's presence; the Christian possibility is always-already available, and may in fact be analogously disclosed by classic narratives of other religions and even non-religious texts. For Frei and Barth, the NT narratives proclaim what God has done in Christ; the NT narratives proclaim the new and impossible possibility of God making himself known as Jesus Christ and acting to save humanity.[33]

Another interpretation might on the one hand ask where Ricoeur says that "the Christian possibility is always-already available" and on the other hand critically explore the implications of John's Prologue for the presence of God to all things and all people, including all religions and all texts, and reflect on the possibility of analogies (or signs, or types, or figures, or illustrations, correspondences, or – a term on which Barth and Ricoeur might agree – parables) to/of the Gospels. It is hard, on the evidence already presented, to imagine Ricoeur disagreeing with the Frei and Barth part of Vanhoozer's third point.

How might the relationship between Ricoeur and Barth be better described? I find an illuminating suggestion in John David Dawson's remarkable work, *Christian Figural Reading and the Fashioning of Identity*.[34] The main part of

---

[32] Ibid.
[33] Ibid., 180f.
[34] John David Dawson, *Christian Figural Reading and the Fashioning of Identity* (Berkeley, Los Angeles, and London: University of California Press, 2002).

the book is a comparison between the theologies of Origen of Alexandria and Hans Frei. The issues at stake are strikingly parallel to those between Ricoeur and Barth discussed earlier (and Frei indeed saw both Origen and Ricoeur as "allegorizing" in their scriptural interpretation). Dawson's complex analyses and arguments, which offer instructive parallels and contrasts to Vanhoozer's (and include a reinterpretation of Origen's allegorizing that is applicable to some of Ricoeur's readings), cannot be rehearsed here, but I will simply use one broad brush conclusion. He suggests that Frei, a convert to Christianity, was centrally concerned with its distinctive identity, as represented above all by the identity of Jesus Christ. Origen, on the other hand, was born a Christian and at ease in that identity, and was more concerned with how the Christian grows in faith, love, hope, and holiness and is transformed through the Holy Spirit. I suggest that there is some analogy with Ricoeur and Barth. Barth's "conversion" was from one type of Christianity (liberal Protestantism) to another, whose identity he largely defined through its focus on Jesus Christ. Ricoeur, so far as I know, went through no such dramatic rebirth and seems to have been a faithful member of the Protestant Reformed tradition all his life. Like Origen, he is especially taken up with human transformation, with the superabundance of the "how much more" that opens up endless possibilities with God.

It is curious that one of Vanhoozer's main theological criticisms of Ricoeur is that he does not do justice to the Holy Spirit. He even claims Ricoeur "lacks an adequate approximation for the Christian teaching about the Holy Spirit."[35] I find the Spirit (largely anonymously) pervading his work. There is a radical sense of divine initiative in that it is God who gives revelation and the human who is first a listener, and many of Ricoeur's favoured terms resonate with language about the Holy Spirit – a transformation, dynamism, intensification, gift and generosity, superabundance, excess, mediation, conscience, faith, freedom, hope, love, imagination, possibility, prophecy, revelation, wisdom, meaning, understanding, and the whole realm of interpretation. Vanhoozer's limited appreciation of this dynamic of the Spirit in Ricoeur the Christian thinker leaves him without a way out of the either/or binary oppositions listed earlier, whereas Ricoeur's implicit pneumatology allows for their mediation into both-and. A notable example of this is the rigour yet generosity of his interpretations of thinkers with whom he differs – a point well made by Vanhoozer in his opening acclamation of Ricoeur's philosophy for "its prime 'theological' virtue: charity."[36]

---

[35] Kevin Vanhoozer, *Biblical Narrative*, 278.
[36] Ibid., 4.

The usual anonymity of the Spirit in Ricoeur might be reflected upon further through our key text the Prologue of John. That was written by the one who also told of the promise of Jesus to give the Holy Spirit that would lead his followers into "all the truth" (Jn. 16:13). Presumably John believed himself in writing his Gospel to be so led by the Spirit. So the Prologue can be read not only as an example of the Spirit leading further into the truth but also as an example of what later followers will be led to go beyond into yet further truth. The Prologue is in fact an extraordinarily daring interpretation of Genesis 1:1 and of Jesus as the *Logos*, going beyond what John ascribes to Jesus himself in the narrative that it introduces. Ricoeur shows analogous daring in some of his interpretations (e.g., of Exodus 3:14 and of the Song of Songs[37]), his conceptualities (e.g., his concept of "oneself as another"[38] and his rethinking of reference in terms of refiguration[39]), his constructive critiques (e.g., of Augustine,[40] Freud,[41] and Levinas[42]), and his challenges (e.g., earlier, on thinking beyond the doctrine of the Trinity and, later, on Christian conscience).

If my parallel with Dawson's account of Origen and Frei is appropriate, then Ricoeur and Barth are richly complementary. This does not mean that they agree on all theological matters (there are many aspects of Ricoeur that are nearer to Barth's great opponent, Rudolf Bultmann[43]) but that, within the capacious tent of John 1:1–18, both Ricoeur's exploration of the *Logos* "in the Spirit" and Barth's massive Christological concentration can be accommodated and can also be in fruitful interplay.

RICOEUR ON JESUS: THREE HIGHLIGHTS

My concern so far has been to summarize Ricoeur's overall position on Jesus and relate it in an exemplary though by no means exhaustive way to the Bible (through John's Prologue) and to Christian theology of his own time

---

[37] LaCocque and Ricoeur, *Thinking Biblically.*

[38] Ricoeur, *Oneself as Another.*

[39] Ricoeur, *Time and Narrative*, trans. Kathleen McLaughlin Blarney and David Pellauer, 3 vols. (Chicago: University of Chicago Press, 1984–1988).

[40] Especially in Ricoeur, *Symbolism of Evil*, and idem, *Time and Narrative.*

[41] Paul Ricoeur, *Freud and Philosophy: An Essay on Interpretation*, trans. Denis Savage (New Haven: Yale University Press, 1970).

[42] Ricoeur, *Oneself as Another.*

[43] Cf. Ricoeur, "Preface to Bultmann," in *Essays on Biblical Interpretation*, and Kevin Vanhoozer, *Biblical Narrative*, esp. chap. 6. One way of putting his – in certain respects – closer relationship to Bultmann is that Bultmann's existentialist interpretation of the Gospel is more pneumatological than christocentric.

(through Barth). I now choose just three examples through which to look in more detail at his understanding of Jesus, with a special concern to illustrate and develop further some of the points made earlier.

Reading the Parables of Jesus

As has been made clear already, Ricoeur keeps together the teaching of Jesus with the teaching about Jesus. The parables of Jesus have especially fascinated him. He has shown how they are "limit-expressions" whose extravagance in placing "the extraordinary within the ordinary" bring about the rupturing of ordinary speech in the interests of realizing the "something more" of the Kingdom of God (cf. the opening paragraph).[44] He later took his interpretation of them a step further in "The Bible and the Imagination" and I will comment briefly on that essay, my main interest being methodological.

The essay explores the imagination (both as "a rule-governed form of invention" and as "the power of giving form to human experience" by redescribing it[45]) as it contributes to the act of reading the Bible, especially its parables. Reading is a dynamic activity that takes further the meanings opened up by the text. In the parables of the Kingdom he finds "the most complete illustration of the biblical form of imagination, the process of parabolization working in the text and engendering in the reader a similar dynamic of interpretation through thought and action."[46] His own key new insight is the significance of the parables being "narratives within a narrative, more precisely narratives recounted by the principal personage of an encompassing narrative."[47] The parables are therefore interpreted intertextually in interplay with the whole Gospel story of Jesus and, more widely, with the Old Testament.

The parables Ricoeur chooses are the only two that appear in all three Synoptic Gospels, those of the Sower (Mark 4 and parallels) and of the Wicked Husbandmen (Mark 12 and parallels). I will not try to summarize the fascinating detail of his interpretations, since my main concern is to portray what it means for him to be what one might call a "biblical philosopher" offering an account of Jesus.

He agrees with H. Richard Niebuhr's description of Christian revelation as the elucidation of all events through the special event of Jesus Christ but finds Niebuhr short-circuiting the way the two are related and undertakes

---

[44] Ricoeur, "Manifestation and Proclamation," in *Figuring the Sacred*, 60f. Cf. Ricoeur, "Biblical Hermeneutics," *Semeia* 4 (1975), 29–148.
[45] Ricoeur, "The Bible and the Imagination," 144f.
[46] Ibid., 147.
[47] Ibid., 149.

a characteristically Ricoeurian detour, this time through parables, in order
to understand it more adequately. He appropriates, but also critiques, A.J.
Greimas's method of narrative structuralist analysis as applied by Ivan
Almeida to the parables. It is a highly technical semiotic discussion that
typically welcomes the structuralist approach while showing that justice can
only be done to the specific content of the Gospels by transcending it. He
complements the structuralism with philosophical analysis and conceptual
construction, with intertextual sensitivity to both the Gospel as a whole and
the Old Testament and with a hermeneutical proposal about how these parables are embedded successively in the Gospel testimony to Jesus, in other
writings down the centuries and in the life of the reader today. In this he
sees us as "accompanying *the interpretive dynamism of the text itself*. The text
interprets before having been interpreted. This is how it is itself a work of
productive imagination before giving rise to an interpretive dynamism in the
reader that is analogous to its own."[48] As regards the Gospel story, he argues
that "what progressively happens in the Gospel is the *recognition* of Jesus as
being the Christ. We can say in this regard that the Gospel is not a simple
account of the life, teaching, work, death, and resurrection of Jesus, but the
communicating of an act of confession, a communication by means of which
the reader in turn is rendered capable of performing the same recognition
that occurs inside the text."[49]

That combines the two sides, identity and transformation, that have
emerged from the discussions of Ricoeur and Barth, Vanhoozer's critique
of Ricoeur, and Dawson's work on Origen and Frei, and which theologically
I have linked to the themes of Christology, soteriology, and pneumatology.
From the standpoint of method the mode of combination is also important:
Ricoeur is a biblical hermeneutical philosopher who is equally at home in "scientific" structuralist analyses of narrative, in philosophical argument about
imagination, in contextually sensitive traditions of ongoing interpretation,
and in the theological thought of H. Richard Niebuhr. I will reflect further on
this combination later.

The Christomorphic Self

Ricoeur's distinctive understanding of Jesus is perhaps best summed up in his
final Gifford Lecture, published as "The Summoned Subject in the School of
the Narratives of the Prophetic Vocation."[50] It is the culmination of a series

[48] Ibid., 161.
[49] Ibid., 162.
[50] Ricoeur, *Figuring the Sacred*, chap. 15.

of lectures on the self, most of which were published in *Oneself as Another*.[51] Since I have engaged at length elsewhere with these as contributions to a theology of the transformation of self,[52] I will here limit myself to points that are relevant to the rest of this chapter.

It is worth first noting what Ricoeur says about the relationship of this explicitly Christian lecture to the other philosophical ones, because it articulates well his nonapologetic and nontriumphalist conception of the relation of his philosophy to his faith:

> I do not want to insinuate that the self, formed and informed by the biblical paradigms, crowns the self of our philosophical hermeneutics. This would be to betray our unambiguous affirmation that the mode of Christian life is a wager and a destiny, and those who take it up are not led by their confession either to assume a defensive position or to presume a superiority in relation to every other form of life, because we lack criteria of comparison capable of dividing among rival claims. The self that here responds, responds precisely to that symbolic ensemble delimited by the biblical canon and developed by one or another of the historical traditions that have grafted themselves to the Scriptures to which these traditions claim allegiance.[53]

As he recognizes, that responsive, "summoned self," situated before the text of scripture and within a tradition of its interpretation, is profoundly different from many philosophical starting points, despite staying in philosophical conversation with them. He moves through a series of "figures of the self" in this tradition: the Old Testament narratives of the prophetic call and vocation with its "mandated self"; the New Testament "christomorphic self" of Paul's Second Letter to the Corinthians; Augustine's figure of the "inner teacher"; and the testimony of Christian conscience in the aftermath of Kant, Hegel, and Heidegger. I will comment briefly on the second and fourth.

Ricoeur starts his Pauline study from 2 Corinthians 3:18:

> And all of us, with unveiled faces, seeing the glory of the Lord as though reflected in a mirror, are being transformed into the same image from one degree of glory to another; for this comes from the Lord, the Spirit.

He sees that picture of conformity to the Christ figure as the New Testament paradigm that comes closest to the mandated self of the Old Testament. He relates it intertextually to the Mosaic prohibition of images, to the Genesis creation of Adam in the image of God, to the glory of the Lord on Mount

---

[51] Ibid.
[52] David F. Ford, *Self and Salvation: Being Transformed*.
[53] Ricoeur, "The Summoned Subject," in *Figuring the Sacred*, 262f.

Sinai according to Exodus and Deuteronomy and then to the transformation of the metaphor of power and the form of glory in the figure of the "Suffering Servant" of Second Isaiah. "The early church confessed the life and death, the death and resurrection of Jesus the Christ as the manifestation of God's glory, by prolonging this figure."[54]

Paul's innovation was to graft

> the extraordinary theme of the transformation of the Christian into this same image. In this way he forged the central metaphor of the Christian self as christomorphic, that is, the image of the image par excellence. A chain of glory, if we may put it this way – of descending glory, it must be added – is created in this way: God's glory, that of Christ, that of the Christian. At the far end of this chain, if the mediation goes back to the origin, the christomorphic self is both fully dependent and fully upstanding: an image "always more glorious," according to the apostle.[55]

Here is Ricoeur's central trope for Jesus: the Jesus who is inseparable both from God and from those created in God's image. It allows for many construals of Jesus, both within the New Testament and in later tradition (he mentions as "the central melody" in books of spirituality that of *The Imitation of Christ* by Thomas à Kempis) and it has a "capacity for renewal" in different periods and cultural contexts while still being "faithful to both the Old and the New Testaments."[56] It also combines the distinctive identity of Jesus Christ with ongoing transformation in the Spirit.

The idea of being "both fully dependent and fully upstanding" is especially important in his fourth figure of the testimony of conscience. Here he reaches back to Paul on conscience (*suneidesis*) and justification by faith, and forward to the Enlightenment's emphasis on human interiority and autonomy:

> It is to the dialogue of the self with itself that the response of the prophetic and the christomorphic self is grafted. In this graft, the two living organs are changed into each other: on the one side, the call of the self to itself is intensified and transformed by the figure that serves as its model and archetype; on the other side, the transcendent figure is internalized by the moment of appropriation that transmutes it into an inner voice.[57]

[54] Ibid., 268.
[55] Ibid.
[56] Ibid.
[57] Ibid., 271.

His uniting of the autonomy of conscience with the obedience of faith involves "a confession of faith in which, in the spirit of hermeneutics, we have discovered a mediate and symbolic structure."[58]

The conclusion is his claim to be both genuinely biblical and genuinely modern (or, perhaps, postmodern – certainly post-Enlightenment) and is his most succinct definition of what it means to be a responsible, intelligent Christian today:

> This articulation of the autonomy of conscience and the symbolics of faith constitutes, I believe, the modern condition of the "summoned self". The Christian is someone who discerns "conformity to the image of Christ" in the call of conscience. This discernment is an interpretation. And this interpretation is the outcome of a struggle for veracity and intellectual honesty. A "synthesis" is not given and never attained between the verdict of conscience and the christomorphism of faith. Any synthesis remains a risk, a "lovely risk" (Plato). To the extent that the Christian reading of the phenomenon of conscience moves from being a wager to being a destiny, Christians can say with the apostle Paul that it is in "good" conscience that they stake their lives on this risk [2 Cor. 1:12]. It is in this sense, after a long journey, that he could place himself in the line of descent leading from the "summoned subject" and could cry out, amid torments that make him a brother of Hamlet, "O my prophetic soul!"[59]

One might add that he had earlier set forth a challenge to theology to work on a theology of conscience. That is certainly a lack in our main dialogue partner, Karl Barth, whose attention to Christian traditions of interiority, whether premodern or later, is scant, so that here too Ricoeur's biblical, hermeneutical Christian thought proves complementary to the theology of Barth.

The End of the Prologue

The third, and briefest, highlight brings us to the final verse of John's Prologue that was earlier suspended at 1:17. Ricoeur's comment on 1:18 is set in the context of a discussion of testimony in John's Gospel. It is Ricoeur's characteristic way of indicating exegetically the mutuality of proclamation and manifestation that was discussed on John 1:14, and it is hard to imagine Barth, or almost any orthodox Christian thinker, dissenting – however different their

---

[58] Ibid., 274.
[59] Ibid., 274f.

terminologies might be. Ricoeur writes:

> The pole of testimony is thus displaced from confession-narration toward manifestation itself to which testimony is rendered. This is the meaning of John 1:18, "No one has ever seen God; the only Son . . . has made him known" (*exegesato*). The *exegesis* of God and the *testimony* of the Son are the same thing. Overwhelmingly testimony rendered by this disciple is regulated in its profound intention by the theological meaning of testimony-manifestation, Christ-act par excellence.[60]

THE CONTEMPORARY CHRISTIAN THINKER AS RATIONAL BIBLICAL PHILOSOPHER

How might one describe the thought of this philosopher who begins by reading the Bible while simultaneously engaging with full sophistication in philosophy and many other disciplines? I see Ricoeur as a prophetic figure for the twenty-first century and will conclude this chapter with some suggestions as to how his example might be followed. But first it is necessary to attempt to place his form of philosophy. Fortunately there exists what I consider a convincing philosophical map on which to situate him, and I will sketch it briefly.

Nicholas Adams in his paper "Narrative, Argument and Pluralism," delivered to a conference on religion and public reason, addresses

> a cluster of vital issues which have come to prominence at various points in the histories of the Abrahamic traditions, whenever scripture has been invoked as an authority higher than the received wisdom of the philosophical schools. Think of Augustine's *City of God*, or Ghazali's *Revival of Religious Sciences* or Maimonides' *Guide for the Perplexed*. The issue is not new, and the radical returns to scripture, in the face of religious crises, by Karl Barth, Franz Rosenzweig and Muhammad Iqbal in the early decades of the twentieth century were not new either.[61]

One issue is the relation of modes of reasoning seeking agreement within a tradition to modes that seek agreement across traditions. He notes the attempts in Western philosophy, such as Spinoza's *Tractatus* (1670), Kant's *Conflict of the Faculties* (1798) and many since, to exclude scripture from the realm of the rational. He responds to them by arguing that the same modes

---

[60] Ricoeur, "The Hermeneutics of Testimony."

[61] Nicholas Adams, "Narrative, Argument and Pluralism," the Claude Ryan Memorial Lecture delivered at McGill University, 14 September 2007; unpublished text (courtesy of the author), p. 1.

of rationality need to operate within and across traditions, but that they need to include the reasoned interpretation of texts.

Adams distinguishes three basic forms of reasoning in modernity and he sees each contributing to "excellent theology."

The first is that of science, understood as "a method for testing rival intuitions," using axioms and hypotheses.[62] "To think scientifically is to know the difference between an axiom and an hypothesis, and to know the rules for action in each case."[63] To think scientifically in theology is to know this in relation to a religious tradition. Ricoeur displays such thinking at many points in his works. In the discussion earlier, it is most evident in his use of structuralist analysis to help interpret the parables of Jesus and also in many strands of discussion of the self in *Oneself as Another*, culminating in the aporetic conclusion quoted earlier as regards the truth question about the self's "other."

The second is that of history. Historical thinking takes a detour toward the truth question by way of acknowledging "that people take different things to be true at different times, and in different places."[64] In order to do justice to their claims one first needs to understand what questions they were trying to answer (Collingwood), and to think triadically – that X does not just mean Y, but X means Y for Z (Peirce). This adds a further dimension of complexity, akin to Ricoeur asking about the meaning of the christomorphic self in Paul, in Augustine, and after the Enlightenment, or to him saying that the doctrine of the Trinity was one epoch's answer to the question of how to name God but not necessarily adequate for our own epoch.

The third Adams calls "the narrative form of religious reasoning – in scripture, in liturgy, in commentary, in preaching," and suggests that it "may well turn out to be as significant as the scientific and historical revolutions for our intellectual life."[65] His definition is: "*To think narratively is to pursue reasoning through commentary on texts and the retelling of stories.*"[66] Here he names Ricoeur as an exemplar, as is clearly appropriate given Ricoeur's insistence on traveling the long route to understanding through interpreting texts and grappling with the commentaries surrounding them.

Adams is Ricoeurian in his resistance to the many attempts to take shortcuts to truth in the religious realm by avoiding one or even two of these modes

---

[62] Ibid., 2f.
[63] Ibid., 3.
[64] Ibid., 4.
[65] Ibid., 7.
[66] Ibid. It might be more appropriate to name this form without privileging a particular genre such as narrative – perhaps "hermeneutical" or "textual" would be preferable.

of reasoning. He holds that whether one is inside or outside a tradition, or somewhere hard to determine, if one wishes to be fully rational one should employ all three. He draws the consequence of this in words that resonate with Ricoeur's insistence on engaging in the full "labour of thought":

> The effort involved in investigating the truth-claims of a person from another religious tradition is titanic. If one is committed to thinking scientifically, historically and narratively, one is agreeing to do a lot of work. It means patient reading of scriptures which may not be authoritative for the investigator, and then reading the relevant commentaries, which are likely to be numerous and difficult. It means reconstructing historically the questions to which various claims are answers, and comparing these with analogous questions which are being asked by the investigator. It means knowing how to handle the axiomatic and hypothetical status that certain claims have, in certain contexts, especially when these statuses change over time or from region to region.[67]

I am reminded by that of Ricoeur's essay on Exodus 3:14 as an example of all three modes being employed in the course of arriving at robust (and sometimes quite polemical) conclusions about a text that rivals John 1:1–18 in its pervasive influence on Christian thought and beyond.[68] Regarding Jesus, whether one agrees with Ricoeur or not, it is hard to deny that the labor of thought in which he has engaged lends his positions a rational authority that is sadly lacking in the less labor-intensive methods of most of his fellow-philosophers in their discussions of this topic.

CONCLUSION: LESSONS FOR TWENTY-FIRST CENTURY PHILOSOPHERS

I have been largely descriptive and comparative in my treatment of Ricoeur. There has not been space to give him the sort of thorough treatment that Adams's threefold rationality would demand. There will, therefore, be innumerable outstanding questions that could only be adequately answered by longer journeys of thought.[69] In conclusion, I will briefly suggest just five lessons that Ricoeur might have to teach twenty-first century philosophers – whether or not they are Christian thinkers – if they wish to think about Jesus.

---

[67] Ibid., 11.

[68] LaCocque and Ricoeur, *Thinking Biblically*, chap. 6.

[69] Elsewhere I have attempted extended answers to some questions in dialogue with Ricoeur, especially about the transformation of the self (in *Self and Salvation*) and about the interrelation of scholarship, hermeneutics and theology in biblical interpretation (in *Christian Wisdom: Desiring God and Learning in Love* [Cambridge: Cambridge University Press, 2007]).

First, and most obvious, is the point just made, drawing on Adams: *travel the long route of scientific, historical, and narrative (or textual) reasoning.*

Second, in line with the lessons of John 1:1–18, *face the full Christian, biblical Jesus* – involving God, cosmos, humanity, history, ethics, politics, other religions, all disciplines, and the full polyphony of the Bible and many Christian traditions through many periods.

Third, if one is to speak of Christian faith, *take into account a faith that is fully rational, has faced the questions raised by the best minds of the past and present, and is imaginative, exploratory, compassionate, and practically responsible in ethics and politics* – a faith such as Ricoeur's.

Fourth, *take seriously the Holy Spirit and the radical challenge of comprehensive transformation in understanding Jesus* – as Ricoeur did.

Fifth, in the inevitable disputes accompanying such a controversial subject as Jesus, *try to be as generous, gentle, and honest with opponents as Ricoeur.*

9

~

Jesus and Forgiveness

Nicholas Wolterstorff

I

Forgiveness plays a prominent role in our moral culture, as do such institutional analogues of forgiveness as pardon, amnesty, and the decision not to file charges for the sake of personal or social good. The prominence of the role of forgiveness and its analogues in our moral culture does not, of course, imply consensus on that role. Where one parent is willing to forgive the abductor of their child, the other is filled with abiding hatred. And whereas social harmony was the aim of the various truth and reconciliation commissions that emerged in Latin America and South Africa over the past several decades, the pardons and amnesties issued by these commissions themselves became the source of social discord. There are even some who argue that forgiveness and its analogues should play no role whatsoever in our moral culture. Forgiveness is always bad, they say; pardon and amnesty should never be granted. But this remains the view of a minority.

Where do the concept and practice of forgiveness and its analogues come from? As with other components of our moral culture, we should not assume that forgiveness is a component of any moral culture whatsoever. The recognition of rights is not a component of every moral culture, certainly not the recognition of human rights. Perhaps the recognition of obligation, and its counterpart, guilt, is likewise not universal to moral cultures. Conversely, whereas shame is prominent in some moral cultures, it has fallen almost entirely out of ours. So once again, what is the origin of forgiveness as a component of our moral culture?

In a well-known section of *The Human Condition*, Hannah Arendt argues for the importance of forgiveness and promising in human affairs, including political affairs.[1] Forgiveness is the remedy for the irreversibility of human action; promising is the remedy for its unpredictability.

> The possible redemption from the predicament of irreversibility – of being unable to undo what one has done . . . is the faculty of forgiving. The remedy for unpredictability . . . is contained in the faculty to make and keep promises. The two faculties belong together in so far as one of them, forgiving, serves to undo the deeds of the past, whose 'sins' hang like Damocles' sword over every new generation; and the other, binding oneself through promises, serves to set up in the ocean of uncertainty, which is the future by definition, islands of security without which not even continuity, let alone durability of any kind, would be possible in the relationships between men (212–3).

Arendt then remarks, "The discoverer of the role of forgiveness in the realm of human affairs was Jesus of Nazareth." She adds, "It has been in the nature of our tradition of political thought to be highly selective and to exclude from articulate conceptualization a great variety of authentic political experiences, among which [are] some of an even elementary nature." This is true of Jesus's discovery of forgiveness. Along with other teachings of Jesus, this has been neglected because of its "allegedly exclusively religious nature." In fact forgiveness is one of those "aspects of the teaching of Jesus of Nazareth which are not primarily related to the Christian religious message but sprang from experiences in the small and closely knit community of his followers, bent on challenging the public authorities in Israel." Thus the fact that Jesus "made this discovery in a religious context and articulated it in religious language is no reason to take it any less seriously in a strictly secular sense" (214–215).

My project in this essay is twofold. First, I will argue, contra Arendt, that Jesus's injunctions to forgive were "primarily related to [his] religious message"; Jesus did not discover the importance of forgiveness in a small group setting and then use religious language to articulate his discovery. In the course of developing this thesis I will spend some time reflecting on the nature of forgiveness. Second, I will argue, in considerably more detail than Arendt herself does, that she is correct in her claim that the origin of forgiveness as a component in our moral culture is the words and deeds of Jesus – with the important addition that the Old Testament/Hebrew Bible is, in turn, the indispensable context for understanding the words and deeds of Jesus.

---

[1] Hannah Arendt, *The Human Condition* (Garden City, NY: Doubleday Anchor Books, 1959), 212–19.

II

Jesus spoke often about God's forgiveness of sins. He instructed his followers to pray that God would forgive their sins. And every now and then he announced to someone that his or her sins were forgiven. Sometimes there had been no prior contact of Jesus with the person; thus he could not be understood as forgiving the person for some wrong he or she had inflicted on Jesus. On at least one of these occasions, some in the crowd understood him to be assuming the prerogative of forgiving the person's sins on behalf of God. The story is told in all three synoptic Gospels. Here is how Matthew tells it:

> And just then some people were carrying a paralyzed man lying on a bed. When Jesus saw their faith, he said to the paralytic, "Take heart, son; your sins are forgiven." Then some of the scribes said to themselves, "This man is blaspheming." But Jesus, perceiving their thoughts, said, "Why do you think evil in your hearts? For which is easier, to say, 'Your sins are forgiven,' or to say, 'Stand up and walk'? But so that you may know that the Son of Man has authority on earth to forgive sins" – he then said to the paralytic – "Stand up, take your bed and go to your home." And he stood up and went to his home. When the crowds saw it, they were filled with awe, and they glorified God, who had given such authority to human beings (Matt. 9: 2–8; cf. Mk. 2:4–7, and Lk. 5:21–26).

In declaring that God forgives sins, Jesus was doing no more than handing on the teaching of the Old Testament. Arendt is correct in her observation that where Jesus went decisively beyond the Old Testament was in his injunction to his followers to forgive those who had wronged them, and in the assumption, behind the injunction, that not only does God have the power to forgive but that we human beings have that power as well (215).[2] Luke reports Jesus as saying, "If another disciple sins, you must rebuke the offender, and if there is repentance, you must forgive. And if the same person sins against you seven times a day, and turns back to you seven times and says, 'I repent,' you must forgive" (Lk. 17:3–4). In Matthew's narrative, Peter seems to have found this saying quite incredible. To check it out he asks, presumably sometime later, "Lord, if my brother sins against me, how often should I forgive? As

---

[2] I think Arendt was mistaken in her further comment that "Man in the gospel is not supposed to forgive because God forgives and he must do 'likewise,' but 'if ye from your hearts forgive,' God shall do likewise." I think the Gospels teach both that we are to imitate God in forgiving and that if we forgive others their trespasses, our heavenly Father will also forgive us, whereas if we do not forgive others, neither will our Father forgive our trespasses (Matt. 6:14–15).

many as seven times?" Jesus's response is, "Not seven times but, I tell you, seventy-seven times" (Matt. 18: 21–2).[3]

What are we to make of this injunction of Jesus to his disciples to forgive those who wrong them when the wrongdoer repents of his wrongdoing? Why did he think forgiveness important? What does it accomplish? Does it accomplish something that nothing else could accomplish? Or is it an alternative strategy for accomplishing something that could be accomplished some other way? In short, what is defective about a moral culture in which forgiveness is missing?

Hannah Arendt, in one of the passages quoted, says that forgiveness "serves to undo the deeds of the past." She cannot mean this literally and strictly, since she also says that forgiveness is the remedy for "the irreversibility of human action." If human action is irreversible, then nothing at all can serve – literally and strictly – to undo the deeds of the past. But if forgiveness does not actually undo the deeds of the past, what is it about the irreversibility of those deeds that it does remedy?

I interpret Peter, in the episode reported by Matthew, as having been mulling over what Jesus enjoined in the episode described in the passage quoted from Luke; could Jesus really have meant to say that one is to forgive a repetitively repentant wrongdoer seven times? In Luke's narration, the injunction comes out of the blue. The sayings of Jesus that immediately precede the injunction offer no interpretative clue, nor do the sayings that immediately follow. And neither does Luke intrude into the narrative to give his own interpretation of what he has reported Jesus as saying.

After replying to Peter that as often as the person who wrongs one is repentant, no matter how many times that may be, one is to forgive him, Jesus goes on in Matthew's narration to tell the Parable of the Unforgiving Servant, the point of which is that if we do not forgive our brothers and sisters from our heart, our heavenly Father will also not forgive us. This, of course, attaches transcendent significance to human forgiveness. But it does not tell us what significance within human affairs Jesus sees in our forgiveness of each other. For that, we have to look elsewhere within the Gospel narratives. I suggest that forgiveness is, for Jesus, an essential component within his ethic of love.

---

[3] What immediately follows in Matthew's Gospel is Jesus's Parable about the Unforgiving Servant: A king out of mercy forgave the very large debt of one of his slaves, whereupon this slave turned around and refused to forgive the minor debt to him of one of his fellow slaves. When the king heard about this, he was angry with the first slave, and ordered him to be punished. "Should you not have had mercy on your fellow slave," he said, "as I had mercy on you?" Jesus concludes the story with these words: "So my heavenly Father will also do to every one of you, if you do not forgive your brother [or sister] from your heart."

III

A highlight of Jesus's ministry, in the narratives of Matthew and Luke, is his proclamation of the Beatitudes. In both narratives, the Beatitudes are followed immediately by Jesus's presentation of the ethic of love in the polemical context of his rejection of what I shall call the *reciprocity code*. I suggest that this polemical context is indispensable for understanding Jesus's ethic of love, at least at it pertains to forgiveness.

Matthew 5:17–48 and Luke 6: 27–36 are among the most provocative and controversial passages in the entire New Testament; even the claim that part of their main point is the repudiation of the reciprocity code will be contested. But if we read the passages as a whole with care, and do not merely snatch at golden nuggets and run with them, I think the polemical point becomes abundantly clear.

"Do not resist an evildoer," says Jesus in the Matthew passage. "If anyone strikes you on the right cheek, turn the other also." Christian pacifists regularly cite the passage in defense of their position of nonviolent resistance. But what the sentence says is not that we should be nonviolent in our resistance to evildoers; it says that we should not resist evildoers. I know of no Christian pacifists who go that far. In the same passage Jesus says, "Give to everyone who begs from you, and do not refuse anyone who wants to borrow from you." Nobody that I know is quite so profligate with his belongings as this sentence says he should be. And no one in my acquaintance has done what the following words of Jesus, in the same passage, say he should do: "If your right eye causes you to sin, tear it out and throw it away. . . . And if your right hand causes you to sin, cut it off and throw it away."

I have spoken thus far of *what the sentences say* – alternatively expressed, of *what the sentences mean*. The question of interpretation that we must address is not that one, however; in this case it is clear enough what the sentences say or mean in the language. The question of interpretation is *what Jesus was saying* with these sentences. These are not to be identified. When one speaks ironically, what one says is (more or less) the opposite of what one's sentence means in the language.

The passages contain two clues to the interpretation of what Jesus was saying with the puzzling injunctions that I have just quoted; there are other, equally puzzling injunctions in the passages that I have not quoted. One of those clues is to be found in both Matthew and Luke; the other is to be found only in Matthew. Let's start with the clue found in both of them, beginning with Luke's formulation of the clue. It is important to quote at some length, lest we miss the clue or not discern its significance.

Love your enemies, do good to those who hate you, bless those who curse you, pray for those who abuse you. If anyone strikes you on the cheek, offer the other also; and from anyone who takes away your coat do not withhold even your shirt. Give to everyone who begs from you, and if anyone takes away your goods, do not ask for them again. Do to others as you would have them do to you.

If you love those who love you, what credit is that to you? For even sinners love those who love them. If you do good to those who do good to you, what credit is that to you? For even sinners do the same. If you lend to those from whom you hope to receive, what credit is that to you? Even sinners lend to sinners, to receive as much again. But love your enemies, do good, and lend expecting nothing in return. Your reward will be great, and you will be children of the Most High, for he is kind to the ungrateful and the wicked. Be merciful, just as your Father is merciful (Lk. 6:32–36).

And here is the passage from Matthew that contains the same clue to the interpretation of the puzzling injunctions. Again, it is important to quote at some length.

You have heard that it was said, "An eye for an eye and a tooth for a tooth." But I say to you, Do not resist an evildoer. But if anyone strikes you on the right cheek, turn the other also; and if anyone wants to sue you and take your coat, give your cloak as well; and if anyone forces you to go one mile, go also the second mile. Give to everyone who begs from you, and do not refuse anyone who wants to borrow from you.

You have heard that it was said, "You shall love your neighbor and hate your enemy." But I say to you, Love your enemies and pray for those who persecute you, so that you may be children of your Father in heaven. For he makes his sun rise on the evil and on the good, and sends rain on the just and the unjust.[4] If you love those who love you, what reward do you have? Do not even the tax collectors do the same? And if you greet only your brothers and sisters, what more are you doing than others? Do not even the Gentiles do the same? Be perfect, therefore, as your heavenly Father is perfect (Matt. 5:38–48).

The reciprocity code has two aspects. If someone does one a favor, then one owes him a roughly equal favor in return.[5] And if someone does one an evil,

---

[4] The translation that I am using, NRSV, has "righteous" and "unrighteous" where I have "just" and "unjust." The Greek words are *dikaios* and *adikos*.

[5] The topic of "exchange" and "the gift," which is all the rage nowadays, is obviously relevant here. But reciprocity is broader than gift-exchange. And though "exchange," by itself, might perhaps be understood broadly enough to be synonymous with "reciprocation," I judge that "reciprocity code" is a more natural and less misleading term for the ethic Jesus is repudiating than "ethic of exchange."

then a roughly equal evil is due him. "Evil" must of course be understood here not as moral infraction but as deprivation of some life-good. In both cases, the positive and the negative, the balance that existed between the two parties before the engagement took place must be restored. The moral order is impaired if balance is not restored. From Jesus's comments one can infer that this code was pervasive in Jewish society of the time. From the texts of pagan antiquity we know that it was also pervasive in ancient Greek and Roman society.

The clue to the interpretation of the puzzling injunctions that Jesus issues to his followers is his attitude toward the reciprocity code. Jesus's attitude toward the first aspect, that if someone does one a favor, one owes him a roughly equal favor in return, is deflationary acceptance. Though returning favors for favors is not always obligatory, it is in general a good thing to do, especially in the interaction of friends with each other. Apart from exceptional circumstances, it's not a good thing among friends if generosity goes entirely in one direction. But there is no point in issuing exhortations on the matter; sinners, tax collectors, Gentiles, all accept this principle. "If you do good to those who do good to you, what credit is that to you?" says Jesus. "For even sinners do the same."

Jesus's attitude toward the second aspect, that if someone does evil to you, then an equal evil is due him, is flat out rejection. Jesus's followers are not to return evil for evil. In all cases, they are to do good; they are to love the other – even when the other is their enemy and has treated them maliciously. "Love your enemies, do good to those who hate you." In so doing, you are like God, who is kind even to the ungrateful and the wicked.

I submit that the puzzling injunctions in these passages are vivid metaphorical and hyperbolic ways of rejecting the reciprocity code and enjoining the ethic of love. If we interpret them with unimaginative literal-mindedness, we miss the point.

If someone strikes you on the cheek, don't try to make things even by hitting him back; offer your other cheek. If someone steals your coat, don't try to make things even by stealing his coat; offer him your shirt. If someone, perhaps a Roman officer, conscripts you into carrying his load for one mile, don't try to make things even by figuring out a comparable evil to impose on him; offer to carry his load a second mile. Vivid metaphorical and hyperbolic ways of making the point that we are to repudiate the code of "making things even" or "getting even," and instead seek to enhance the well-being even of those who have imposed some evil on us. It's easy to carry on with metaphorical and hyperbolic examples from present-day society of the same point. If someone steals your bicycle, don't try to make things even by stealing his bicycle; offer him your car. If someone discovers your social security number, don't try to make things even by learning his; offer him your credit card. If someone steals your electronic gadgetry, don't try to make things even by stealing his; offer him your silver plate. And so forth.

Jesus is not enjoining nonresistance to evil in these passages, though of course that is what the English sentence "Do not resist an evildoer" means. And certainly he is not permitting resistance but enjoining that it be nonviolent. One is at a loss to understand why anyone has ever thought he was doing that. No one interprets everything that Jesus says in these passages literally. But if one nonetheless singles out the sentence "Do not resist an evildoer" and insists on understanding Jesus as speaking literally with that sentence, then what Jesus is enjoining is not *Do not resist an evildoer with violence,* but *Do not resist an evildoer,* period.

Though the most vivid and extensive rejection of the reciprocity code in favor of the ethic of love occurs in these two passages from Matthew and Luke, Jesus explicitly rejects the code on a good many other occasions as well. On one occasion he even spoke critically about the positive side of the code. Luke reports that Jesus was invited on a Sabbath day to a dinner at the home of one of the leaders of the Pharisee party. It soon became clear to Jesus that, apart from himself, the invited guests were friends and relatives of the host. That led Jesus to remark to his host:

> When you give a luncheon or a dinner, do not invite your friends or your brothers or your relatives or rich neighbors, in case they may invite you in return, and you would be repaid. But when you give a banquet, invite the poor, the crippled, the lame, and the blind. And you will be blessed, because they cannot repay you, for you will be repaid at the resurrection of the just (Lk. 14:12–14).[6]

Jesus's rejection of the reciprocity code is carried forward into the epistolary literature of the New Testament. "Do not repay anyone evil for evil," says Paul in his letter to the Romans, "but take thought for what is noble in the sight of all" (12:17). And in 1 Peter 3:9 we read, "Do not repay evil for evil or abuse for abuse; but, on the contrary, repay with a blessing."

The second clue to interpreting the puzzling injunctions is found only in Matthew. "Do not think that I have come to abolish the law or the prophets," says Jesus. "I have come not to abolish but to fulfill" (5:17). What then follows is a series of five paragraphs, each introduced with the formula "You have heard that it was said,... but I say to you." One of these five is a passage

---

[6] Where I have "just," the NRSV has "righteous." The Greek is *dikaioi.*

already quoted: "You have heard that it was said, 'An eye for an eye and a tooth for a tooth.' But I say to you, do not resist an evildoer." The point in each case appears to be that what one finds in the law and the prophets is the bare minimum of what the ethic of love requires. The ethic of love does not repudiate the Torah; rather, it catches it up into a much more challenging ideal. Though love does indeed underlie the Torah, for the most part its expression there is minimalist.

"You have heard that it was said to those of ancient times, 'You shall not murder'; and 'whoever murders shall be liable to judgment.' But I say to you that if you are angry with a brother or sister, you will be liable to judgment; and if you insult a brother or sister, you will be liable to the council" (Matt. 5:21–22). Of course you should not murder; murder is incompatible with love. But when you discern the love requirement that underlies the command not to murder, you will realize that not only should you not murder but you should not even get angry with your brother or sister or insult them.

"You have heard that it was said, 'You shall not commit adultery.' But I say to you that everyone who looks at a woman with lust has already committed adultery with her in his heart. If your right eye causes you to sin, cut it out and throw it away" (5:27–29). Of course you should not commit adultery; adultery is incompatible with love. But when you discern the love requirement that underlies the command not to commit adultery, you will realize that not only should you not commit adultery, but you should not even lust after a married woman. Get rid of your lust. Cut it out.

"You have heard that it was said, 'An eye for an eye and a tooth for a tooth.' But I say to you, Do not resist an evildoer" (5:38–39). Many commentators have suggested that the formula "An eye for an eye and a tooth for a tooth" should be heard as a repudiation of blind vengeance and the affirmation of a system of punishment in accord with the reciprocity code. *No more* than an eye is to be exacted for an eye, and *no more* than a tooth for a tooth. I think it likely that that is how Jesus understood it. If so, then what he is saying is that of course you should not engage in blind vengeance; blind vengeance is incompatible with love. But when you discern the love requirement that underlies the prohibition of blind vengeance, you will realize that not only should you refrain from blind vengeance, but you should repudiate the reciprocity code's way of dealing with being wronged. Being wronged should be answered not with proportionate evil but with good.

I suggest that Jesus's injunctions to forgive should be seen as an integral part of his repudiation of the reciprocity code and his affirmation of the alternative ethic of love. The reciprocity code says that I am to even things up with the wrongdoer – restore the prior balance – by seeing to it that he is subjected to hard treatment roughly equal to the harm he did me. Forgiveness is one component in the alternative ethic of love.

IV

One cannot distribute forgiveness for wrongdoing hither and yon. To forgive someone is to forgive him for the wrong he did one. Hence one can only forgive the person who has wronged one, and only for the wrong he has done one. We must not be myopically individualist, however, in our understanding of when we are wronged, and hence in our understanding of when forgiveness is a relevant possibility. I may be wronged not because I personally was attacked but because I am a relative of the one attacked, or a friend or associate.

Forgiving someone for the wrong he did one presupposes that one recognizes that he has wronged one; if one does not recognize that one has been wronged, then forgiving the one who wronged one is impossible. Forgiveness presupposes the moral judgment that one has been a victim of wrongdoing. Given that situation, forgiveness is then the foregoing of something or other. Forgiving is not forgetting that one has been wronged, nor is it forgetting who it was that wronged one. Forgiveness is not putting out of mind the moral judgment that one made. Forgiveness is foregoing, not forgetting.

What is it that one foregoes when one forgives? I suggest that there are two main components to the foregoing that constitutes forgiveness. In the first place, one foregoes the negative feelings one has toward the malefactor on account of his having wronged one, especially one's feeling of anger. The natural response to the recognition that someone has wronged one is anger at him for what he did to one. Forgiveness is the relinquishing of that feeling – not the relinquishing of the moral judgment that he has wronged one, but the relinquishing of one's anger at him for having done so. Usually this takes time. Forgiveness, in general, is not an event but a process.

The second component of forgiveness, so I suggest, is the foregoing of retributive punishment. Some reflection on the rationale for punishment is required if we are to see how and why this is so. It is widely held – correctly, I think – that the various rationales that have been offered for punishment reduce to four. Three of these appeal to life-goods that punishment is thought capable of achieving. Punishment can be a deterrent to wrongdoing, punishment of certain sorts can protect society from hardened criminals, and punishment of certain sorts can reform the wrongdoer. The fourth rationale, retribution, is different from these in that it makes no reference to goods that punishment is thought capable of bringing about, be it in the life of the malefactor or in the lives of members of society.

The thought behind the retributive rationale for punishment is that punishment of the right sort evens things up. Forget about life-goods that punishment might bring about. Someone has imposed an evil on me; what this calls for is that things be evened up between us by the imposition of a comparable evil on him. If part of the thought behind the formula "An eye for an eye and a tooth for a tooth" was *no more* than an eye for an eye and *no more* than a tooth for a tooth, then the formula reflects the transition from the old vengeance system, with its uncontrolled cycle of revenge and getting even, to a system of punishment based on retribution. Jesus treats such a system as the negative side of the reciprocity code.

Jesus tells his followers that they are to reject the negative side of the reciprocity code. Instead of evening things up by imposing on the wrongdoer an evil equal to the evil that he imposed on me, I am to seek his good; I am to love even my enemies. Jesus, it seems clear, is instructing his followers to reject retributive punishment. Instead of paying evil with evil, they are to seek the good of the wrongdoer.

The question remains whether rejection of retributive punishment is an intrinsic component of forgiveness, as I have suggested, or whether it is something that Jesus instructs his followers to do in addition to forgiving the wrongdoer. Is it possible to forgive someone who has wronged one – genuinely and fully forgive him – while at the same time seeing to it that he is punished so as to even things up? Does the foregoing of retributive punishment go beyond what is essential to forgiveness?

To answer this question, we must take note of a puzzle that has been looming over our discussion for some time now. How is it possible to overcome my negative feelings toward the person who wronged me without putting out of mind my negative judgment about what he did to me? The wronging of me was not an event without a subject. It was an act; and the subject of the act was that person. The wronging did not just happen; *he* did it. So how can I possibly overcome my negative feelings toward him without eradicating my negative judgment concerning what he did? How can I forgive the sinner without forgetting the sin?

The ancient Stoics held that as long as one believes that someone has deprived one of a true good, it is impossible not to be angry with that person. Yet they also held that we should aim at eliminating anger from our lives, and negative feelings in general. Emotional tranquility is to be our goal. Their solution was that we must alter our ordinary judgments as to what is truly good and bad for a person. The only true good in a person's life is virtuous action on his or her part; and it is entirely up to oneself whether one does or does not act virtuously in a certain situation. When a husband abuses his wife, it remains up to her whether she will act virtuously in this difficult situation; he can neither make her act virtuously nor make her act "viciously." In abusing her as he did, he did not deprive her of any genuine life-good. Hence she has no cause for anger. Or if she does have cause for anger, it will be anger at herself for not acting virtuously in this situation. Naturally she prefers that he not abuse her; she may take steps to stop him from doing so. But any anger she may feel toward him is a sign that she has mistaken the merely preferable situation of not being abused for a genuine good.

Jesus was not a Stoic. Being abused by one's spouse is a genuine evil in one's life; to be abused is to be wronged. Yet Jesus urges forgiveness – not forgetting but forgiveness. And forgiveness includes overcoming one's anger. How is that possible?

I suggest that forgiveness – overcoming one's anger at the doer while continuing to condemn the deed – is possible only if one believes that there was then, or that there is now, a space, a distance, between the doer and the deed. He did not know what he was doing. Or he did know but could not help himself, so that he's not accountable for what he did. Or though he was accountable for what he did, he has now repented of his misdeed; he is now a different person, in the relevant way, from the person who performed that misdeed. This is the significance of Jesus's references to repentance. The person who repents of what he did has dissociated himself from the one who performed that misdeed, put a space between them. Hence it is possible for me not to hold it against him even though I do not dismiss bygones as bygones.[7]

A persistent topic of discussion in the literature on forgiveness is whether we should forgive even those who show no sign of repentance. The discussion assumes that it is possible to forgive an impenitent agent who was fully accountable for what he did. I judge that assumption to be mistaken. If a central component of forgiveness is overcoming one's anger at the wrongdoer while not forgetting the wrong done, then forgiveness is impossible if the agent was fully accountable in the first place and now in no way distances himself from the deed done.

Let us now return to the question posed but not yet answered. Is foregoing retributive punishment an intrinsic component of forgiveness, or is it something that Jesus enjoins on his followers in addition to forgiveness? Well, suppose that I have overcome my anger at the person who wronged me without forgetting that he did indeed wrong me. This is possible, I have

---

[7] The idea that true forgiveness requires a "space" between the person and the deed is thoroughly developed by Jean Hampton in her contribution to Jeffrie G. Murphy and Jean Hampton, *Forgiveness and Mercy* (Cambridge: Cambridge University Press, 1988).

argued, because I no longer hold the deed against him. But if I no longer hold the deed against him, then evening things up between us by imposing on him an evil comparable to the evil he imposed on me is no longer relevant. Foregoing retributive punishment of the one who wronged one is an essential component of forgiveness.

My argument, that the foregoing of retributive punishment is intrinsic to forgiveness, must not cause us to lose sight of the fact that Jesus enjoins his followers to forego retributive punishment even when the wrongdoer is unrepentant and forgiveness is consequently impossible. I am to foreswear the reciprocity code even in my engagement with my enemy. Jesus does not say that I am to forgive my enemy; he does say that I am to seek his good. The enemy is unrepentant of the wrong he did me; hence he remains my enemy. So I remain angry at him. Given that he is unrepentant, there is not sufficient distance between his deed and his present self for me to make the overcoming of my anger possible. I could overcome my anger only if I forgot what he did to me – and forgetting is not forgiving. Yet I am to seek his good – to love him. Obviously this is a difficult path to tread: seeking the well-being of someone with whom one is angry. Jesus instructs his followers to tread that difficult path.

V

Does forgiveness require foregoing nonretributive as well as retributive punishment of the wrongdoer? Well, if it is possible for me to overcome my anger toward the wrongdoer because he has repented of what he did, then punishment aimed at making him penitent is irrelevant; that reform has already taken place. No need for a penitentiary. But the assumption behind the reform-rationale for punishment is that an act of wrongdoing is typically not a one-off deed but the manifestation of a character flaw that can be expected to yield other acts of wrongdoing of roughly the same sort. And a person might genuinely repent of what he did to me while yet possessing the character flaw that led him to do it. In that situation, I might judge that even though I have forgiven him, punishment of the right sort would be for his own good.

The same sort of thing is to be said concerning punishment whose rationale is the protection of society. Suppose I am no longer angry with the person who wronged me, because I judge that he has genuinely repented of what he did; I may nonetheless believe that what he did was the manifestation of a serious character flaw, and that unless he is reformed he is likely to do the same sort of thing again. I may then recommend that he be punished in such a way as to secure the good of protecting society – until such time as he has been reformed and is no longer a social menace.

Lastly, if one believes that a system of punishment secures the social good of deterrence, one might forgive a penitent wrongdoer while at the same time recommending that the rules of the system be applied to him.

I conclude that though forgiveness is incompatible with retributive punishment, it is not incompatible in principle with punishment aimed at securing the good of reform, the good of protecting society, or the good of deterrence. Of course, when deciding whether or not the wrongdoer whom one has forgiven should be subjected to some sort of punishment, one cannot remain at the level of what is true in principle. One has to assess whether or not the proposed punishment is in fact likely to reform the wrongdoer, whether or not it is in fact likely to protect society from the wrongdoer as long as he is not reformed, and whether or not it is in fact likely to deter others from similar wrongdoing. Punishment as applied in present-day American society all too often fails these tests or, conversely, continues long after the goods have been achieved.

VI

In Luke, Jesus says that "if another disciple sins, . . . and if there is repentance, you must forgive" (17:3). What is the force of the "must" in this injunction? Is Jesus saying that I have an obligation toward the repentant brother who has wronged me to forgive him? If I did have such an obligation toward him, he would have a correlative right against me to my forgiving him. Were I not to forgive him, I would then wrong him. Is that what Jesus is saying? Does God have an obligation toward the penitent person who has wronged him to forgive him, and does that person have a correlative right against God to God's forgiving him? Is forgiveness of the repentant wrongdoer by the one who has been wronged a matter of justice? When God forgives, is it God's justice or God's mercy that is to be praised?

Without now citing passages in support of the point, I think it abundantly clear that in the moral vision of Christian scripture, the wrongdoer never has a right against his victim to be forgiven by the victim, not even if he repents for what he did. Justice to the wrongdoer does not require that the penitent wrongdoer be forgiven; forgiveness goes beyond what justice to the wrongdoer requires. Forgiveness is generosity, mercy.

But if the victim has no moral obligation toward the wrongdoer to forgive him, then nonforgiveness is morally permitted with respect to the wrongdoer. In general, if one is not obligated not to do something, then one is permitted to do it. On account of having been wronged, I now have certain permission-rights with respect to the wrongdoer: I am within my rights in being angry with him and in insisting on retributive punishment. Forgiveness consists of foregoing the exercise of those rights.

More important is the opposite side of what Jesus was saying: retributive punishment is not required – permitted but not required. One of the most deeply entrenched components in the moral code of human beings, both ancient and modern, is that wrongdoing must be punished lest the moral order be upset.[8] Jesus rejects the assumption. Though retributive punishment is permitted, it is not in general required. A good deal of traditional Christian theology has failed to absorb what Jesus taught and implied on this point. And if the various goods that punishment of the wrongdoer are thought to achieve have already been achieved, or if there is no obligation to achieve them, then no punishment of any sort is morally required.[9]

So what, then, did Jesus mean when he said to his disciples that they *must* forgive the brother or sister who has wronged them and is repentant? There are two possibilities; on this occasion I will not choose between them. One possibility is that Jesus is setting before them a better way to go, a way that goes beyond what duty and justice require, a way in tune with the ways of our Father in heaven, the way of supererogatory love. The other possibility is that he is declaring that they have an obligation toward Jesus and our Father in heaven to forgive the repentant wrongdoer. This would be a so-called third-party duty; they have a duty *toward* Jesus and the Father *with respect to* their fellows to forgive them. Correlative to this third-party duty would be a third-party right: Jesus and the Father have a right against them with respect to their fellows, to forgive their fellows. If they do not forgive the brother who has wronged them and is repentant, they wrong not the brother but Jesus and the Father.

VII

Let me now turn to Hannah Arendt's claim that "[t]he discoverer of the role of forgiveness in the realm of human affairs was Jesus of Nazareth." I do not

---

[8] Describing the tradition of Greek antiquity, Martha Nussbaum says that human life was seen as something "that can be invaded, wounded, or violated by another's act in many ways. For this penetration, the only remedy that seems appropriate is a counterinvasion. . . . And to right the balance truly, the retribution must be strictly proportional to the original encroachment." "Equity and Mercy," *Philosophy and Public Affairs* 22, no. 2 (1993), 89.

[9] In my essay "Does Forgiveness Undermine Justice?" (in *God and the Ethics of Belief*, eds. Andrew Dole and Andrew Chignell [Cambridge: Cambridge University Press, 2005]), I discuss the claim, made by Kant among others, that failure to punish the wrongdoer is immoral.

interpret Arendt as meaning to deny that one may occasionally find positive references to forgiveness in the writers of pagan antiquity; what she means to say is that forgiveness plays no systematic role in their moral thought. I think she is right about that.

This is not the place for a comprehensive survey of what the writers of pagan antiquity had to say about forgiveness, nor am I competent to offer such a survey. Let me instead look at what two representative figures said, Aristotle and Seneca – Aristotle as a representative of the Peripatetic school of ancient eudaemonism, Seneca as a representative of the Stoic school.

In Book IV, section 5, of the *Nicomachean Ethics*, Aristotle discusses the ethics of anger. Following his usual strategy of explaining a virtue by locating it at the midpoint between extremes, he declares that "good temper is a mean with respect to anger" (1125b 27). "Good temper," he says, is his own term for the virtue in question. In ordinary speech "the middle state [is] unnamed," as are the extreme states – though "the excess might be called a sort of irascibility" (1125b 28–30).

Aristotle then goes on to say that the good-tempered man is "the man who is angry at the right things and with the right people, and further, as he ought, when he ought, and as long as he ought" (1125b 31–32).

> For the good-tempered man tends to be unperturbed and not to be led by passion, but to be angry in the right manner, at the things, and for the length of time, that reason dictates; but he is thought to err rather in the direction of deficiency; for the good-tempered man is not revengeful, but rather tends to forgive.
>
> The deficiency, whether it is a sort of inirascibility or whatever it is, is blamed. For those who are not angry at the things they should be are thought to be fools, and so are those who are not angry in the right way, at the right time, or with the right persons; for such a man is thought not to feel things nor to be pained by them, and, since he does not get angry, he is thought unlikely to defend himself; and to endure being insulted and to put up with insults to one's friends is slavish (1125b 33–1126a 8).

Anger at the person who has harmed one is a good thing, provided it be of the right duration, intensity, and so on; not to feel such anger would be "slavish." Aristotle offers no hint whatsoever of conditions under which it would be good to work toward overcoming such anger. He does say that the good-tempered man "tends to forgive." But this tendency in the good-tempered man is described as something to be blamed. Good-tempered people have a regrettable tendency to get less angry than they should.[10] And Aristotle

---

[10] Aristotle speaks in a rather similar way about our tendency to forgive in *Nicomachean Ethics* VII, 6; 1149b 4–6.

says nothing about foregoing retributive punishment. That was no accident. To forego retributive punishment would be an act of injustice. That is the clear implication of his account of retributive punishment and its relation to justice in Book V of the *Nicomachean Ethics*.

In a transaction in which one party "is in the wrong and the other is being wronged, and . . . one inflicted injury and the other has received it," injustice has the character of an "inequality." So "the judge tries to equalize it; for in the case . . . in which one has received and the other has inflicted a wound, or one has slain and the other been slain, the suffering and the action have been unequally distributed; but the judge tries to equalize things by means of the penalty, taking away from the gain of the assailant" (1132a 4–10). Retributive justice consists of this equalizing of gains and losses; to forego it would be unjust.

VIII

The likeliest place to find an affirmation of "the role of forgiveness in the realm of human affairs" by a writer of pagan antiquity would be Seneca's *On Mercy* (*De Clementia*). In fact it's not there. The reason it's not there is not that Seneca overlooked it but that forgiveness is impossible within a Stoic framework.

In the first place, foregoing retributive punishment has no place in a Stoic framework. Seneca says a good deal about punishment in both *On Mercy* and *On Anger* (*De Ira*); in both texts it is clear that he thinks about it exclusively in terms of the natural goods (preferables) to be secured, not in terms of evening things up by repaying evil for evil. The reason is clear. If virtuous action is the only true good in one's life, and if acting virtuously is entirely up to oneself, then no one can inflict any true evil on me, nor can I inflict any true evil on anyone else. The concept of retribution simply lacks application in a Stoic framework, and so, of course, foregoing it lacks application.

Could Seneca and the other Stoics have thought of retributive punishment in terms of returning one dispreferable for another, rather than in terms of returning evil for evil? Possibly. But it's hard to see what rationale a Stoic could give for thinking along these lines. And in fact, as I mentioned earlier, Seneca thinks of punishment exclusively in terms of the natural goods, the preferables, to be achieved by punishment.

Overcoming one's rightful anger likewise has no place within a Stoic framework. If no one other than myself can inflict any true evil on me, then there is nothing for me to get angry about in how I am treated by others. If I do get angry with someone other than myself, that is an indication that I have mistakenly judged that he inflicted an evil on me – when at most he did something to me that I would prefer he not have done. The thing to say to the person who is angry at someone is not that he should stand ready to forgive the one who wronged him but that he should correct his mistaken judgment that he has been wronged.

De Clementia was addressed by Seneca to the young Nero. Book I, which is most of what we have, consists of a multifaceted argument, with many examples, for the conclusion that clemency in punishment by a ruler yields all sorts of natural goods (preferables) in society. In the fragment of Book II that we have, Seneca tells us what clemency is.

Clemency is mildness in the imposition of the punishment that is due a person. When a range of punishment is specified for misdeeds of a certain sort in a legal or quasi-legal system, from more lenient to more harsh, clemency consists of choosing the more lenient. "The following definition will meet with objections," says Seneca, although it comes very close to the truth. We might speak of mercy [clemency] as "moderation that remits something of a deserved and due punishment." The cry will go up that no virtue ever gives any one less than his due. But everyone realizes that mercy is something which "stops short of what could deservedly be imposed."[11]

Clemency possesses what Seneca calls "freedom of decision." "It judges not by legal formula, but by what is equitable and good. It can acquit or set the damages as high as it wishes. All these things it does with the idea not of doing something less than what is just but that what it decides should be the justest possible." Clemency is thus what the Greeks called *epiekeia*, usually translated as "equity," and explained by Aristotle as follows:

> The equitable is just, but not the legally just but a correction of legal justice. The reason is that all law is universal but about some things it is not possible to make a universal statement which will be correct. In those cases, then, in which it is necessary to speak universally, but not possible to do so correctly, the law takes the usual case.... When the law speaks universally, then, and a case arises on it which is not covered by the universal statement, then it is right ... to correct the omission.... Hence the equitable is just.... And this is the nature of the equitable, a correction of law where it is defective owing to its universality....
>
> It is also clear from this what sort of person the equitable person is. For a person who chooses and does such things, and who is not zealous for strict

---

[11] Seneca, *On Mercy*, II. 3, in *Seneca: Moral and Political Essays*, eds. and trans. John M. Cooper and J. F. Procopé (Cambridge: Cambridge Press, 2003), 160.

judgment in the direction of the worse, but is inclined to mitigation, even though he can invoke the law on his side – such a person is equitable and this trait of character is equity, being a kind of justice and not a distinct trait of character (*Nicomachean Ethics* 1137b34–1138a3).[12]

Aristotle describes equity as attending to the full particulars of the case and then correcting the applicable law so as to achieve justice in this particular case; Seneca describes clemency as attending to the full particulars of the case and then choosing the milder of the punishments that the law permits so as to achieve justice in this particular case. I dare say that Aristotle would want to include what Seneca describes as clemency under his concept of equity, and that Seneca would want to include what Aristotle describes as equity under his concept of clemency.[13]

To elucidate his concept, Seneca offers the following examples.

In one case, [the clement person] may simply administer a verbal admonition without any punishment, seeing the man to be at an age still capable of correction. In another, where the man is patently labouring under an invidious accusation, he will order him to go scot-free, since he may have been misled or under the influence of alcohol. Enemies he will release unharmed, sometimes even commended, if they had an honourable reason – loyalty, a treaty, their freedom – to drive them to war. All these are works of mercy [clemency] (II.7; p. 164).

Seneca is at pains to emphasize that clemency is neither forgiveness nor pardon. "Forgiveness... is failing to punish what in your judgment should be punished, while pardon is the remission of a penalty that is due" (II, 7; p. 164). "The wise man does nothing that he ought not to do and omits nothing that he ought to do. So he will not excuse a punishment which he ought to exact" (ibid.). He may "do the same as he would if he forgave them – but without forgiving, since to forgive is to confess that one has left undone something which ought to have been done" (ibid.).

Seneca is likewise emphatic in saying that clemency is based on moral reasoning concerning what is the most just punishment, not on pity. Pity is

---

[12] The translation of the last paragraph of this passage is from Nussbaum, "Equity and Mercy," 92.

[13] An implication of Seneca's discussion that he does not take note of is that making punishment just by fitting it to the particulars of the case will prove to be leniency in punishment. Nussbaum, in "Equity and Mercy," has an interesting discussion of why in fact this will usually prove to be the case. Another implication of Seneca's discussion is that the natural social goods that ensue from the more lenient punishment is a factor in making it the most just punishment; Seneca also does not take note of this implication.

a vice, not a virtue, something that all good men will avoid. "The fault of a petty mind succumbing to the sight of evils that affect others...is a feature very familiar in the worst kind of person. There are women, senile or silly, so affected by the tears of the nastiest criminals that, if they could, they would break open the prison. Pity looks at the plight, not at the cause of it. Mercy [clemency] joins in with reason" (II, 7; p. 161).

I take it as obvious that in praising clemency as he does, Seneca is not praising forgiveness. Of course we cannot draw this conclusion from Seneca's insistence that clemency is not forgiveness, since Seneca's concept of forgiveness is different from that which I have articulated. But being lenient in punishment, so as to achieve the punishment that is just because it takes account of all the particulars of the case, is clearly not the same thing as overcoming one's anger at the person who wronged one, upon his repentance, and consequently foregoing his retributive punishment.

IX

I quoted Hannah Arendt as saying that forgiveness is the remedy for the irreversibility of human action. It is "the possible redemption from the predicament of irreversibility," for it "serves to undo the deeds of the past." I then observed that when Arendt says that forgiveness serves to undo the deeds of the past, she cannot intend her words to be taken literally and strictly, since she herself says that we are unable to undo what we have done. But what then is forgiveness the remedy for? What does it redeem us from? What is deficient about a moral culture that does not affirm the importance of forgiveness? What is the point of forgiveness? I have argued that Jesus's injunctions to forgive were a component within his more comprehensive ethic of love. To love the neighbor is to care about her, to seek her well-being, and to honor her worth. How does forgiveness fit into this? What is the good that forgiveness achieves?

Forgiveness opens up the possibility of reconciliation with the one who has wronged one; reconciliation is the *telos* of forgiveness. Forgiveness achieves other goods as well – the good of getting rid of one's festering anger, for example. But forgetting that one was wronged also achieves that good. And sometimes forgetting is the best we can do. If there is no sign of distance between the deed done and its doer, then the only way to get rid of one's anger is to forget what was done. But forgetting does not open up the possibility of reconciliation. That is the unique office of reconciliation.

Retributive punishment has been visited on the wrongdoer; things have been evened up between us. But if that is the end of the matter, then I still hold it against him that he wronged me, and if I still hold this against him, we cannot be reconciled. We may get on with things, but we are not reconciled. Pagan antiquity never faced up to this deficiency in punishment. With his message of forgiveness, Jesus did.

Jesus Christ and the Meaning of Life

Charles Taliaferro

What is the meaning of life? In the West, this question was considered profound and important in the 1960s through the 1970s in the heyday of exis-
tentialism and the popular quest to shape or define one's personal identity
outside of conventional categories. Many philosophers subsequently backed
away from the question on the grounds that it made no sense: it may be
proper to ask questions about the meaning or purpose behind different
individual projects, some argued, but to ask about the meaning *of* life is
to commit a category mistake or to assume some discredited philosophy
according to which life itself was created to serve a great purpose. Some
philosophers revel in there being no meaning or further purpose of life.
For example, in *The Meaning of Life*, Terry Eagleton recommends we see
meaning in an understanding of personal interaction modeled after a jazz
ensemble, making music simply for its own sake and not for any other
purpose.

> What we need is a form of life that is completely pointless, just as the jazz
> performance is pointless. Rather than serve some utilitarian purpose or
> earnest metaphysical end, it is a delight in itself. It needs no justification
> beyond its own existence. In this sense the meaning of life is interestingly
> close to meaninglessness.[1]

In this essay I shall argue that the meaning of our delight or sorrow in
life depends very much on the truth of some "earnest metaphysical end" or
framework. First, I hope to show that the question (what is the meaning of
life?) is altogether sensible, and then to consider how Christian belief and the
person of Christ may impact how such a question should be answered.

[1] Terry Eagleton, *The Meaning of Life* (Oxford: Oxford University Press, 2007), 174.

QUESTIONING LIFE'S MEANING

A question about the meaning of something calls for different types of answers. If you see some dark clouds and are asked, "What does that mean?" you are probably quite right in offering a blend of meteorology and advice ("We better find shelter before the storm comes"). And if you say, "Let's meet at the bank," and are asked what you meant, you are probably being asked to disambiguate your sentence (is the meeting at a river bank or a financial institution?). A question about the meaning of life itself is more like the first question than the second. In ordinary, informal terms I suggest that "What is the meaning of life?" is best understood as questions like "What is happening?" "What is the significance of what is happening?" and "What should we do about it?" when these questions are articulated in very broad terms about the roles of human life (and other life forms) in general. The history of philosophy may plausibly be understood as an effort to answer such questions.

Consider three different responses to the question "What is the meaning of life?": Christianity, Theravada Buddhism, and secular naturalism. How would the truth or falsehood of these worldviews impact life's meaning?

If Christianity is true, then "what is happening" is that we, and the cosmos as a whole, are continuously conserved in existence by an all-good, omnipotent, omniscient God.[2] Moreover, this purposive divine reality has been revealed in human history as both just and merciful. According to this revelation, God is not indifferent to cosmic evils and goods, but is affectively responsive to these values, sorrowing over evil and taking pleasure in good. If this revelation is veridical (as understood in accord with the church's ecumenical councils), then Jesus Christ is both God and man, offering redemption and healing creation. Our ultimate fulfillment, on the Christian view, lies in good, fruitful relations with fellow creatures and in relationship (union) with God. In this framework, *the meaning or significance of one's life rests partly with respect to one's relationships with creation and the Creator and Redeemer of creation.*

---

[2] The version of Christian theism I am addressing is articulated in my *Consciousness and the Mind of God* (Cambridge: Cambridge University Press, 1994). Although contemporary self-described Christian theists may differ on some divine attributes (the scope of omniscience, divine simplicity, eternity, etc.), most hold that God is (in some sense) the creator and conserver of the cosmos, omnipotent, omniscient, all good, free, incorporeal, everlasting, and necessarily or essentially existing. I am employing a theistic philosophy, of special relevance to the next section of this chapter, according to which God is passable. On this view, God is affectively responsive to the values of creation. This view is opposed to traditional impassabalism. See my "The Passability of God," *Religious Studies* 25 (1989), 217–24.

Consider now an alternative state of affairs in which Christian theism is false and secular naturalism is true. There are many forms of secular naturalism. For present purposes let us engage a broad naturalist framework according to which there is no God, no afterlife, but human beings are believed to be conscious, sentient agents who possess some freedom and values. Although contemporary secular naturalists, Christian theists, as well as Theravada Buddhists agree on many things – from the atomic theory of matter to the importance of the Golden Rule – they differ radically on some key points. So, imagine that secular naturalism is true. What does that mean for practicing Christians? It means that when Christians believe they are praising, petitioning, or experiencing God, no such thing is actually occurring. Instead, Christians are praising what they (wrongly) project or envisage as God; they are (vainly) petitioning what turns out to be a bare idea of God, and they are not actually having a direct or mediated awareness of a loving transcendent reality, but only of some surrogate (e.g., the love of humane companionship). I suggest that the meaning of Christian theistic practice would in fact be different if secular naturalism were true.

How might the truth of Theravada Buddhism impact the meaning of the lives of secular naturalists or Christians? Because Theravada Buddhism is either atheistic or unconcerned with the issue of God, secular naturalists will not be wrong in their rejection of theism, and insofar as Christians truly extol a life of selfless compassion, they too will share some valued practices with their Buddhist friends. But if the Christian and secular naturalist believe that the self is a substantial individual, existing identically as the same being over time, both are courting an illusion, and insofar as the Christian and the naturalist believe that it is good to nurture the desires of their substantial selves, both are engaged in a harmful practice that will leave them, in the end, trapped in a world of rebirth, and thus re-death.

I propose that the truth or falsehood of any of these three major worldviews directly impact the meaning of virtually all our actions, desires, emotions, and so on. Take any trivial event, such as a birthday party or giving a stranger directions to a hotel. The Christians will see these (*ceterus paribus*) as interactions with persons who are made in the image of God. The first event may be an occasion to be grateful to the Creator; the second would be an example of *caritas*, a charity that is a faint reflection of the love that made the cosmos. The Theravada Buddhist and naturalist will not see such divine signification. For the naturalist, the party may be an occasion for a thoroughly stratifying humane exchange of earthly (i.e., nonsacramental) love, and giving directions may be seen as honorable, civic humanism. Some naturalists might even link such kind treatment of strangers to pre-Christian Homeric roots in which hospitality (*xania*) is a key virtue. The Theravada Buddhist will not see birth as the beginning of a radical substantial individual who will exist for a time and then perish at earthly death. Instead, the self is a cluster of impermanent components with sufficient continuity to establish self-reference but not in the fashion that is (from a Buddhist point of view) wrongly desired by some Christians and naturalists; thus the significance of the birthday party is radically altered. Buddhists might see the kind treatment of a stranger as a matter of compassion and merit, but in no way linked to Christian *caritas* or Homeric, pagan hospitality.

I submit that insofar as Christianity, naturalism, and Theravada Buddhism are conceivable, intelligible worldviews, we seem to have ample ways of articulating how each would impact the meaning of life. Consider two objections before taking a closer look at Christianity and then Jesus in light of the meaning of life. These objections have been influential in turning some philosophers away from meaning-of-life questions, but I suggest they are unpersuasive.

The Skeptical Objection: What if we do not know whether any of these three worldviews or any other one is correct? What if our best arguments leave us in a state of deep agnosticism about the truth of theism, naturalism, Buddhism, and so on?

If Christianity or Buddhism or certain other worldviews are correct, then agnosticism will not be perpetual. There will come a time when you will know or have justified true beliefs involving reliable modes of reasoning that God or karma and so on exist. But there is nothing about some worldviews, such as naturalism, that guarantees we will avoid skepticism. If in fact we are not in a position to know the truth (or have a reasonable belief about the truth) of these overriding metaphysical worldviews, then we will lack knowledge or reasonable belief about the meaning of our lives. That does not mean our lives lack meaning; it means we simply do not know what that meaning amounts to. This predicament is no stranger than any action wherein you lack an ability to verify how it is interpreted. Imagine you are a professor and you provide what certainly seems to you to be a brilliant lecture to a full classroom. Did you accomplish some good teaching? You may never know. Presumably, in order for there to be teaching, there has to be some learning stemming from your presentation (the source is pivotal, for students may learn things from you – such as *philosophy is less practical than engineering* – that you did not actually teach). You may know some things (that there was an effort to teach) without knowing the full story. Arguably, highly skeptical practicing theists like Louis Pojman prayed and worshiped without *knowing* whether they were actually praying to or worshiping God. Pojman famously defended the thesis that in the religious life it suffices simply to hope for the truth of religious beliefs.[3] For him, then, the full meaning of his acts was not knowable during his lifetime. If skepticism or agnosticism is vindicated, then we may never know the full meaning of life, but that does not mean that there is no meaning.

The Internalist Objection: Arguably, the way the meaning-of-life question gets adjudicated between the three great worldviews overlooks the fact that, most fundamentally, what constitutes the meaning of someone's life is his or her own beliefs, desires, and values. So, imagine you repudiate grand metaphysical schemes (religious and secular) but have a loving family, fulfilling career, and so on. Why think the meaning of you life depends on the truth of some theoretical framework? More radically, some philosophers have contended that the meaning of one's life depends crucially on what one cares about. On this view, if you cared about nothing at all, your life would be without meaning.[4]

In reply, I agree that the presence or absence of one's interior, subjective states – one's intentions, desires, wishes – all need to come into play in a comprehensive understanding of the meaning of one's life. But I suggest it is profoundly implausible to think that the whole story can be settled with only such interior references, without taking on board the truth of a person's beliefs, the fittingness of his or her intentions, and so on in light of a broader understanding of reality.

Imagine a person with no cares at all, but who was brought to such a state because of trauma caused by battle fatigue. Given this scenario, I think it would be more reasonable (*ceterus paribus*) to see this person as a casualty – certainly a meaningful category – rather than as someone who lacks meaning. As for the contented person who has no concern for "the big picture," it is also unreasonable to think that the big picture has a little or no bearing on the meaning of his or her life in matters both great and small. Imagine Christianity is true. This means that (in terms of momentous events) the death of loved ones is not their annihilation and (in terms of small events) even modest courtesies between persons are a reflection of divine love insofar as the God of all creation has made us for loving relationships. It is vital to note, in this thought experiment, that part of the meaning of *that* person's life would have to include *indifference to the meaning of events beyond his or her immediate domain*. Additionally, it remains true that someone being uninterested in X

---

[3] See Louis Pojman, "Faith Without Belief?" *Faith and Philosophy* 3 (1986), 157–76.
[4] See Harry Frankfurt, *The Reasons of Love* (Princeton: Princeton University Press, 2004).

(whatever it may be) does not suffice to show that X is uninteresting.[5] It may not interest our internalist whether Theravada Buddhism is true, but if it is true, he is headed for rebirth, whether or not he finds the topic boring.

THE MEANING OF CHRISTIAN LIFE

If it turns out that classical Christianity is true, then there are at least two dimensions of meaning that have a bearing on our lives: an expansion or magnification of ordinary values and the introduction of what may be called extraordinary values.

In the first paragraph of this chapter, I cited Terry Eagleton's remark that life should be seen as pointless, in the way that we see a jazz ensemble as pointless. Consider again his comment and his further observation about religious views of meaning:

> What we need is a form of life that is completely pointless, just as the jazz performance is pointless. Rather than serve some utilitarian purpose or earnest metaphysical end, it is a delight in itself. It needs no justification beyond its own existence. In this sense the meaning of life is interestingly close to meaninglessness. Religious believers who find this version of the meaning of life a little too laid-back for comfort should remind themselves that God, too, is his own end, ground, origin, reason, and self-delight, and that only by living this way can human beings be said to share in his life. Believers sometimes speak as though a key difference between themselves and non-believers is that for them, the meaning and purpose of life lie outside it. But this is not quite true even for believers. For classical theology, God transcends the world, but figures as a depth within it. As Wittgenstein remarks somewhere: if there is such a thing as eternal life, it must be here and now. It is the present moment that is an image of eternity, not an infinite succession of such moments.[6]

Eagleton's point is correct that if one recognizes God's intrinsic value, rather than seeing God as meaningful only because he serves some further purpose,

---

[5] Similarly, just because someone finds X interesting, it does not follow that it is interesting in the sense that the person *should* have an interest in X. The view of meaning I am advancing in this chapter is realist in terms of values and metaphysics. That is, I hold that there is a fact of the matter whether something should (normatively) interest a subject whether or not the subject cares about matters or who has any care at all. I defend realism in several publications, e.g., *Contemporary Philosophy of Religion* (Oxford: Blackwell, 1998), chaps. 2 and 8.

[6] *The Meaning of Life*, 174–5. Incidentally, Wittgenstein's observation about eternal life may be found in the Gospel of John. The Jesus of the fourth Gospel in the here and now is plausibly understood as affirming eternal life as realized in this life and the next (Jn. 10:28). Where Wittgenstein may depart from the Jesus of the Johannine tradition is that he thinks of eternal life as only in one's earthly life.

then one should not complain when someone claims that some terrestrial form of life has intrinsic value and is not meaningful because it serves a further purpose. But what Eagleton refers to, and yet does not develop, is the way in which the truth of some religious beliefs (here my focus is on Christian theism) radically expands and deepens other creaturely goods. Given Christian theism, jazz performances are valuable in themselves and because they reflect the goodness of a Creator who made creatures for the sake of their goodness. This divine goodness (the goodness of God's creation as well as the good of God's delight in the goods of creation) is not so much "outside" the cosmos, but it is an expansive additional scope of goodness that is not available in, say, secular naturalism.

The first thesis, then, is that the truth of Christian theism magnifies the significance of created goods. The goods and thus the meaning of friendship, justice, and compassion have intrinsic value as well as the value of being intended by (and delighted in by) an all-good God. This is not to quantify meaning and to propose that theism offers, say, precisely double or triple the meaning that is acknowledged by naturalists. Metric scales of degrees are not always needed to secure claims of greater or lesser meaning. Winning a race may have greater meaning if it is done in front of proud parents rather than indifferent strangers, but there is no clear way to quantify such differences.

The expansion of meaning predicated on the truth of Christian theism supports a general magnification of values, both positively and negatively. So, if there is a God who is affectively responsive to the values of creation, the goods of creation are the subject of divine pleasure and the ills of divine sorrow. To put matters simply, the reality of a passabilist God entails there is more good and ill than there would otherwise be, partly because of the magnification of sorrow and delight.[7] Philosophers sometimes overlook this deepening of goods and ills because they set up a false dichotomy between theism and their favored, nontheistic alternative. In *What's It All About? Philosophy and the Meaning of Life*, Julian Baggini offers the following curious juxtaposition between "the humanist" and a person who looks for the "transcendental support" essentially found in theism:

> The humanist, who sees this life as providing the only available source of meaning, accepts all [of life's limitations], just as she accepts the claims of morality without transcendental support and the existence of mystery

---

[7] I defend this magnification of values, given theism, in *Contemporary Philosophy of Religion*. My underlying theory of values follows F. Brentanno, G. E. Moore, Roderick Chisholm, and others (including Augustine), who hold that taking pleasure in the good is itself good and that (*ceterus paribus*) it is good to feel sorrow over evil.

without seeing it as a placeholder for the divine. The transcendentalist, in contrast, wants what is of value in life to be underwritten by a high order. Love isn't good enough unless it is all-conquering and can triumph even over death. Morality is not morality if it is rooted only in human life. Mystery is intolerable if it merely reflects the limits of human understanding. The transcendentalist's desire for something more is understandable, but the humanist's refusal to succumb is, I believe, a sign of her ability to confront and accept the limits of human understanding and, ultimately, human existence.[8]

What seems misleading in this portrait is that Baggini casts the transcendental theist as disparaging natural goods such as love between persons, a morality that is rooted in human nature, and an appreciative humility over the limits of human cognition and aspirations. I suggest that theism deepens and intensifies the meaning or significance of such matters by claiming that although morality is indeed grounded in nature, both nature and morality are further grounded in a divine transcendental reality. Evil, then, is a violation of natural goods as well as sacrilege. This broader outlook may be clarified in contrast with secular naturalism. In his famous essay on suicide, David Hume remarked, "The life of man is of no greater importance to the universe than that of an oyster."[9] Perhaps a reasonable humane morality does not need a caring universe to have normative authority, but compare a Humean naturalist who holds that natural evils are necessary given all antecedent and contemporary events and the laws of nature, with a Christian theist who holds that such evil stems from free action that is *not* necessary and that stands in profound violation of the Creator.[10] In terms of meaning, the point is not that "the humanist" cannot have a meaningful ethics, but that, given theism, such an ethic has greater or wider meaning that extends within and transcends the world. Moving on to Baggini's other points, why shouldn't the theist hold that the love between persons is deeply valuable and would suffice to make life profoundly meaningful even if there is no higher order of love? What still needs to be appreciated is the magnification or intensification available if theism is true. The truth of theism would mean that the love you have for your beloved is something that need not end, but may instead participate in the

---

[8] Julian Baggini, *What's It All About? Philosophy and the Meaning of Life* (Oxford: Oxford University Press, 2004), 184.

[9] David Hume, "Of Suicide," in *David Hume; Writings on Religion*, ed. A. Flew (Chicago: Open Court, 2000), 44.

[10] Here I am assuming a libertarian account of agency. For a defense of theism and agency against naturalism, see S. Goetz and C. Taliaferro, *Naturalism* (Grand Rapids: Eerdmans, 2008).

Creator's eternal divine love. Without such a transcendent ground, human love suffices, but with transcendent love human love can be part of a deeper, more comprehensive love.

This magnification of values is worth emphasizing when confronting cases like Baggini's, in which there is a failure to appreciate how theism impacts the question of life's meaning. In *Meditations for the Humanists; Ethics for a Secular Age*, A. C. Grayling writes:

> A secular moralist would say: If love (in the sense of the Greek term *agape*: in Latin, *caritas*, hence "charity") is the reason for being moral, what relevance does the existence or non-existence of a deity have? Why can we not be prompted to the ethical life by our own charitable feelings? The existence of a god adds nothing to our moral situation, other than an invisible policeman who sees what we do (even in privacy and under cover of night), and a threat of post-mortem terrors if we misbehave. Such additions are hardly an enrichment of the moral life, since the underpinning they offer consists of fear and threats of punishment: which is exactly what, among other things, the moral life seeks to free us from.[11]

There are a host of assumptions to challenge here. A chief point to highlight in reply is that theists can (and virtually all do) insist that creaturely *caritas* suffices to be a bona fide good and that the goodness of charity does not in any way hang on whether there is punishment for the lack of charity. But Grayling's stress on the centrality of *caritas* raises the further question of what you and I would or should hope for if we do truly have love for other persons.

Let us assume (as Grayling does not) that the theistic worldview is a credible alternative to secular humanism and that it is possible, in this life and the next, to find redemption and healing of wrongs through the compassionate, creative power of God. Under these conditions, why would one treat the possibility of such value as irrelevant or hold that it "adds nothing to our moral situation"?

Imagine the veridical awareness of God's loving presence is no mere chimera, but that one may truly apprehend the profound care of God in Christ. Imagine further, what many testify to in religious experience, that the experience deepens the love and desire to heal world harms.[12] Grayling's description of what the meaning of life must amount to for theists is deeply at odds with the central tests and testimony of the tradition. Is the following

---

[11] *Meditations for the Humanist; Ethics for a Secular Age*, A. C. Grayling (Oxford: Oxford University Press, 2002), 101.

[12] See the constructive philosophical work on religious experience by R. Swinburne, W. Alston, J. Gellman, Caroline Franks, and W. Wainwright.

testimony of the fourteenth-century English mystic Julian of Norwich a plausible portrait of Julian longing to encounter an invisible policeman who sees
us always in order to threaten us with postmortem terrors?

> We ought to highly enjoy that God dwells in our souls; and even more so we
> ought to enjoy that our souls dwell in God. Our soul is made to be God's
> dwelling place, and it dwells in God who is the first and only Creator . . . .
> God is God and our nature is both created and part of God. For the almighty
> truth of the Trinity is our Father, since He made us and keeps us in Him. And
> the deep wisdom of the Trinity is our Mother, in whom we are enclosed. And
> the high goodness of the Trinity is our Lord, and in Him we are enclosed
> and He in us. We are enclosed in the Father, and we are enclosed in the Son,
> and we are enclosed in the Holy Ghost. And the Father is enclosed in us, the
> Son is enclosed in us, and the Holy Ghost is enclosed in us, all power, all
> wisdom, and all goodness, one God, and one Lord. And our faith is a virtue
> that arises from our nature, which our soul perceives by the power of the
> Holy Ghost. By faith all our other virtues come to us – for without it no man
> may receive them, for it is nothing more than a true understanding with
> genuine belief and trust of our being existing in God and He in us, although
> we cannot see it.[13]

I cite this at length, as this testimony to unity with God will bear on the
third section of this chapter. But I hope considering that this text here (as one
representative example among millions) suffices to point out that Grayling's
depiction of God as an invisible police officer is wide off the mark.[14] The
metaphor of an invisible policeman does not take us beyond thinking in terms
of the permissible and the forbidden, supervised freedom and incarceration,
whereas Julian articulates a vision of profound, expansive goodness both
within and transcending the world.

---

[13] Julian of Norwich, "Revelations of Divine Love," in *Medieval Women Writers*, ed. K. M.
Wilson (Athens: University of Georgia Press, 1984), 284–5.
[14] Though I do not at all disparage the key theistic tenet that God will indeed bring about a
fitting justice involving the exposure of evildoing. One more example of how the truth of
theism magnifies values may be helpful. I know of a mother who rescued her two children
from a car that had caught fire. The children survived without injury, but the mother suffered
permanent, deep scarring on both hands. Imagine this action on her part was done out of
selfless love and not due to any morally compromising factors, e.g., she did not light the
fire. Now imagine years later the children are in college and contemplating experimenting
with dangerous psychotropic drugs that could cause permanent brain damage. Clearly they
should not fall into temptation based on the merits of the case and on the grounds of self-
preservation. Granted all that, but the mother's loving sacrifice will naturally magnify these
other considerations. One of the children may well reason: my mother's love for me was
so deep, surely I should also have sufficient self-love not to endanger the very life that she
rescued.

Apart from the expansion or magnification of value and meaning, the truth of Christian theism also implies that there is a dimension of meaning available that would not be if Christianity were false. In part, this involves the meaning of acts and desires already referred to: given the truth of Christianity, prayer and adoration of God actually mean what religious believers contend: the actual praise and petition of the living God. Prayer, adoration, and similar values may be thought of as extraordinary, because they offer a more extensive distinct realm of value than offered by naturalism.

The truth of Christianity would also imply that God has offered in Christ an occasion for radical forgiveness and merciful restoration and redemption for wrongdoers. Apart from the benefit of such goods, this would also mean that the neglect or rejection of such mercy will loom large as a central feature of what someone's life is about. Consider an analogy: Imagine you grievously and wrongly harmed someone whom you cared about and eventually came to regret this, but you nevertheless remain unwilling to confess the wrong or do anything to bring about restitution or reconciliation. Imagine further that you never reach a resolution to achieve any kind of atonement with the person, and you end your life in despair. And yet, had you taken the time to confess and repent, the person you harmed would embrace you with a love that is so overwhelming that your life would have been healed (the toxic vices you cultivated would have been vanquished) and you would have experienced a profound joy in a restored relationship. Under these conditions where you do not seek reconciliation and end your life in despair, I suggest it would be plausible to claim that one of the things your life was about was a missed opportunity. This accords with a natural reading of Shakespeare's tragedies and comedies. *Othello* is about (among other things) a man who is bewitched by a "friend" to wrongly and unfairly suspect his wife of infidelity. The life of Othello is the life of a person who has a dangerous, imperfect love of a woman whom he is led to kill. What Othello missed was recognizing the deceptive motives of Iago, keeping faith with Desdemona, and restraining his passion for revenge. The meaning of his life amounts to both his vile action and also what he missed. Alternatively, *The Tempest* is about Prospero's restraint of his passion for revenge and the success of love between Miranda and Ferdinand, a rich opportunity taken. If these cases are credible descriptions of when a life can be about either rejecting or accepting a great good, then the truth of Christianity would imply that one's recognition and acceptance, rejection, or ignorance of one's relationship to God in Christ would have a bearing on what one's life is about. I am not taking a stand here over whether salvation itself rests on a recognition of, and an overt redemptive relationship with, Christ in this life. I am suggesting a more modest but still substantial point: if there is an extraordinary, unparalleled redemptive good to be found in a relationship with Christ, then it is plausible to think that either finding it or missing it is (in part) what one's life is about and, thus, part of the meaning of one's life.

JESUS CHRIST'S MEANING

The last section considered how the truth of Christianity would impact the meaning of one's life in two general ways. In this section, let us consider how the truth of Christianity can shape one's individual life in a corporate communion with the person of Jesus Christ.

New Testament and Christian tradition speaks of how individual followers of Christ are called to make up the Body of Christ (e.g., 1 Cor. 12:27). Augustine spoke of the church as acting out and displaying God's love in bodily terms. "What outward appearance, what form, what stature, and hands or feet has [divine] love? No one can say; and yet love has feet . . . (and) love has hands which give to the poor, love has eyes which give intelligence to him who is in need."[15] For New Testament authors, Augustine, and other church fathers, living in Christian community constitutes a coordinated faith and practice that functions as Christ's body in the world. The Christian community is not somehow metaphysically identical to the corporeal body of Jesus, but it is to be in the world in a way that reflects the mind of Jesus Christ. How might it be the case that an individual could come to be part of the Body of Christ, a process by which the meaning of one's life would come to be shaped by Christ's very identity?

I offer here a general account that would require refining depending on specific Christian traditions about the church, sacraments, the scriptures as the Word of God, and the office of priests, ministers, and so on. As a general account, I suggest that what it would involve for the meaning of your life to be composed, in large part, by being part of the Body of Christ would involve five elements: cognition, intentions, a rite, an affective identification, and deliberate acts of *caritas*. As this is advanced as a general overview rather than a detailed defense, I shall treat each of these elements succinctly.

(A) *Cognition*. While some Christian communities (such as my own, which is Anglican) allow for infants to be fully recognized as part of the Body of Christ, an account of an adult being such a member requires an at least modest grasp and acceptance of the basic elements of Christian theism. An utter failure to recognize that Christianity includes acknowledging the

---

[15] Augustine, *Homilies on the First Epistle General of St. John*, VII, 10.

existence of God or the belief in Jesus Christ as the author of salvation would seem to be a failure to recognize Christianity. Such a failure is portrayed in one of the more amusing passages in David Hume's *The Natural History of Religion*.

> A famous general, at that time in the Muscovite service, having come to Paris for the recovery of his wounds, brought along with him a young Turk, whom he had taken prisoner. Some of the doctors of the Sorbonne (who are altogether as positive as the dervishes of Constantinople) thinking it a pity, that the poor Turk should be damned for want of instruction, solicited Mustapha very hard to turn Christian, in this world, and paradise in the next. These allurements were too powerful to be resisted; and therefore, having been well instructed and catechized, he at last agreed to receive the sacraments of baptism and the Lord's supper. The priest, however, to make every thing sure and solid, still continued his instructions, and began the next day with the usual question, *How many Gods are there? None at all,* replies Benedict; for that was his new name. *How! None at all!* cries the priest. *To be sure,* said the honest proselyte. *You have told me all along that there is but one God: And yesterday I eat him.*[16]

I suggest that unless one grasped that taking the sacraments did not annihilate God, one has not grasped the fundamental teachings of Christianity.

Philosophers disagree over whether belief in Christian teaching is essential to be part of the Christian community and thus part of the Body of Christ. As noted earlier, Louis Pojman thought it would suffice simply to hope Christian teaching is true. Be that as it may, I think it plausible to contend that at least some awareness of Christian teaching is essential.

(B) *Intentions.* For adults, entry into the believing community must be intentional. Virtually all denominations today insist on this and regard incidents of compulsory conversions (e.g., the Spanish monarchs insisting that Jews convert or be exiled in the late fifteenth century) as horrifying aberrations, incompatible with the teaching and nonviolent life of Jesus. Involuntary or enforced entrance into the Body of Christ is plausibly interpreted as injuring that Body and violating its very structure of voluntary love.

(C) *A Rite.* Almost all self-described Christian communities recognize the rite of baptism as a process or means of entrance into the Body of Christ. In virtually all Christian denominations, the rite of baptism involves a coordination of physical action and intentions. The one doing the baptizing is to understand himself or herself as blessing a person with water in the name of

---

[16] Hume, *David Hume; Writings on Religion,* 155.

the Triune God, setting the one baptized apart as a member of the Body of Christ.[17]

(D) *An Affective Identification.* The New Testament and large tracts of Christian tradition call individual Christians to so identify with the community of believers as a whole that they displace narrow self-concern. In New Testament terms, functioning as the Body of Christ involves noncompetitive, collaborative sharing to care for fellow Christians and to reach out in hospitality to those in need (1 Cor. 12). This may be thought of as persons coming to have the minds or perspective of Christ. The passage cited earlier from the revelations of Julian of Norwich portrays in dramatic terms the ideal enfolding of a person's life into the higher life of God.

(E) *Deliberate Acts of* Caritas. The fifth element involves action. This is the central charge of Augustine, cited earlier. Christian denominations have disagreed historically on the relationship and importance of faith and works, but there is near unanimity that (*ceterus paribus*) faith that does not at least lead to or is accompanied by good works is sterile or incomplete.[18] Acting as part of the Body of Christ should lead to the cultivation of the acts of mercy enjoined by the Christ in his New Testament teaching.

Clearly, this is no more than a sketch of a philosophy of the meaning of life as part of the Body of Christ. The five elements that are involved would come into play upon leaving the Body of Christ. Such a departure can be affected by a loss of belief, a voluntary dissociation with the Christian community, the renunciation of one's baptism, the repudiation and withdrawal of coordinated sharing of activities, and the dissociation of any acts of charity as flowing from the mind of Christ. The important point to consider, whether in entering and composing or in leaving the Body of Christ, is that *the meaning of one's actions is substantial and structured.* It is quite different from the portrait of the meaning of life one gets in books like *What's It All About?* Baggini offers this portrait of a person of faith:

> If we merely trust that God has a purpose for each of us and that this purpose will prove satisfying for us, we are effectively saying, "I don't know what the purpose of life is and I'm not going to worry about it. I'm just going to leave it to God to make it known to me in its own good time." A person who

---

[17] I develop an account of Christian ritual in "Rites and Christian Philosophy," in *Ritual and Philosophy*, ed. Kevin Schilbrack (London: Routledge, 2005).

[18] The *ceterus paribus* caveat is included to allow for the integrity of religious faith for those who are otherwise severely damaged or impaired and thus not in a position to perform corporeal acts of mercy.

believes that has no greater understanding of the purpose of her life than an atheist who rejects the possibility that purpose can come from God.[19]

I am inclined to agree with Baggini that if a Christian theist were to say this, then he or she may be no better or worse than Baggini's atheist. But I am disinclined to think that a mature Christian would have no idea of the magnified and extraordinary value that comprise a meaningful life, nor realize that the calling to be part of the Body of Christ is an immediate call in the present rather than something to discover when God may someday make it known.

Although my aim in this third section is to offer a fuller picture of meaning than, say, we find with Baggini, I close by suggesting a further point linking the outline of being part of the Body of Christ with an outline of being Jesus Christ, in accord with traditional Christology.

The five components involved in a person's life coming to be caught up in the meaning of the life of Jesus Christ are themselves present in a traditional understanding of Christ's life as the God-man, the incarnation of God as a human being. Traditionally, the incarnation is thought of as the second person of the Trinity assuming severe limitations of cognition; it was voluntary; Christ submitted to baptism; Christ sought to foster a community that proclaims the Kingdom of God involving selfless concern for others; and the incarnation involved action with respect to teaching, healing, submitting to death, and resurrection. If there is this parallel role for cognition and so on, then the meaning of the incarnation of Jesus Christ involves some of the same components in the meaning of a person's life who desires to become part of the Body of Christ.[20]

---

[19] What's It All About?, 43.
[20] I thank Tricia Little for her assistance in preparing the text.

Index